Ritual Encounters

▸ ▸ ▸ ▸ *Interpretations of Culture in the New Millennium*

Norman E. Whitten Jr., General Editor

A list of books in the series appears
at the end of the book.

Ritual Encounters

Otavalan Modern and Mythic Community

Michelle Wibbelsman

University of Illinois Press · Urbana and Chicago

Manufactured in the United States of America
1 2 3 4 5 C P 5 4 3 2 1
∞ This book is printed on acid-free paper.

Library of Congress Cataloging-in-Publication Data
Wibbelsman, Michelle
Ritual encounters : Otavalan modern and
mythic community / Michelle Wibbelsman.
p.   cm. — (Interpretations of culture in the
new millennium)
Includes bibliographical references and index.
ISBN 978-0-252-03397-1 (cloth : alk. paper) —
ISBN 978-0-252-07603-9 (pbk. : alk. paper)
1. Otavalo Indians—Social life and customs.
2. Otavalo Indians—Rites and ceremonies.
3. Otavalo mythology.
4. Imbabura (Ecuador)—Social life and customs.
I. Title.
F3722.1.O8W53   2009
305.898'323—dc22   2008027199

Contents

To my abuelo, *Hugo Vicente Moncayo Crespo*

.

Preface

Ritual in the highlands of northern Ecuador is ubiquitous. It marks the cadence of life in indigenous communities. Among Otavalan indigenous people of Imbabura province, ritual is defined by the deep knowledge that emerges from an oscillating rhythm of everyday life and celebration, and from a sustained conversation with beings in other realms of existence. It is in these ritual contexts of physical and metaphysical encounter that Otavaleños invoke their mythic and historical past as integral to the formation of their ethnic and moral identity as a modern community.

Mayman Ringui? Choosing a Field Site

I arrived in Imbabura by a winding path that first took me away from my native country and then returned me to it. I was born in Quito, Ecuador, in 1968 to an Ecuadorian mother and a North American (U.S.) father. In 1981, a period of political and economic transition in Ecuador, we relocated to Texas. I was brought up in the urban Ecuadorian private educational system, and yet knew little about my own country. It was not until I entered college in the United States that I became truly aware of the multiethnic and multilingual diversity in Ecuador. This sparked my desire to return to the Andes for research purposes. While completing my master of arts degree in Latin American studies at The University of Texas at Austin, Dr. Gerard Béhague encouraged me to visit Otavalo and put me in contact with Ecuadorian ethnomusicologist Carlos Coba at the Instituto Otavaleño de Antropología. In the summer of 1995 I traveled to an Ecuador I had never known before.

Ethnographic fieldwork requires the researcher as a curious observer to be open to random encounters and the opportunities they extend. Ethnography is a method insofar as we gain glimpses of culture in details we are often not looking for, but are fortunate to witness and trained to notice. At the heart of these anthropological pursuits lies an ability to discover similarity across differences. This is how in 1995 I came to meet Blanquita and her family—by chance and mutual curiosity. *Nos simpatizamos,* as one would say in Spanish, and this affinity more than any preconceived research agenda defined the circumstances of my fieldwork.

I met her in a craft workshop, where she wove handbags along with other Otavalan women. During our brief exchange, she extended an invitation to a family baptism in the community of Ilumán Bajo. It was something I could have just as easily dismissed as polite conversation as followed through with. This was the first time I would venture outside the city of Otavalo at night. I stumbled along the old railroad tracks following the irrigation channel, per Blanquita's directions, equipped only with her father's nickname, "Cuchara," as a sort of password that validated my presence in the community and en- sured help along the way.

When I arrived, I was put immediately to work in the kitchen as another pair of hands. My task of frying enormous quantities of chicken integrated me into the informal interaction and agitated pace of production behind the scenes, and allowed me to cut through the awkwardness of being received as a special guest. After the excitement of serving dinner to the new godparents was over, I ate in the kitchen with the rest of the women. As it got late, I was invited to spend the night at Blanquita's house. I piled into a bed with her two youngest siblings, and slept soundly on a reed mat under heavy wool blankets. Little did I know that five years later, this would be my home.

The process of moving away from Ecuador and returning periodically to rediscover it in a different light has guided the evolving insights I share in this book. My initial research trip led to subsequent summer visits in 1997 and 1999 and to my extended doctoral investigation in 2000 and 2001.

I lived in Ilumán with Blanquita's family for fourteen months in 2000–2001. My research aimed to investigate indigenous ritual practices and to analyze the ways by which their interconnected and progressive character offers a unique perspective on Otavalan identity, morality, and modernity. As a single woman, I initially operated in the private sphere of the home. I gained invaluable insight into the daily lives of my indigenous family as I became involved in cooking for work parties, taking animals to pasture, attending school meetings and helping children with their homework, washing clothes in the spring, and planting and harvesting crops. I attended mass, sat in on community meetings, and partook in private rituals including family house cleansings, baptisms, funerals, and prayer sessions. I also sold chickens and guinea pigs at the live animal market and hunted for june bugs in the highland moor when they were in season. This is what anthropologists call deep immersion in a culture through the method of participant observation. It is these day-to-day experiences that provided the context for cultural interpretation and theoretical framing of my research on ritual and identity.

As my research developed a comparative dimension, I extended the geographical scope of my project. Another friend by mutual liking and chance encounter, Luis Pacífico Fichamba, "Paci," involved me with a second-tier indigenous organization in the town of Cotacachi. There I met Segundo Anrrango, Rumiñahui Anrango, and Edy Zaldumbide, among many other dedicated *compañeros*. I volunteered at UNORCAC (Union of Indigenous Organizations of Cotacachi) as a member of a team charged with documenting area cultural traditions as part of a sustainable development project funded through the Inter-American Foundation. UNORCAC oversees forty-two communities in Cantón Cotacachi. Working for this organization extended my opportunity to do collaborative work with community members. In addition, it provided introductions and transportation to distant communities, many of them accessible only by motorcycle. I was also invited to participate in collecting oral narratives on regional traditions for a project at Jambi Mascaric, a holistic medicine center affiliated with UNORCAC. Director Magdalena Fueres and I met and talked often. She provided important insights regarding my observations, as did local researchers Carlos Guitarra and Rosita Ramos, whom I accompanied, on occasion, on field interviews throughout the canton.

Mayman ringui? Until I figured out that when people asked where I was going, the appropriate response was *kaygullaman rini* (just over here), or *kaygumanda tigramugrini* (I am coming back from just over there), I would explain where I was headed. People were intrigued by my desire to learn about local practices and public festivals, and, somewhat surprisingly, they would often decide spontaneously to come with me. This is how, from time to time, I gained valuable translators and cultural guides. Similarly, I learned to allow time in my schedule to take people up on invitations for me to tag along.

Working in different places gave me perspective on important cultural nuances throughout the Otavalo and Cotacachi areas. It also provided insight into regional politics and allowed me to develop a better understanding of organizational relations and coalitions on local and national levels. There were, in addition, practical considerations for conducting research in various locations. Sometimes I experienced problems gaining access to information or recruiting participation. At first I pursued all opportunities diligently, doing my best to overcome bureaucratic and local political obstacles. Eventually, I felt more comfortable doing research where I was welcomed. There, I found rewarding opportunities, enthusiastic collaboration, and a mutual interest in establishing enduring professional and personal ties.

Festive and ritual events often took place simultaneously throughout the area, presenting unique opportunities for comparative research (for instance, my analysis of two different renditions of the Stations of the Cross on Holy Friday in Cotacachi, chapter 6). Multisited fieldwork, in addition, ensured a backup plan. Celebrations were sometimes canceled or postponed without prior notice. On one occasion, a cow in the pasture surrounding San Juan Pogyo, a sacred spring where many public events for the communities of Ilumán and Pinsaquí take place, tripped over an electrical wire, jeopardizing the cultural activities scheduled for that afternoon. Another time, roadblocks along the Pan American Highway erected as part of a national indigenous political protest influenced a decision to reschedule the San Pedro Festival in Peguche. A flexible approach to research location allowed me to focus more aptly on the flow of people along social networks and in relation to festive rituals as moveable feasts.

Today my field site is expanding. Blanquita was in Switzerland for most of 2000–2001 and continues to reside there. Her siblings, Anita and Walter, eventually followed her to Europe. Through them I learn about the legal, financial, and cultural challenges of making a living abroad. My godchild, Martha, is studying in Ibarra. She is the first in her family to attend university. Two good friends from Peguche, Roberto Lema and his wife, Blanquita Lema, have joined a community of more than one hundred Otavaleños living in Chicago. They keep me informed about Pawkar Raymi and Inti Raymi celebrations in Peguche and abroad. My *compadres* from Chimbaloma have also migrated and call me occasionally from Chile. Yet our transnational lives continue to revolve around a unique association with this place called Imbabura, and the pace of our diverse existences is marked by its ritual seasons.

Acknowledgments

My thanks go to the many people in the Otavalo and Cotacachi area communities who granted me interviews, invited me to participate in their activities, and enriched my research in innumerable ways. My greatest debt is to my *compadres,* Segundo Yamberla and Carmen de la Torre, and to their children, Blanquita, Anita, Walter, Martha, and Edwin Yamberla de la Torre. They took me into their home in Ilumán with warmth and allowed me to share in their joys, their sorrows, and their daily reflections.

A heartfelt *Dius si lu pagui* goes to the many people who contributed to my investigation in Ilumán, especially to Alberto Yamberla Conejo, president of UNICOBICI (Unión de Comunidades y Barrios Indígenas y Campesinos de Ilumán) in 2001; recently deceased artist Segundo Conejo Morales, whose eye for detail captured vividly the lives and the memories of his community; Remigio Cáseres Yamberla; members of the Asociación de Yachaqs de Ilumán; José de la Torre Morales, Teniente Político of Ilumán in 2001, and his family; Anita Yamberla de la Torre and Brishit Tocary Caiza Yamberla, my dedicated Quichua teachers; neighbors and friends in Ilumán Bajo, especially the Caiza Yamberla family; and the children who learned my name and greeted me with enthusiasm every day upon my return from work.

In Cotacachi my thanks go to Luis Fichamba, Segundo Anrrango, Rumiñahui Anrrango, Edy Zaldumbide, and other *compañeros* at UNORCAC not only for a stimulating work experience but for the enduring friendships that resulted from it. At Jambi Mascaric, I especially thank Magdalena Fueres, Carlos Guitarra, and Rosita Ramos. My gratitude also goes to Carmen Haro at the Museo de las Culturas (Fundación Raices) in Cotacachi; Alfonso Maygua, director of the Taller de Artesanías in La Calera; members of SIGNE (Servidores de la Iglesia Católica de las Nacionalidades Indígenas del Ecuador); members of CICUJ (Comunidades Indígenas Católicas Unidas con Jesucristo); indigenous catechists; and Padre Gonzalo Flores at the Church of La Matriz.

In Otavalo, I am grateful to José Manuel Quimbo Amaguaña for involving me in UNAIMCO (Unión de Artesanos Indígenas del Mercado Centenario de Otavalo) planning sessions for Inti Raymi 2001 and for our continuing friendship and collaboration on his trips to the United States. I owe many thanks to staff at FICI (Federación Indígena Campesina de Imbabura) and to members of ASHIM (Asociación de Shamanes de Imbabura). Carlos Coba welcomed me to the Instituto Otavaleño de Antropología (IOA) and facilitated an institutional affiliation in 1995. I am also obliged for the hospitality and help I received from Frank Kiefer and Margaret Goodhart, longtime residents of Otavalo and owners of the Ali Shungu hotel.

Roberto and Blanquita Lema in Peguche and Chicago have been my friends since we first danced together on the eve of San Juan in 1995. They have always offered me a place to stay in Peguche and openly shared with me their interpretations of festival practices. In Peguche, my appreciation also goes to Don Pacho Lema, Mario Conejo Cotacachi (Kalimán), José Amado Lema, Jorge Fabián Tuquerres Panamá (Fujimori), Narcizo and Fanny Conejo, Rafaél Pinsaq and Rebeca Guaján, native anthropologist Luis Enrique Cachiguango, and members of the Pawkar Raymi Peguche Tio organizing committee.

Kristine Latta, a graduate student in anthropology at Princeton University, and her husband Orlando Cachiguango were in Peguche during 2000–2001 as well. Kristine and I exchanged information about our respective investigations, discussed our findings, commiserated about our research frustrations, and collaborated in filming several festival events. I am particularly grateful for the moral support and encouragement I received from them and from other anthropologists in Ecuador during the time of my fieldwork, including Chris Krupa, Liz Lilliott, Avi Tuschman, Jeroen Windmeijer, Dagmar Schweitzer de Palacios, and Lynn Meisch. I feel privileged to have met these colleagues and to have benefited from their provocative scholarly engagement in the field.

In Quito, I would like to thank Diego Quiroga at Universidad San Francisco de Quito and Fernando García at the Facultad Latinoamericana de Ciencias Sociales (FLACSO) for providing institutional affiliations in 2000–2001 that gave me access to library resources, guest lecturer opportunities, and scholarly exchanges with Ecuadorian intellectuals. The executive director of Comisión Fulbright, Susana Cabeza de Vaca, and her staff extended help with practical matters and involved me in a dynamic intellectual community at the commission.

Many people I interviewed wished to be recognized for the knowledge they contributed to this project. I have left their names unchanged with their permission. For anyone who preferred to remain anonymous, I was careful to omit any identifying annotation, but certainly want to acknowledge their important contributions.

My fieldwork was funded through a Fulbright-Hays Doctoral Research Grant (2000–2001), Tinker Foundation Grant (1995, 1997), University of Illinois Dissertation Travel Grant (1999), and an assistantship under a Beckman Institute and University of Illinois Research Board Grant (1999). My thanks and acknowledgments go to these institutions for enabling my research. My appointment as research fellow at the Lozano Long Institute of Latin American Studies has been indispensable in ensuring my access to library and other resources at The University of Texas at Austin in the final writing stages of this book manuscript.

Nils Jacobsen, Andrew Orta, Mahir Saul, Arlene Torres, Tom Turino, and Norman Whitten at the University of Illinois at Urbana-Champaign offered constructive comments in the early writing stages. I received feedback on select chapters from Jorge León Trujillo, participants on a 2006 American Anthropological Association panel organized by Kathleen Fine-Dare, faculty at a research presentation at Stephen F. Austin University, and members of the communities of La Calera and Turuku who attended research talks I delivered in the summer of 2007. Kristine Latta corrected several details in chapter 2 based on her own research on the Pawkar Raymi festival. Finally, my friend and colleague Matei Costinescu offered invaluable comments on final drafts of the entire book manuscript. His penetrating analysis and compassionate criticism helped me avoid important theoretical pitfalls.

In addition, Ketty Wong, ethnomusicologist at the University of Kansas, helped me with musicological analysis. Eva Pajuelo, a graduate student in Andean archaeology, and graphic designer Jeff Clarke generated the maps that appear in the book. Maritsa Córdova did an exceptional job with tape transcriptions. Delia Quilumbaquí, a native Quichua speaker from Cotacachi now living in Austin, Texas, corrected Quichua orthography and several details in the Calendar of Festive Rituals in the Imbabura Area. Staff and anonymous readers at the University of Illinois Press helped bring this ethnography into completion. Their hard work improved the book considerably. I, of course, accept responsibility for any mistakes or omissions.

I am grateful for the unfailing support of my family in Quito, especially my grandfather, Hugo Vicente Moncayo Crespo. My *abuelo* not only offered encouragement but engaged my research project in spirited discussions over coffee. I am also deeply thankful to my family in the United States. I owe an enormous thank-you to Christopher Layden, my husband, who has been my most steadfast supporter through the writing phase of this book.

Thank you, Chris, for nurturing a stable and loving environment in our household and for your patient understanding of the idiosyncrasies that come with academic life. My mother, Cecilia, has provided help on multiple levels throughout my academic career. I thank my brother, Nick, for inspiring my work environment with his art. A very special acknowledgment goes to my sister, Caroline, who read the chapters as they progressed and engaged my analysis from her own disciplinary perspective in transpersonal psychology. Caroline also accompanied me to the field on several occasions as an inspired photographer and a capable field assistant. Her natural rapport with people made a lasting impression in Imbabura. My father, Frederick Wibbelsman, has played an enduring role in my life. The principles he instilled in me, his passion for intellectual engagement, and his insatiable curiosity about the worlds we live in have guided my academic and personal pursuits.

It was Dr. Gerard Béhague who embarked me on this research path. I remain indebted to him for the support and friendship he extended throughout my professional development. A simple thank-you is insufficient to express my immense gratitude to Norman Whitten, series editor. I am but one of many scholars who have been deeply influenced by his prolific scholarship on Ecuador and by his dedicated mentorship.

Note on Orthography

Spanish and Quichua words and phrases appear throughout the book. Both are set off in italics in the text, and I have provided a list of Quichua and Spanish terms and acronyms in the appendix. All translations are mine unless noted otherwise.

Although Spanish orthography is standard for the Americas, contemporary written styles of Quichua, originally a spoken language, are largely inconsistent. Ecuadorian Quichua, *Runashimi,* belongs to the broader linguistic family, Quechua, spoken by an estimated ten million people throughout the Andes. Recent efforts to standardize Quichua orthography under a format known as "Kichwa Universal" have only been partially successful. Different orthographies in Ecuadorian Quichua reflect regional preferences. Discrepancies in spelling also appear within regions. Two or sometimes three different orthographies are often apparent in a single written document. Within a single family, individuals spell their name differently (for example, Anrrango and Anrango). Similarly, an individual might choose to spell his or her name differently on different occasions. Native anthropologist Luis Enrique Cachiguango is a case in point. In publications his name appears variously as Cachiguango, Kachiguango, or Kachiwango. These variations reflect the rapid transformations Quichua is undergoing as a living language and capture the politics of language behind the messy transition from oral tradition to written form.

The orthographic consistency I have imposed here may not always reflect local preferences for spelling. My choice of orthography takes into consideration readability for non-Quichua speakers, with a focus on eliciting correct pronunciation especially from English-speaking readers. General rules of my transcription adhere to use of k (for q, c, and for j at the end of words) and w (for hu, gu). Beyond this, the use of j at the beginning of a word, for example *jatun*, designates an English h sound. Ch after a consonant carries a zha sound, as in *puncha* (variably spelled in other texts as *punja, punlla, pun-zha*). Vowel sounds in Quichua correspond to the Spanish a, i (with a range from e to i), and u (with a range from o to u). Y is generally used instead of i where two vowels appear in succession (karay rather than karai). The suffix *kuna* added to any singular noun forms the plural.

In Quichua, the adjective comes before the noun in the sentence structure, as in English. Influences from the Spanish language sometimes reverse this order, placing the adjective after the noun. I have transcribed expressions as I heard them. In all other contexts I have retained the Quichua construction. When Quichua speakers communicate in Spanish, I have left the syntax unchanged, rather than forcing their expression into "correct" Spanish. I have also retained colloquialisms both in Spanish and Quichua. Proper names appear in their original form (for example, Urcuciqui, Cuicocha, Jambi Marcaric) and I have respected alternative spellings when citing other authors. Finally, I have made exceptions for certain words, such as Quichua, which is more recognizable in its conventional international spelling.

List of Illustrations

Ritual Encounters

Introduction:
Otavaleños at the Crossroads

Imagine a place, nestled in the dramatic landscape of the Andes, where technology intersects with religion and myth, where an international highway cuts across pastoral landscapes connecting rural agricultural laborers to global communities and metropolitan centers, where the indigenous people of the area use systems of local barter and trade just as expertly as they participate in worldwide market trends. This place is Otavalo, a culturally and geographically unique area in northern Ecuador. It is home to Quichua-speaking highland indigenous people known as Otavaleños or Otavalo Runa, people who span an extraordinary heterogeneity of experience and yet maintain a strong sense of community and ethnic identity. Otavaleños are among Ecuador's most traditional people in the sense that they maintain in the twenty-first century their native costume, indigenous language, cultural practices, and ritual expression. They are also among the most internationally traveled and cosmopolitan populations of Latin America.

This book is about the moral, mythic, and modern crossroads at which Otavaleños stand, and how, at this junction, Otavalo Runa come to define themselves as millennial people. Otavaleños refer to themselves as a *pueblo milenario* (millennial people) and affirm their native traditions as *wiñay kawsay* (our millennial culture). These allusions, along with a more common identification as Runakuna, "fully human beings," evoke the cultural and political self-determination that Norman Whitten (2003:x) ascribes as central to millennial identities. *Ritual Encounters: Otavalan Modern and Mythic Community* highlights the ritual and mythic dimensions of Otavalan daily lives as fundamental for understanding contemporary Otavalo Runa, their sense of community, their production of ethnic and moral discourses and identities, and their expectations for individual and collective action. The book thus exposes a crucial side of Otavalan society often overlooked by contemporary emphasis on the economic success and political achievements of Otavaleños. I show how in the thick of globalizing, deterritorializing trends, annual rituals provide critical opportunities for periodic encounter and constitute increasingly important contexts for community building. It is here that in an era of dramatic transition people can come together in spite of their differences and geographic dislocations to exercise a rhythm of shared conversation and to affirm their inclusion as part of a single, yet diversifying, community.

Modern Otavalan existences develop against a backdrop of metaphysical conditions—those abstract conceptions concerned with principles of existence, causality, and truth. The mythic dimension of the Otavalan community alludes to knowledge and power that derive from an ability to move back and forth among primordial time, historical past, and present (Reeve 1988:27). Placing the mythic alongside the modern draws attention to the vitality of alternative narratives, structured through myth and ritual, in shaping the historical consciousness of South American peoples (Trouillot 1995, Hill 1988:2, Cohn 1981). The notion of past and future "imaginaries," which as Whitten (2003:xi) describes are central to group memory and to the possibility of approaching objective conditions "with transformative hope," is pivotal to an appreciation of the modern and mythic community as a single and emergent condition.

More specifically, through annual rituals, Otavaleños open and maintain not only the channels of human exchange but also those of otherworldly intercommunication. Ritual enables people to gain access to the domain of mythic time-space wherein all life forces converged in a single realm of existence and interaction (Reeve 1988:26, Whitten 1976: 48, 51). Continual interchange among people, and also with the realms of nature, the divine, and the dead, lies at the heart of Otavalan collective experience. As contexts of heightened reflexivity, ritual and mythic encounters invite people to ponder the order of the universe and to contemplate their central position at its metaphysical crossroads.

A journey through memory, myth, and ritual to the cosmic intersection, the moral and mythic Andean *chakana,* marks our point of departure and of periodic return throughout this ethnography. The *chakana* stands for the interrelatedness of everything and the interpenetrability of different time-spaces. It is the center upon which all essential modes of being converge and where communication and even passage between realms of existence is possible (see Lawrence Sullivan 1988:130 on *axis mundi*). In time, it marks a moment of transition toward the future and of convergence between the past and the present. The *chakana* has been described in Andean literature as a cosmic bridge or a giant cross. Sometimes it is referred to as a ladder or as the Andean steps (see, for example, Sullivan 1988, Estermann 1998, Rodriguez 1999). Regardless of how it is depicted—as ladder, cross, bridge, or steps—in every case the *chakana* is a cosmic intersection where the connections between principles of vertical (divine) correspondence and horizontal (mundane) complementarity are affirmed (Estermann 1998:156). It is not so much a map of the Andean cosmos as it is a symbol of the principles of dialogical interplay that underpins the Otavalan modern and mythic community.

In the ethnographic account that follows I outline the types of dialogue that unfold through ritual, and describe the nature of this unifying principle of ongoing communication as it extends to conversations with otherworldly beings. The configuration of the *chakana* provides an organizing framework for the chapters in the book—each dealing with communication and interchange particular to the realms of the living, the dead, nature, and the divine. The metaphor of the *chakana*, in addition, establishes an oscillating rhythm in the book defined by an expanding and centralizing cadence that follows the periodic departure and return of the migrants, the passage through social change and the progression in time through memory and historicity, the dynamic between continuity and change, the movement between ritual and everyday life. Insight gained by way of this rhythmic oscillation is what Otavaleños claim as *Ñawpa Yachaykuna,* described as knowledge that derives from looking forward into the past in all of its dimension. This is the "deep knowledge" that Otavalo Runa sustain through ritual as the creative soul of their ethnic community.

El Lechero: Signpost at the Cosmic Intersection

On June 22, 2001, I was invited by members of SIGNIE (Servers of the Catholic Church of the Indigenous Nationalities of Ecuador) and members of ASHIM (Association of Imbaburan Shamans) to join them for a ritual known as Inti Watana (the tying of the sun). The shamans explained that they would call "Shamuy Inti (come sun). We will tie you so that you will wait here," symbolically lassoing the sun in a perpendicular position to the equator. It would be an act of human intervention to arrest the movement of the cosmos, if only momentarily.

For more than a decade, members of ASHIM have organized an annual ritual offering at the site of the sacred Lechero on the occasion of the summer solstice. Previous to this time, indigenous ritual experts, referred to as shamans and locally known as *yachaks* (literally, ones who know), suffered persecution and practiced their rituals clandestinely. Between 1532 and 1660, native peoples throughout the Andes suffered an intense evangelizing campaign aimed at eradicating idol worship. During this early colonial period, pre-Hispanic *wakas* (sacred ancestors) were destroyed and indigenous spiritual leaders were targeted as *hechiceros,* witches (Vinicio Rueda 1982a: 69). It was only in the late twentieth century, beginning with the General Conference of Latin American Bishops in Medellín in 1971 and later the Latin American Episcopal Council in Bogotá in 1978, that the Catholic Church sanctioned popular religions, allowing a gradual public resurfacing of traditional ritual practices (Vinicio Rueda 1982b:26–27).

On the morning of the ritual, Alfonso Cachimuel, president of SIGNIE and member of ASHIM, addressed the crowd of participants gathered in Plaza Bolivar, the main square of the city of Otavalo. Standing in front of an enormous stone bust of Rumiñahui, which honors the principal military strategist of Atahualpa, the Inka of the north, Cachimuel thanked a variety of organizations that had supported this ritual effort. The list is revealing of the syncretisms, reconciliations, and alliances that have developed around traditional indigenous practices in the twenty-first century: the shaman's association (ASHIM), the indigenous Catholic Church organization (SIGNIE), an intercultural and bilingual educational establishment, the Ecuadorian Foundation for the Recovery of Indigenous Centers, the municipality of Otavalo, and the nonprofit Friends of the Lechero Project. After honoring *Yaya* (Grandfather) Rumiñahui, from whom the Otavalos claim direct descent, with a red headband, the shamans prayed for strength, protection, and wisdom on this pilgrimage, imploring *Intiyaya* (Sun Grandfather), *Allpamama* (Earth Mother), and *Jisucristu* (Jesus Christ). Although the Lechero site was only a few kilometers away across relatively friendly terrain, the prayers prepared people for a pilgrimage across a mythic map that involved moving from one mode of being to another in a journey of transformation.

Shamans, both male and female, dressed in multicolored beads, feathers, crosses, and headbands, wearing T-shirts that advertised SHAMAN in big letters across the back and carrying lances and staffs, led the pilgrimage. In addition to local specialized knowledge, their ritual paraphernalia reflected intercultural and interregional borrowings ranging from Native American healing traditions to ritual knowledge from the Ecuadorian Eastern Lowlands, known as the Oriente. Dorothea Whitten (2003:259–65) explains that rather than appealing to easy acculturation or new age hype, this blending of contemporary and traditional themes, in fact, constitutes the basis of the geographic, psychological, socially expansive, and deep knowledge of powerful indigenous visionaries. She underscores the indigenous belief that "power

Taita Churu honoring Yaya Rumiñahui

resides in the acquisition of distant knowledge" and that it is, in fact, the ability to control knowledge from broad networks of people and ideas that forms the base of shamanic authority (D. Whitten 2003: 253–54).

A crowd of schoolchildren, indigenous people of various backgrounds, mestizo participants, an *Aya Uma* ("spirit head": a traditional festival character that wears a mask featuring a face on both the front and the back, with multicolored horns or "serpents" on top), a couple of musicians, an ice cream vendor, and an anthropologist walked at a fast clip behind the shamans to the music of the twin flutes. As we left town, a drunkard mistook the procession for a parade in honor of Catholic Saint John, whose feast day is also celebrated in late June, and cheered us on, babbling, *¡Viva mi rey! ¡Viva mi rey! ¡Viva San Juanito!* (Long live my king! Long live my king! Hurray for San Juanito!)

The gusty San Juan winds picked up as we pilgrimaged up Reyloma to the sacred Lechero tree in the community of Pucará Alto. This enormous lechero (*Euphorbia laurifolia;* commonly named for its milky white sap) overlooks Lake San Pablo and must be hundreds of years old. It stands alone at the top of the hill with its thick branches outstretched against the arresting background of Mount Imbabura. The Lechero tree, for many Otavalo Runa, is, along with other *wakas* such as the *urkumamakuna* and *urkutaitakuna* (the female and male mountains) and the *pukyukuna* (springs), a living being with personality and gender attributes, and with physical needs like those of any other person. The honorific titles *Taita, Mama,* and *Yaya* are commonly used in Quichua in deference to elders and ancestors, including divinities embodied in the natural landscape. Prayers and offerings to the Lechero capture the personable interaction people maintain with these divine and natural beings, emphasizing a relationship of mutual dependency between Otavalo Runa and their environment.

The ascent to Reyloma was informal in character as people talked and children played along the way—behavior that characterizes most indigenous rituals. On the last stretch of the journey the shamans asked participants to remove their shoes and *alpargates* (local sandals), and encouraged the congregation to approach the Lechero barefoot as a sign of respect. It was a clear day for viewing the volcanoes. José Manuel Vásquez, head shaman and president of ASHIM, better known as Taita Churu, saluted each mountain individually by name: Cayambe to the south, Imbabura to the east, Cotacachi to the northwest, Yana Allpa and Fuya Fuya to the southwest, and collectively called on them as *ñukanchikpak Yayakuna* (our Grandfathers).[1] One of the shamans blew a conch. And Taita Churu, now standing in the shade of the sacred Lechero, announced, *gulpi kaypi kanchik* (we are all here).

Lawrence Sullivan (1988:131–33) writes of a cosmic tree, the guardian-of-the-world tree in South American religions, its branches spread throughout the world-planes, drawing the different realms together, marking the center of the universe. It is significant that the Lechero on Reyloma is at zero de-

Yachaks in front of sacred Lechero tree

grees latitude (0° 14" to be exact), almost directly on the equator. The site marks the precise location of a pre-Inka Pucará religious and astronomical temple (Caillavet 2000:39). Its counterpart is the temple site on Araque hill just south of Lake San Pablo. From the vantage point of the ancient settlement of Otavalo along the western shores of Lake San Pablo, also known as Imbacucha, these sites line up accordingly with the two most important volcanoes in the area—Reyloma in a direct line with snowcapped Cotacachi (4,936 m.) and Araque in a direct line with Mount Imbabura (4,557 m.) (Caillavet 2000:39). In addition to the significance of these geographical coordinates, the existence of a symbolic center, argues Sullivan (1988:130), is essential to the possibility of a meaningful cosmos.

Rituals performed by Otavalo Runa render sacred sites meaningful as living, acting, and interacting agents in the community. In the animated and transmogrifying Andean landscape, the Lechero is an embodiment of Taita Imbabura and occasionally of the Catholic God himself. As such, he commands a central place in many ceremonies. People, moreover, snap off branches from the sacred Lecheros to take home and plant, in essence bringing the divine into the realm of everyday uses. These everyday lecheros occupy a central location in indigenous homes. Everything can be missing from an indigenous household except for a lechero. The lechero stands as a sentinel in the patio of each household (*un waka protector de las casas*) and also guards the family *chakra* (small subsistence field). Lechero branches are commonly staked around farm fields as fence posts. Some say that the energy they emanate fends off wrongdoers. Others say that the milky sap is a natural acid that burns the skin, deterring intruders, both human and animal, from trespassing through the branches. One characteristic of this tree is that no matter how it is pruned, the leaves always grow back. Planted bare stems eventually set roots and become live fences as they branch and intertwine. This is, in part, why the lechero is known as the tree of eternal life.

Taita Alfonso Anangonó, *yachak* from the community of La Joya in the Otavalo area, tells me that the lechero is also used to prepare medicine for healing a variety of illnesses. He often prescribes a lechero potion for curing deafness, toothaches, eye problems, liver cirrhosis, and *nervios* (nerves). He most commonly applies the milky acid to get rid of bacterial and fungal skin infections. *Euphorbia laurifolia,* according to Taita Alfonso, is also effective for cleaning the intestines because the sap is a natural laxative. But this medicine, if not administered properly, can also kill. A few *yachaks* in the area and a number of the older *parteras* (midwives) still know how to handle the lechero to induce abortions.

Sullivan (1988:138) writes that although the world-tree facilitates communication between various regions of the universe, its inner nature is noxious. As the tree of life and of death with the powers both to heal and to kill, the Lechero stands as a complex symbol of the cycle of life at the Andean crossroads. Its branches and roots extend laterally and perpendicularly, tracing the framework of the mythical *chakana,* outlining the connections among the different worlds that make up the Andean universe. Marco Vinicio Rueda's (1982a:93) observation of indigenous perceptions of Christian crosses elsewhere in the Ecuadorian Andes as a sort of "landing platform" for souls underscores the prevalence of this symbolism. In addition to assembling the people who accompanied the procession to the Lechero, Taita Churu's pronouncement of the words *gulpi kaypi kanchik* (we are all here) was a powerful verbal act affirming the convergence of beings from multiple realms on this sacred spot.

"Rimarishpa, Rimarishpa Kawsanchik"

As we listened to Taita Churu's stories at the top of the hill, we were reminded by the shamans that these stories and the rituals we performed that day were also for the benefit and enjoyment of the otherworldly beings present on this occasion. Sacred beings are often protagonists in narratives ranging from children's rhymes and pedagogical fables to mythico-religious and historical accounts, and even to pseudoscientific explanations. A popular story told by one of the *yachaks* about the Lechero involved a romance between a young man, Watalquí (*Amarre del Sol*, Tying of the Sun), and a young woman, Ninapacha (*Tiempo de Fuego*, Time-Place of Fire). A time of drought had fallen upon the area, and people decided to perform a ritual known as *Wakcha Karay* to bring rain. In those days, the story goes, this ceremony required the sacrifice of a *ñusta* (a beautiful young woman), and Ninapacha was chosen as the victim. Watalquí, who was in love with Ninapacha, convinced her to run away with him. As they were escaping, Taita Imbabura struck Watalquí with a lightning bolt on Reyloma and transformed him into the Lechero tree. Ninapacha was transformed into a natural spring whence flowed the water that flooded what is today Lake San Pablo.

In a different version of the origin of Lake San Pablo, God himself floods the valley to punish the rich landowners who lived there for turning him away when he, as an embodiment of Taita Imbabura, showed up at their door disguised as a beggar. Distinct versions of these stories abound in the Otavalo Valley. Interpretations vary and narrators selectively present these stories as truth, fact, or creative fiction. The fantastical nature of these stories and their inherent ambiguity render them unfailing catalysts for lively discussion and ongoing speculation.

Storytelling among Otavalo Runa is polyphonic, meaning that several people simultaneously participate in recounting a tale or an event. The multitude of voices blends in the collective narrative. This, however, does not necessarily indicate agreement. "None of these symbolic processes takes place in a simple, unambiguous way," writes Roger Rasnake (1988:214), adding that "the multivocality of symbols ensures the flexibility of meanings. . . ." Meaning making is a messy process that involves imaginative interpretation, improvisation, and transformation with every new narrative or ritual performance. The multivocality apparent in Otavalan expressions and interpretations does not lead to chaotic dissonance, though. Competing versions of these stories contribute to a negotiated development of basic metaphorical

Taita Imbabura, Lake San Pablo in the foreground

and symbolic referents. It is these symbolic moorings that, in turn, provide an evolving cultural repertoire that can elicit mutual recognition among the people who share that repertoire. Frank Salomon (1981a:172) suggests that ritual events provide opportunities for people to "explore, in a setting of heightened and yet disguised consciousness, the question of how people in a state of potential discord can live together." The aim of this ritual interaction, he adds, lies in a progressive understanding of this dilemma, and not in its resolution or removal (Salomon 1981a:202).

People in Otavalan communities often told me, *"rimarishpa, rimarishpa kawsanchik"* (talking, talking we live). This statement, along with Salomon's observation, made me aware that the purpose of storytelling among Otavaleños is to keep people imagining together, talking about differing opinions and interpretations. This ongoing and productive engagement constitutes a generative tension that by its very nature keeps people's conversation with one another open-ended. In addition to signaling the importance of continuing dialogue among people, the expectation of an ongoing conversation includes the constant interaction people maintain with beings from other realms of existence.

Familiarity and *cariño* (affection) capture the tone of discourse with and about otherworldly beings. Regular use of the diminutive both in Spanish and in Quichua is a marker of this type of intimacy. God is not the fear-inspiring, punishing god of the Old Testament; he is *Taita Diusitu, Achiltaitiku* (literally, Dear Great Father). The powerful, menacing Imbabura is *Yayitu* Imbabura (Little Grandfather Imbabura) or *Taita* Imbabura (Father Imbabura). There is some variation in vocabulary across generational and linguistic differences, but generally this principle of affective and familiar language holds true.

Telling stories about the origin of the *wakas*, their embodiment of different gods and their transformations, or gossiping about them as though they were neighbors, effectively draws the sacred into the space of casual discourse in the community and reveals a comfortable relation with sacred beings. A number of people commented in a gossipy tone, for example, that when Volcán Cotacachi has ribbons of snow on its peak, it is because that rascal of Taita Imbabura has been visiting Mama Cotacachi again and has decorated her with glittery gifts. Mama Cotacachi's full Christian name is María Isabel Cotacachi de las Nieves, also known as Rasu Warmi, Snow Woman. These anthropomorphic characterizations add to the discursive layering that renders deities more personable.

Horizontal Complementarity in the Andean Universe

In addition to embodying a conversation about and with the divine, the Lechero signals a reciprocal relation between human beings and nature in what Estermann (1998) calls "horizontal complementarity." The foundation of this complementarity is respect, reciprocity, collaboration, appreciation, and *cariño*. Mistreatment of the earth is equated with the abuse of a person, of one's own mother, in fact. *No hay que hacer que esté solo pariendo y pariendo la Allpamama* (We should not expect the Earth Mother to be giving birth continuously), commented Luis Enrique Cachiguango, who is both a respected *yachak* and anthropologist from the community of Cotama. This idea resonates deeply among people who work closely with the earth as agriculturists in the rural areas and who take their metaphorical and interpretive cues from their daily labor in the fields. Cachiguango's statement reflects a generalized belief that forms of exploitation involve not only forcing excessive production but also impersonal treatment, neglect, and failure to acknowledge or thank the Earth for what she provides.

Countless hours are devoted to caring for the family animals and fields. Tremendous effort and sacrifice go into ensuring their survival and well being.

Mama Cotacachi, Lake Cuicocha in the foreground

Camino de la Madre, *by Blanquita Lema, local artist from Peguche. Oil on canvas, 60* ×90 cm., 1994

Material concerns account in part for the attentiveness people demonstrate toward crops and domestic animals. The death of a cow or a pig, the theft of a chicken, or the failure of a harvest can be economically devastating to an indigenous household. The relationship with nature, nonetheless, runs deeper than just an interest in protecting an investment. People with whom I talked on our way to take the animals to pasture sometimes referred to their animals as friends whose company they enjoyed and with whom they learned to communicate over the years. When one of our neighbors' bulls fell into a ravine and died, it was evident that the owner's grief was not just a reflection of ruinous financial consequence but an emotional expression of personal loss.

Plants and even seeds are treated with similar tenderness. From an early age, children are socialized to care for all living things. A friend of mine from one of the communities in the Cotacachi area shared a story about how when he was a child his mother would tell him to pick up the poor little *porotos* (beans) when he swept the floor of the house. She prompted him to have pity on these orphaned *porotos,* left behind, defenseless, and in need of care. My friend says that to this day he cannot sweep the floor without picking up stray kernels or beans and saving them in his pocket for preparation later. Another person who related to this experience added that their grandfather would warn in a more severe tone, "if you neglect to pick up a *poroto,* you are throwing away life itself. For this little *poroto* is life!" I noticed similar upbringing among the children in my compadres' household in Ilumán, and was always intrigued that pennies, nickels, and even dimes might be overlooked when sweeping, but never a *poroto.*[2] Select seeds carefully wrapped in carrying cloths are even brought to hear mass and receive the priest's blessing (see also Camacho 2006:161). I witnessed this on Easter Sunday in Cotacachi. Although the priest's blessing is desirable for ensuring a good harvest, there also seems to be a sense of moral responsibility for people to intervene as Christian caretakers and bring the seeds or *wakas* that depend on them to hear mass.

At the other extreme of this horizontal interaction is the world of the dead, where communication and dependency similar to that with nature exist between human beings and *las almas* (the souls). People explained to me on various occasions that the souls of those who have died depend upon the living for nourishment, conversation, and creativity that will literally keep them alive. "The dead," writes Mircea Eliade (1963:121) "are those who have lost their memories." Many people believe that Runa souls continue living only as long as relatives visit their graves. The number of days devoted to visiting the cemetery and celebrating the ritual of Wakcha Karay (the offering to the poor, the orphaned, and the dead) reflects the importance Otavalo Runa give to the community of *las almas*. Throughout the Otavalo and Cotacachi areas, Wakcha Karay is celebrated at least four times during the year: on Holy Thursday or Good Friday during *Semana Santa* (Holy Week); on the day of San Pedro, June 29; on *Finados* (All Saints Day), November 2; and on New Year's Day, January 1. Beyond this, every Monday and Thursday are dedicated to venerating the dead. Crowded cemeteries on these days reveal the prevalence of this practice among Otavalan households.

In addition to food offerings, dreams play a vital role as conduits for communication with the deceased and also with nature. Soon after the death of her mother, my *comadre* explained that if one does not visit the grave of a relative often enough, especially during the first year after the death, the *difunto* (deceased person) will call on people in their dreams telling them to bring to the grave a little bit of *tostado* (roasted corn) or a plate of *champús* (sweet soup) because they (the deceased) are hungry. Though there are degrees of interpretation, dreams are generally taken seriously and treated as important messages from the world beyond. Even outspoken skeptics of the practices of feeding the dead will often respond to dreams as a precaution, preparing food and taking it to the cemetery the very next Monday or Thursday, and hiring *rezadores* (prayer experts) to pray over the soul of the *difunto*. Reverence for the dead and the social habits of dream interpretation are not superstitions that people talk about as idiosyncratic folklore. In rural communities, these are lived practices that are considered essential for proper living and for a healthy social, personal, spiritual, and physical existence among Otavaleños (see also Butler 2006:51).

Andean Time-Spaces

A total of four worlds, or *pachas* (time-spaces), make up the universe in Otavalan perspective. The human realm where Otavalo Runa live is known as *Uku Pacha* (the world below or within).[3] Christian saints, deities, and spirits, including *supay* and *ayas*—spirits of ambiguous moral character—coexist in the space of the world above, known as *Jawa Pacha*. Nature exists in *Kay Pacha,* which means "this world." Finally, *Chayshuk Pacha,* literally, the other world (also referred to as *Chusku Pacha,* or the fourth world) is reserved for the dead. The dialogical relation among these four realms is partially captured in a graphic representation of the *chakana* as a square cross, offered by Luis Enrique Cachiguango at an UNORCAC workshop in 2001. The key to interpreting this diagram is the intersection among worlds it depicts:

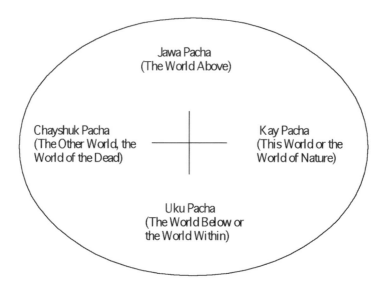

Andean Chakana by Luis Enrique Cachiguango

Fantastical or mythical as these realms of existence may appear to outsiders, there is little doubt that they are intrinsic to Otavalan everyday realities. Those who know Otavalo, or are Otavaleños themselves, would likely agree that, as Rowe and Schelling (1991:105) have observed about the indigenous Andes more generally, belief cannot be separated as folkloric vestige from practice, just as magic in this part of the world is inextricable from technology.

This tour of the Andean universe was part of the passage through memory and myth that people undertook during their pilgrimage to the sacred Lechero that day. People did not just talk about the order of things; through their participation, they effectively enacted the progression of the universe and rehearsed the dialogical connections that sustain it. In Quichua, space and time are linked as part of a single phenomenon, wherein the past is conceived of as lying in front of us, and the future as lying behind us. As people pilgrimaged forward across the physical terrain, they journeyed backward in time through memory, myth, and historicity to the origin of all things. The pilgrimage was a return to first concepts and ultimate grounds; to questions of time, space, being, causality, existence; and to ideas about origins and the limits of human knowledge. Through ritual actions, people revisit these metaphysical and epistemological questions, and in doing so they periodically locate the symbolic center of the cosmos and assert their participation in it as meaningful.

As the metaphor of the *chakana* unfolds, it is possible to see how Uku Pacha, the world that people inhabit, evolves through this human effort from the physical world below to the introspective world within. In a three-dimensional representation of the *chakana*, Uku Pacha is the first sphere in a series of concentric realms. It is surrounded by the world of nature and the world of the dead, all of which are circumscribed by Jawa Pacha, the world of the divine. Jawa Pacha is in turn enveloped by Pacha Mama, the Andean universe. Uku Pacha, the space of human life, the place where Otavalo Runa exist and come to achieve their potential as "fully human beings" or Runakuna, ends up being at the generative center of the mythical universe.

Standing at the juncture of this metaphysical crossroads, Runakuna, explains Josef Estermann (1998:198), are in essence cosmic bridges themselves— human *chakanas*—indispensable for their mediating ability to present the universe in rituals and, through a celebration of the cosmic order, come to know the universe and conserve it.

Meaningful communication among these realms sustains the quality of Runa experiences along the combination of physical, economic, social, religious, historical, mythical, and cosmological vectors. It is the keystone that holds the universe together in productive tension. The phrase *rimarishpa*,

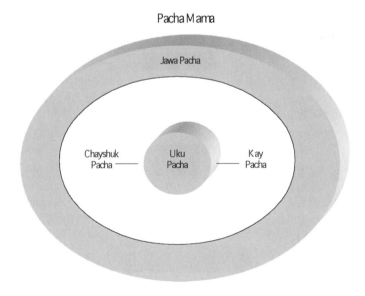

Three-dimensional Chakana

rimarishpa kawsanchik, which characterizes Otavalan life in terms of a continuous conversation, emerges as a statement not only about what people do and how they live, but also about who they are and how they come to reproduce the vitality of the universe through their ritual and everyday actions.

Modern Crossroads

Rituals constitute dramatic attempts to shape and present particular interpretations of social reality in a way that imbues them with a sense of plausibility and legitimacy. As such they belong to the structuring side of the cultural-historical process (Moore and Myerhoff 1977:3–8). Public ceremonies indeed seem to stand as declarations against indeterminacy (Moore 1975), as "models for" understanding and social action (Geertz 1973). These conceptual and strategic models come into particular relief in the context of yet another crossroads at which Otavaleños stand.

Modern Otavalans are poised at the intersection of national and international cultural confluence, political confrontation, global trade, thriving local mixed economies, corporate interests, historical struggles, and cutting-edge technology. Many Otavaleños engage in intercontinental travel, participate in worldwide business networks, and master new technologies. An increasing number of young Otavaleños adopt elements of foreign clothing fashions, drive the latest model Chevrolet trucks, carry cell phones, speak Quichua as a second language, reside in national and Latin American urban centers, and often complete their education abroad. Many Otavaleños are involved in traditional craft and music production ventures abroad.

In the last decade, the growing Otavalan international "trade diaspora" (Kyle 1999) has become the subject of several scholarly publications (see, for example, Meisch 1997 and 2002, Windmeijer 1998 and 2001, Kyle 1999 and 2000, Colloredo-Mansfeld 1999). These analyses for the most part note the resilience of Otavalan ethnic identities in the context of dramatic change, and focus on the economic success, the global marketability of Otavalan ethnicity, and the resulting accumulation of social capital as an explanation for the vitality of an Otavalan collective identity. It is worth noting that the Otavalan diaspora has surpassed its exclusive designation as a trade phenomenon. Otavaleños also leave the valley in pursuit of professional careers, higher education, or wage labor opportunities in metropolitan areas. Though this "wider set of 'possible' lives" (Appadurai 1991:198) produced by the breadth of Otavalan experiences certainly fuels a sense of opportunity and ambition, or an impression of collective achievement, it has, nonetheless, brought

Otavaleños unevenly into the fold of global processes and opportunities (Colloredo-Mansfeld 1999). Many Otavalans continue to subsist on agricultural and small-craft production with methods similar to those used by preceding generations. They plow their fields with a team of oxen, operate nonmechanized craft workshops, manage self-sustaining households, and function within minimal cash-flow economies. They do not fit the profile of the jet-setters of the growing diaspora. Yet they, too, form an integral part of modern Otavalan identities.

This extraordinary diversity of Otavalan individual experiences frames an appreciation of rituals as crossroads where globetrotters meet subsistence agricultural workers, and where together they periodically overcome generational and occupational differences and affirm their inclusion as part of an ethnic community. As shifts in the social terrain lead to a proliferation of Otavalan lifestyles, ritual practices operate as increasingly important contexts for the formation and expression of contemporary collective identities. Otavaleños have not maintained ritual practices *in spite of* modern transformations, but rather *because* ritual is uniquely suited for symbolically capturing cultural changes, and for exploring them critically and celebrating their originality. Otavalan ritual practices hardly correspond to definitions that focus on the

Otavalo Runa agricultural worker

formal, repetitive dimensions of ritual as elements of "culture lag" (Goody 1977:32), nor do they exclusively satisfy agendas of nostalgic, romanticized, or commercialized image making. Among Otavaleños, rituals emphasize transformative experience and are performed as creative, progressive cultural forms of representation and action.

Transnational experiences and new economic opportunities have certainly affected the ways Otavaleños see themselves and are perceived by others. An analysis of Otavalan identities, however, remains incomplete without an understanding of the mythic, religious, and cosmological vectors that complement the economic and social influences on Otavalan daily realities. The approach I propose reveals a dynamic of individual and collective transformation that projects Otavaleños outwardly as agents in increasingly diverse social roles and simultaneously draws them back, through ritual, toward a common origin.

"Community is Where Community Happens"

Arjun Appadurai (1991:196) has articulated the challenge of modern ethnography as the task of unraveling the conundrum of human mobility and the nature of locality as lived experience in a globalizing, deterritorialized world. Martin Buber's quote (cited in Turner 1995 [1969]:127), "Community is where community happens," seems to provide an apt response to this dilemma and serves as a springboard for the analysis of socially integrative processes presented in this book. Buber explains that by community he means the condition of "being no longer side by side but *with* one another of a multitude of persons." This is what anthropologist Victor Turner calls *communitas*—a spontaneous, immediate, self-generating interrelatedness (Turner 1995 [1969], 1974).

Festive rituals descend boisterously upon place and become contexts of spontaneous dialogue, reflexivity, and human intimacy. Lipsitz (1994:6) describes such spaces of encounter as the "crucibles for complex identities in formation that respond to the imperatives of place at the same time that they transcend them." Hundreds of Otavaleños time their periodic returns to the Otavalo area from metropolitan and international destinations with the festival seasons. They come back in greatest numbers for the Pawkar Raymi in February (chapter 2) and for the Inti Raymi celebrations in June through August (chapter 3). Although these festivals have traditionally marked planting and harvest seasons in the agricultural cycle, in contemporary context they have become occasions for welcoming travelers home and for returning migrants to reunite with other travelers. During these mass repeat-return migrations to the Otavalo area, the city and the surrounding hamlets become the contexts of community.

Rituals abroad fulfill a similar function as focal points of encounter and meaningful localities of community experience. They are celebrations of Otavalan ethnic presence around the world. Otavalan anthropologist Patricio Lema (personal communication, 2001) has documented on video Inti Raymi events among migrant Otavalan populations in various European, Canadian, United States, and Latin American cities. Similarly, www.OtavalosOnLine .com, a Web site owned and operated by Otavaleños, regularly posts images and text of Otavalan festive rituals around the world. This proliferating virtual Otavalan community adds yet another ethnographic and analytical dimension to Appadurai's challenge.

Otavaleños are protagonists in their own story, reflexive in their endeavor, shrewd in their beliefs. They engage with the philosophical and existential implications of these questions of shifting localities, ritual, and community at the same time that they live these experiences on a daily basis. As Otavaleños travel away, the geographical, technological, and social dislocations they experience seem to produce a renewed awareness of their cultural and mythic heritage, leading them back through ritual and memory toward an understanding of centralizing concepts that contribute to their sense of commonality. This outward thrust of Otavaleños from their homeland, countered by the introspective cultural journey of return toward a mythic center, generates the multivocal discussions that are fundamental to people's sense of participation and belonging, and to their evolving notion of who they are as *social persons* (Smith 1999:206).

Organization of the Book

The organization of the chapters follows the broad outline of the *chakana*, which allows for an exploration of the dialogical interaction with and within the different realms of existence in the Otavalan universe. This structure reflects the dynamic between the world of people and the parallel time-spaces of nature, the divine, and the dead. As the sequence of rituals that take place throughout the year unfolds, the deep interrelations among these realms become apparent. Attention to the annual progression of ritual events as interconnected activities, in addition, yields an evolving understanding of the ritual process itself. This comprehensive view takes into account Otavaleños' experience of rituals as extended periods of symbolic engagement and allows the weight of ritual practice as system of social critique, vehicle for reflexivity, mechanism of political action, and guide to moral behavior to come into relief.

An initial working definition of ritual as cultural performance and representation in the symbolic realm gives way to an emphasis on ritual as action. Each successive chapter develops an appreciation of ritual as lived experience and action that is consequential for the universe. The chapters increasingly draw on semiotic analysis as a heuristic of emotional understanding, and apply this theory as an effective complement to symbolic analysis in exploring ritual as practice and as transformative experience.

The aim of this book is not to catalogue all rituals celebrated over the course of the year. Readers can refer to appendix 2 for an overall view of the cycle of rituals. A glance at this list reveals the intensity of ritual activity in the Otavalo and Cotacachi areas. My objective here is to anchor an analysis of ritual in the northern Andes in ethnographic examples that will illustrate clearly the relationship among ritual, historicity, power, and identity. In conjunction with this, I critically assess the advantage of the distinct questions and methods that the study of ritual contributes to an understanding of millennial identities, including the potential for collective political mobilization they imply.

I present theoretical insights together with the anthropological detail and historical context from which they emerge in an attempt to render transparent the ethnographic process of observation, data collection, analysis, reflection, and written representation. Two guiding theoretical objectives, nonetheless, bear mentioning up front as general motifs. First, I challenge the widely held assumption that festive rituals are bounded events that merely punctuate the calendar. I have framed this ethnography in terms of ritual seasons and festival complexes to draw out not only the intensity of ritual activity and the extended duration of Otavalan ritual events, but also the critical interrelation among rituals throughout the year. Second, I feel that *Ritual Encounters* makes an important contribution to the literature on ritual by challenging the presumed dichotomy between ritual and everyday life. I demonstrate how, in the Otavalo area, ritual effectively overlaps with and ultimately comes to operate within daily life. Breaking with these two traditionally held theoretical tenets is not only imperative for presenting an accurate depiction of Otavalan reality, but essential for developing fresh theoretical and methodological perspectives that avoid the pitfalls of either/ or setups and modern/traditional divides.

Brief Outline of the Chapters

Chapter 1, entitled "Uku Pacha: The World Below," offers an overview of the geographical, social, political, and historical coordinates of the world of the living. It introduces contemporary Otavaleños and their cultural practices as products of this sociohistorical context. I also locate the world of academics in this realm given that the paradigms we present as cultural analysts influence the ways in which the world is perceived, represented, and experienced.

We remain in the World Below for chapter 2, "Return of the Migrants," to explore the intricacies of the world Otavaleños constitute socially and politically. My analysis centers on the practical aspects of sustaining the rhythm of conversation among members of one highly diasporic community. This ethnographic narrative offers insights into the broader social circumstances, complexity of human networks, enduring relations, and political disputes intertwined with the production of public festivals. I focus on the dynamics of joint conceptualization of events, problem solving, gossip, and virtual participation in community celebrations from abroad through Internet access, and show how the challenges of producing an event contribute to development of a distinct sense of ethnic and cultural community.

In chapter 3, "Encuentros: Dances of the Inti Raymi," I enter the realm of ritual symbolism with the dances of the Festival of the Sun. This chapter reveals the symbolic layering of ritual performances and the concurrent processes of identity formation that take place in a single event. Ethnic and class dynamics are represented and metaphorically inverted by dancers in the racially charged context of the historical Conquest and the legacy of social inequalities it left behind. Heightened reflexivity achieved through ritual performance elevates the notion of dialogue to encounters of different types, ranging from discursive and symbolic to physical and violent interchanges, as participating groups assert their presence and reposition themselves socially and politically in relation to other indigenous communities and interethnically vis-à-vis urban mestizos. The dances draw on historical and modern symbols of power, and incorporate shifting definitions of authority as the Inti Raymi tradition is transposed onto new sociopolitical circumstances both in Ecuador and abroad.

Beyond the human interactions they depict and symbolically recast, the dances of the Inti Raymi also embody a conversation with nature. Stomping on the ground wakes up the Earth Mother. The vigor of the dance as well as the blood sacrifice expected during the violent confrontations that characterize this ritual in certain areas are considered by Otavaleños as ways of reciprocating with nature. The analysis of violence, pain, and ritual sacrifice in chapter 4, "Mythico-Religious Encounters—The Clash of *Aciales*," brings forth a discussion of how participants in a trancelike state essentially become conduits for communication between otherworldly dimensions or time-spaces.

Chapter 5, "Conversations with the Dead," details the practice of feeding the souls. I show how the social responsibility of charity among Otavaleños toward members of their communities extends to the dead, as beings who depend upon the living for nourishment, conversation, and creativity that will keep them active as influential members of the community. The practice of feeding the souls takes place in the context of extended celebrations and presents a female counterpart to male activities that unfold in the public sphere. In this chapter I bring forth an indigenous emphasis on ritual *practice* through a theoretical distinction between commemorative sites of memory and interactive contexts of memory. My analysis not only comments on ethnic differences manifest in indigenous and mestizo memorial customs, but also raises the critical issue of place and locality as dynamic spaces of ritual interaction, especially in the wake of intensifying Otavalan migration. Fulfillment of the obligations to the deceased ultimately sustains a moral discourse critical of mestizos, who do not regularly visit their dead. This moral discourse is also projected onto new generations of jet-setting Otavaleños who are no longer around to feed their ancestors.

In chapter 6, "Stations of the Cross—The Eternal Return to Existence and Hence to Suffering," I draw on semiotics in an analysis of emotional and embodied understanding in order to illustrate the process of memory and ritual representation as lived experience. My description of an indigenous rendition of the Stations of the Cross during Holy Week informs a discussion on empathetic memory and shared suffering. The focus on practice and embodied understanding in the indigenous interpretation of this Catholic ritual supports a moral discourse of indigenous devotees as brothers with Christ in a community of shared pain and sacrifice. As the biblical story maps onto contemporary Ecuadorian realities, semiotic associations in place allow this moral claim to give way to political indignation and a call to action.

My conclusion, "Threshold People of Imbabura," returns us to Uku Pacha as an evolution of the human world of interaction achieved through human effort and introspection. The Quichua self-designation, Runakuna, becomes the fulfillment of Otavaleños' potential as complete human beings in Uku Pacha as the world within. I point out the tremendous amount of energy and resources Otavaleños allocate to maintaining ritual intensity throughout the year and conclude that with each successive ritual experience, people develop increasingly complex conceptual frames that allow for an intensifying sense of interrelatedness or *communitas.*

(Part of this chapter was originally published as Wibbelsman, Michelle, "Otavaleños at the Crossroads: Physical and Metaphysical Coordinates of an Indigenous World," *Journal of Latin American Anthropology,* Vol. 10, No. 1 [April 2005]: 151–85. © 2005 by University of California Press for the American Anthropological Association.)

1

Uku Pacha—The World Below

This chapter provides physical and historical bearings for the world that humans inhabit and shape through their actions. I situate Otavalo and Cotacachi geographically and provide a brief overview, based on secondary sources, of key historical circumstances that have propelled Otavaleños into myriad roles and occupations in the twentieth and twenty-first centuries. Historical precedents explain, in part, the dramatic transfiguration of the social topography Otavaleños navigate today. This historical sketch assigns time depth to an understanding of the diversity within contemporary Otavalan society, the variety of cultural and political influences in the valley, and the social and geographic dispersal of individuals.

As a domain shaped by human intervention, the world below seems like an appropriate place to situate the ethnographer as well. In the second part of the chapter, I contextualize my observations on ritual and festival in the broader literature on this topic and sketch a theoretical frame of reference for the ethnographic examples explored in chapters 2 through 6. Scholars enter the dialogue on culture at the intersection of representation and analysis. The theoretical constructions and culturally influenced perspectives that we bring to bear on an understanding of the Andean world function as conceptual frameworks that, to some extent, define those realities and ours. More than three decades ago, Stanley Diamond (1974:93) suggested anthropology was "the study of men in crisis by men in crisis." His observation acknowledges the very human ways in which we relate to and understand the people among whom we study. This too is part of the cumulative intellectual and experiential method of ethnography—a process that ideally leads from Uku Pacha as the objective world below to its evolution as the perceptive and compassionate human world within.

Physical and Historical Coordinates of the Otavalan Experience

The town of San Luis de Otavalo lies nestled between two volcanoes—Imbabura (4,557 m.) and Cotacachi (4,936 m.)—in a valley 2,805 m. (9,203 ft.) above sea level, 110 kilometers (sixty-five miles) north of Quito, and 150 kilometers (ninety miles) south of the Colombian border. Located in the province of Imbabura, it is the largest market town in the northern Andes, with a mixed mestizo (people of combined Spanish and indigenous descent), indigenous, Afro-Ecuadorian, and foreign population of approximately 26,000 (in 2001). Approximately seventy-five rural communities surround Otavalo. The total population of Cantón Otavalo is 90,188 (INEC 2001), with 30,965 people living in urban areas and the remainder in rural areas. The population of Otavaleños throughout Imbabura province and, beyond that, worldwide as a diaspora is estimated at seventy thousand (Meisch 2002, Kyle 1999). Cotacachi, capital city of a large canton by the same name, lies at the foot of the volcano Cotacachi. The total population of the canton is 37,215 (INEC 2001). The rural population is 29,726, approximately half of whom self-identify as *indígenas*. The remainder are mostly mestizos, with a small population of Afro-Ecuadorians residing especially in Intag, an area that slopes westward toward the northern Ecuadorian coastal province of Esmeraldas. The city of Cotacachi is home to 4,685 people, who are predominantly mestizo. Their primary source of income is the manufacture and sale of leather goods. Tourism largely sustains the service sector and small family-owned businesses. Communities adjoining Cotacachi city are mostly indigenous.

As is the case with many colonial reduction towns (settlements founded with the purpose of concentrating Indian populations to better assimilate them into European culture and religion), Otavalo and Cotacachi have historically been divided along socially constructed "racial" lines, with whites or mestizos (nonindigenous Ecuadorians) living in and around the center of town, and indigenous people inhabiting settlements in the urban periphery or outlying rural communities. The indigenous urban population in both towns has grown especially rapidly in the last couple of decades, however, as indigenous people relocate to the city in pursuit of education, labor opportunities, and business ventures (Pallares 2002:74; see also, for example, INEC 2001). Elsie Clews Parsons (1945:10) writes that in the early 1940s, "no

Indians except a few in domestic service live(d) in Otavalo." By the 1960s, an urban trend was already underway, with several hundred Otavaleños, mostly connected to the textile trade, residing in the city of Otavalo (Andrew Pearse, cited in Kyle 1999:431). The Otavalan urban phenomenon in the 1980s and 1990s drew so much attention that it was, as Kyle (1999:439) reports, the subject of a video documentary aptly entitled *The Reconquest of Otavalo,* which aired on national Ecuadorian television in 1993.

Similar demographic trends occurred beyond Imbabura province, with increasing numbers of Otavaleños moving to Quito and other large cities around the country. As for transnational migration, David Kyle's (1999, 2000)

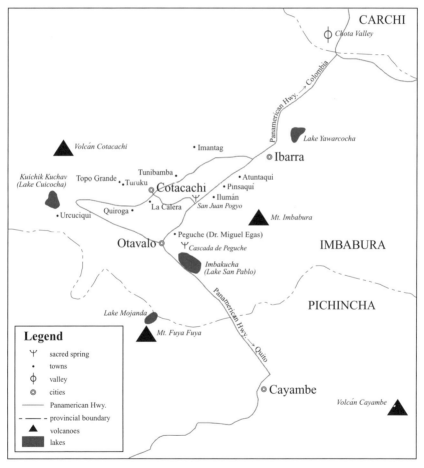

Otavalo and Cotacachi area map by Jeff Clarke

Map of Imbabura Province by Eva Pajuelo

Map of Ecuador by Jeff Clarke

and Lynn Meisch's (2002) excellent studies provide detailed information. Kyle's analysis reveals that modern Otavalan travel to international urban destinations throughout Latin America, Europe, and the United States began as early as the 1940s. Rosa Lema's diplomatic Goodwill Cultural Tours to the United States in 1949 and the incursions of Otavalan dance troupes and music groups onto the world stage in the 1960s and 1970s laid original paths that would facilitate extensive networks of international travel for Otavaleños in the latter part of the twentieth century. A broader Ecuadorian emigration trend, which between 1996 and 2001 increased to more than 378,000 people, or 3.1 percent of the total population (Santiago Izquierdo Office of Social Affairs, Ecuador http://www.csdo.cs/sif/conference2004.nsf), began much later, in the late 1970s, during Ecuador's oil-led export boom, according to Brad Jokisch (1998:7; see also Ann Miles 2004).

Lynn Meisch's (2002:164) estimates for the beginning of the twenty-first century indicate that approximately four thousand Otavaleños are permanent transnational migrants, and another six thousand travel abroad for short-term trips (that is, 15 percent of the total Otavalan population). This figure actually seems conservative in light of higher numbers reported by other authors for Europe alone (see, for example, Windmeijer 2001). Although modern migration has drawn attention because of its magnitude and success, long-distance commercial travel among Otavaleños harks back much further.

Frank Salomon (1986) has documented a thriving native economy in the northern Andes, prior to the arrival of the Spanish, propelled by long-distance trade specialists known as *mindaláes*. In the fifteenth century, before the Inka invasion of the northern Andes, Caranqui inhabitants of the valley that is today Otavalo specialized in weaving and trade (see, for example, Parsons 1945; Salomon 1981b, 1986; Colloredo-Mansfeld 1999:13). *Mindaláes* eventually enjoyed special privileges as royal weavers and merchants under the Inka, under local *caciques* (local lords), and subsequently under the Spanish Crown. *Mindaláes* from the Otavalo area persisted in their trade practices well into the seventeenth century in spite of heavy Spanish colonial tribute requirements. In Cayambe, a neighboring market town just south of Otavalo, Colloredo-Mansfeld (1999:123) reports that *mindaláes* show up in official registers as a distinct group as late as 1782. Although Antonio Males (1989:96) (and Joanne Rappaport in a translator's note) identifies *mindaláes* as an institution characteristic of northern Andean Ecuador, Salomon (1986:102–5) presents evidence of "merchant Indians" as part of a broader, interzonal economic and political articulation. Citing Collier and Buitrón (1949:163) and John Murra (1946:794), Salomon (1981b:434) affirms that in addition to traveling the north-south Andean corridor, before the European conquest or the coming of the Inkas, Otavalo weavers, for example, traded for cotton with people from the Amazonian area. Though the scope of pre-Hispanic trading paths remains the subject of ethnohistoric research, there does not seem to be disagreement over the fact that a long-standing craft tradition, namely weaving, to a great extent propelled this human mobility.

Global Processes in the Colonial and Post-Colonial Eras

In the late sixteenth and early seventeenth centuries, Spanish colonial authorities singled out, under the system of indentured labor known as *huasipungo,* a number of Otavalan villages for *obrajes,* or weaving factories (Kyle 2000:15). These became the primary suppliers of cloth for colonial ventures on the new continent, namely for the silver mines in Potosí (Sempat Assadourian 1983). In 1582 Rodrigo de Salazar founded the Obraje Mayor of Otavalo with 490 tribute-paying Indians (Rueda Novoa 1988:57). This *obraje* continued under the control of the Royal Crown after de Salazar's death in 1584, underwent several administrative transformations, and remained in production through the nineteenth century. The textile mill of San Joseph de Peguchi was founded in 1622, at the height of the second silver production era in Bolivia (Andrien 1995). Although the Spanish Crown had prohibited intercolonial commerce in 1630, effectively ending the textile boom, it made an exception for the cloth produced in the Audiencia de Quito owing to the reliable supply of wool from the enormous flocks in Riobamba and the extraordinary quality of the weavers in Otavalo (Korol and Tandeter 1998:50–58). In the seventeenth century, *obrajes* in the Otavalo area continued under a rent agreement that established these weaving factories as property of the community under the supervision of an administrator (Rueda Novoa 1988:78–79). Although the Crown's original intention may have been to protect indigenous people from excessive labor requirements, under the rent system, the administrators sought to maximize profits for themselves (Rueda Novoa 1988:79–80). One strategy for ensuring higher yields at less expense to the administrators was the apprenticeship system, justified under the argument that this practice had been customary under the Inka system of textile production. Of the three hundred Indians assigned to the *obraje* of San Joseph de Peguchi, 150 of them were young apprentices (*muchachos*) between the ages of twelve and eighteen. This *obraje* was also assigned twenty-four *mitayos* (workers conscripted for periods of six months at a time; an institution described by Salomon [1981b:439] as a functional equivalent of slavery). Apprentices and *mitayos* represented cost savings for administrators because they were paid significantly less than *indios de entero* (full-time Indian workers) (Rueda Novoa 1988:75–87).

In 1634, upon discovering flagrant extortion on the part of administrators, the Crown suspended the position of administrator and placed the mills in the hands of local ethnic lords. Two aspects of this history of the *obrajes* are particularly relevant to the development of modern Otavalan cottage-industry craft production. First, the apprenticeship system, which ensured perpetuation of textile production skills and endures to this day; and second, placement of *obraje* administrative responsibilities in the hands of indigenous *alguaciles, alcaldes,* and *quipocamayos* (constables, mayors, and guardians of the *kipus*—a pre-Hispanic system of accounting and documentation) after termination of colonial administrators. I speculate this promoted industry management skills within the community. Of similar importance was the presence of European specialists in cotton textiles and master carpenters brought from Italy and Spain in the late eighteenth century, when the *obraje* of San Joseph de Peguchi was under the private ownership of Don Miguel de Jijón León (Rueda Novoa 1988:126). These specialists were hired to teach indigenous laborers new weaving techniques and the manufacture of high-quality looms.

Although they were the unintended outcome of a colonial (and later privately owned) production and export system based on exploitation of indigenous labor, the factors mentioned above arguably contributed to indigenous control over the *means of production* of textiles. Salomon (1981b:427, 431–32) argues that it is precisely control over the means of craft production that allowed Otavaleños in the twentieth century to preserve their way of life by using their textile expertise toward the goal of reconquering the land. The flood of cheap English textiles on the market after independence led to the ruin of the *obraje* industry in Ecuador. In this competitive market context, Indian weavers working outside hacienda workshops found a profitable niche selling to other Indians (Salomon 1981b:441). These individual inroads into the market eventually gave rise in the early twentieth century to the farming-weaving complex that Salomon considers key to the perseverance of Otavalan traditional lifestyles.

A historical turn of events in the second decade of the twentieth century provided an additional boost to Otavalan cottage-industry textile production. During World War I, German U-boats effectively blocked English trade ships, creating a shortage of English fabric on the world market. In 1917 Otavalan-made "English tweed" exploded onto the international arena to fill market demand and propelled Otavaleños into an era of modern transnational trade (Kyle 1999:428). Kyle (1999:424, 426) concludes that the social capital derived from Otavaleños' striking ethnic appearance, combined with their expert craftsmanship and a relentless entrepreneurial spirit, accounts for the unique opportunities and noteworthy success of Otavalans in the twentieth century. As Kyle observes, these historical experiences extended urban social networks, heightened international interest in the region, and set the stage of indigenous modernization. They created opportunities for Otavaleños above those available to other indigenous ethnic groups in Ecuador.

Several developments in the latter twentieth century contributed to expanding trends in the Otavalo Valley. In 1954 Dutch artist Jan Schroeder coordinated craft workshops financed by the United Nations and taught interlocking tapestry weaving in forty highland indigenous communities, including Otavalo (Kyle 1999:432). His stylistic influence is still visible in Otavalan tapestries. Similar workshops took place in Salasaca (an indigenous community in Tungurahua province in the southern highlands of Ecuador) in 1957 under the international aid agency known as the Point IV Program (Casagrande 1981:268; Norman Whitten, personal communication, 2004). In the early 1960s United States Peace Corps volunteers encouraged the formation of craft cooperatives in both locations. By the 1970s they were introducing pre-Colombian motifs as well as Amazonian and North American Navajo designs in Otavalo for greater appeal and marketability of crafts to foreign tourists (Meisch 1987: 292). These "cultural borrowings," as Kyle (1999:439–40) describes them, are, in fact, characteristic of Otavalan commercial strategies. Indeed, when I visited Otavalo in 2000–2001, weavers were consulting Abercrombie and Fitch catalogues for sweater design ideas. Otavaleños' open disposition toward the integration of new ideas and new technologies is nothing new and affirms Salomon's (1981b:443) reiteration of Sol Tax's claim that "traditional populations will innovate readily, provided that innovation promises to be useful within the context of already accepted norms."

Three circumstances combined in the 1970s to trigger what was initially a slow trickle of visitors to the valley but would soon become a healthy stream of tourists and also vendors, businesspeople, extended guests, scholars, and governmental and nongovernmental organization volunteers and workers. First, the Organization of American States (OAS) declared 1972 "Tourism Year of the Americas" and offered incentives for increased air travel from Europe to Ecuador (Meisch 2002:84). Cuenca and Otavalo were promoted as must-see destinations in OAS advertising. In 1973, as part of the national infrastructure development project, paving of the Pan-American Highway was completed. That same year, the Plaza de Ponchos (an open-air tourist craft market in Otavalo) was paved with financial support from the Dutch government. Previous to that, the unpaved Plaza Centenario (later renamed Plaza de Ponchos) was the location of an open-air fair since the mid 1930s. It catered to local, mostly indigenous, not tourist, clientele (Meisch 2002:33; see also, for example, Collier and Buitrón 1949:15, 25 and Parsons 1945:30–31). Meisch (2002:37) reports that, in fact, relatively little tourism infrastructure existed in Otavalo when she first visited the area in the 1960s. This all changed with the 1970s developments, which bolstered Otavalan commercialization at a global level.

Foreign tourism to Ecuador escalated dramatically in the following decades. Meisch (2002:84) reports 508,713 visitors and almost $343 million in tourism revenues for the country in 1999. By 2005 the number of tourists increased to 860,784 (Ministerio de Turismo Ecuador 1/19/2006, www.ecuadorvirtual .com). Tourism is now the fourth largest source of national income. More than one-fourth of the tourists who visit Ecuador stop through Otavalo and Cotacachi. The next largest attraction to the Plaza de Ponchos is the Cotacachi-Cayapas Natural Reserve, especially the crater lake, Cuicocha. These two destinations are generally visited in combination as a day-trip excursion from Quito.

As tourist routes to Otavalo increased, so did trade paths out of the valley. The establishment of Transportes Otavalo in 1950, with a bus line that serviced Otavalo, Ibarra, and Quito, and, a decade later, of Transportes Los Lagos, with a line that ran between Otavalo, Quito, and Esmeraldas, were indicators of growing regional trade and mobility (Meisch 2002:37). These regional bus routes were precursors of a developing trade infrastructure that flourished into the presence and proliferation of shipping companies, travel agencies, exchange houses, and money transfer services beginning in the mid to late 1980s (see, for example, Meisch 2002). In 1986, the first international travel agency opened in Otavalo. Meisch (2002:113) reports that by 1995 there were nine such establishments with the dual purpose of providing services for foreign tourists and catering to Otavalan travel needs with airline ticket sales on credit, help with travel documents, money transfer services, and airfreight shipping worldwide.

According to anthropologist Jeroen Windmeijer (2001:299), among those who took advantage of these international services were the five thousand Otavaleños who lived in Europe in 1992. One-fourth of them settled in the Netherlands, with more than five hundred Otavaleños living in Amsterdam alone. They asserted such a visible presence in the city that Amsterdam came to be known affectionately as *klein* Otavalo (little Otavalo) or *het* Otavalo *van Europa* (the Otavalo of Europe). Otavaleños in the heart of Amsterdam live with their music, cuisine, native costume, Quichua language, and with the traditions of the Otavalo Valley that lies across the Atlantic Ocean. Windmeijer (2001:299) states that musicians dressed in ponchos, white trousers, sandals, and hats, and wearing long hair in a single braid have, in fact, become a familiar sight in many European cities. Communities of Otavaleños all over the globe, mostly in urban settings but also in far-flung areas, carve out cultural niches in the most diverse environments, creating spaces for the production of unique, but always recognizably Otavalan, identities.

Mobility into and out of the valley lends the communities in Imbabura a cosmopolitan air. Although exposure to foreign visitors and influences is not new to Otavalo, as even a brief history of the area reveals, international trends have certainly accelerated. For those who do not travel abroad, the world comes to them through tourists and repeat-return migrants (*viajeros*). *Viajeros* bring back impressions, experiences, souvenirs, pictures, videos, new forms of knowledge, and different languages. Even for people who have never ventured farther than the limits of Imbabura province, the names of foreign cities roll off their tongues as easily as those of neighboring hamlets. Cutting-edge telecommunications technology in the form of cellular phones and Internet access adds a virtual layer to this mobility and contributes to the sense of worldly familiarity. These technologies also allow travelers to remain connected to their home communities.

Human mobility defines geography in relational terms. In many ways, Otavalo has moved experientially closer to European and North American cities along entrepreneurial networks and through greater participation in global consumer and marketing trends. It also remains intimately connected to other forms of knowledge and experience along and across the Andean cordillera. Exchange routes that crosscut the Andes toward the east and the west have channeled both products and information from the Oriente and the Pacific Coast (see, for example, Villamarín and Villamarín 1999:652 and Salomon 1981a:192–94, 1986). Worthy of particular mention are the networks of ritual experts or *yachaks* that have historically interacted along these inter-regional corridors. Dorothea Scott Whitten's (2003:249–54) description of the multinational and multicultural nature of Ecuador's shamanic healing practices captures these patterns of interaction. Her analysis of Tigua paintings from Cotopaxi province in the Ecuadorian Sierra reveals the extraordinary syncretism of Andean and Amazonian symbolism in artistic representations of healing ceremonies.

In spite of their intense global mobility, access to land remains a priority for most Otavaleños, and not merely as a nostalgic reference to a distant homeland. Salomon (1981b:441–43) describes the emphasis on independent landownership among Otavaleños in the nineteenth century as "the only reliable and autonomous way of earning a living" and the only way to ensure "full participation in Indian society" (see also Salz 1955:198–200). The premium placed on landownership persists among Otavaleños for the same reasons today. Practices of land inheritance in the nineteenth century, with land willed from parents to children, guaranteed a parcel for each child. Salomon explains, however, that as the plots grew smaller with each generational partition, this arrangement eventually precipitated a land crisis. In response, in the middle or late nineteenth century, indigenous free peasants began buying land. By 1909, "the trend toward land buying by Indians had gone far enough to alarm the anonymous author of Otavalo's municipal history," who clearly identified indigenous investment in both land and independent labor as a path to well-being for the "Indians," and a threat to available labor for *latifundistas* (large landholders) and government projects (Salomon 1981b:442). By the 1940s Elsie Clews Parsons (1945:8) reports, "of 122 households, only 3 households are 'hacienda Indians,' tenants working out their rent on the hacienda. Economic independence is generally true of the Indians throughout the valley, who are more distinctively landowners than other mountain Indians in Ecuador."

The 1964 laws of land reform and the final abolition of the *huasipungo* system of de facto debt peonage broke up twenty-seven haciendas in the valley—all owned by whites or mestizos. This made more land available both to indigenous hacienda laborers and non-hacienda Otavalans. Meisch (2002:36) writes that two thousand hectares were distributed in Imbabura under the new law, but that, in addition, many large landholdings were voluntarily divided and distributed or sold.

Beyond the local strife, shared histories of disenfranchisement and identification with land struggles across Latin America infused this ethnic community with a broader sense of power and historical purpose. These webs of experience explain national and regional political activism revolving, to a great extent, around the unremitting quest for land. Land was a catalyst behind the institutionalization of peasant and indigenous resistance, first in the late 1920s with rise of the PSE (Ecuadorian Socialist Party) and later, in the 1940s and 1950s, with the establishment of Communist Party–backed FEI (Ecuadorian Federation of Indians) and other local peasant and indigenous cooperatives. Political involvement continued in the 1960s with Otavalan presence in FENOC (National Federation of Peasant Organizations), which focused on land reform. On the regional level Otavaleños participated in UNORCAC (Union of Peasant Organizations of Cotacachi), established in 1977, and in FICI (Indigenous and Peasant Federation of Imbabura), launched in the mid 1970s (Pallares 2002:12–14, 73–76). On the national level, indigenous activism, which as Pallares (2002) argues developed particular momentum after 1964, has resulted in the election of indigenous mayors in the late twentieth century in both Otavalo and Cotacachi, adding a new layer of empowerment and mainstream political participation for Otavaleños. National-level organizations include ECUARUNARI (Ecuadorian Indian Awakens), the first regional Indian organization in the highlands, created in 1972, and CONAIE (Confederation of Indigenous Nationalities of Ecuador), which led an unprecedented national indigenous uprising in 1990, subsequent uprisings in 1992 and 1994, and created in 1995 a viable political party—Pachakutik-Nuevo País (Pallares 2002:17–69).

The most visible political posts occupied by Otavaleños include Mario Conejo Maldonado, who was voted mayor of Otavalo in 2000 and reelected in 2004. That same year, native anthropologist Luis Enrique Cachiguango was elected as a member of the Otavalo city council. Auki Tituaña Males became mayor of Cotacachi in 1996, and was reelected with overwhelming (80 percent) support from both indigenous and mestizo constituents for a second four-year term in 2000, and a third term in 2004. Tituaña Males was courted as a presidential candidate by the indigenous political party, Pachakutik-Nuevo País, in 2006. José Manuel Quimbo became elected provincial counselor (*consejero*) to the governor of Imbabura in 2003. Other local leaders that stand out include Blanca Chancoso, Carmelina Yamerla, and Pedro de la Cruz. On the national level, Otavaleña Nina Conejo Pacari Vega became vice president of the National Congress in 1998. She served as foreign minister (*canciller*) in 2001, during the early stages of Lucio Gutiérrez Borbúa's presidency. Currently she is a member of the permanent forum of the United Nations.

As Rudi Colloredo-Mansfeld (1999:28) notes, Otavaleños have "use[d] material culture as a social medium to produce networks of identity and power." These nonfinancial resources have also played a critical role, Kyle (1999:424) argues, in motivating many Otavaleños to become independent merchants, and in developing "the *expectation* that they would succeed on a global scale." However, the same circumstances that have brought exceptional achievement to some have planted the seeds of unequal opportunity for others. An anecdote from Colloredo-Mansfeld's (1999:223–24) epilogue captures the uneven modernization that has taken place within this ethnic community:

> "What is the third world?" asks an Otavalan international merchant from the community of lower Ariasucu, east of Otavalo, where Colloredo-Mansfeld lived and conducted extended fieldwork. After careful deliberation, Colloredo-Mansfeld replies, "When people use the term, they usually are talking about places where people do not have water, where many babies die when they are small, where people do not have electricity." He pauses and then adds, referring to the neighboring community 500 meters up the path, "Many people would think upper Ariasucu is the Third World." Colloredo-Mansfeld reports that this answer amazed and upset his friend. "Really?" she asked, "In upper Ariasucu they do not have electricity? Are you sure?"

The contrast of Otavalan experiences is wide-ranging and pronounced, not just based on diversity generated by global possibility but also on differences produced by historical, economic, racializing structures in place that constrain or deny opportunity. Dramatic changes locally, nationally, and internationally in terms of mobility, economy, politics, and social relations redefined the Ecuadorian social terrain in the twenty-first century. Changes at a national level have included momentous sociopolitical shifts brought about by the upsurge of national indigenous movements throughout the 1990s led primarily by CONAIE (Confederation of Indigenous Nationalities of Ecuador), Ecuador's most important first-tier indigenous organization; political instability leading to three presidential ousters between 1995 and 2005; economic instability marked by high rates of devaluation; and currency transition to the dollar in 2000, which initially resulted in exorbitant inflation and led to mass emigration of skilled laborers and professionals.

The complexity of "cultural dynamics in the vortex of globalized power" (N. Whitten 2003:xiv) requires a rethinking of previously assumed underpinnings of Otavaleño identity. As intraethnic class divisions, such as those described by Colloredo-Mansfeld, reveal contrasts in quality of living among Otavaleños and expose social rifts in the collective experience of the community, identifying new axes of cultural affinity and collective representation becomes essential to understanding a persisting unified Otavalan ethnic identity.

Theories, Analysts, and the Unending Struggle for the Possession of the Sign

A resurgence of indigenous cultural politics characterized the end of the twentieth century and beginning of the new millennium in Ecuador (Whitten, Whitten, and Chango 2003, D. Whitten 2003). As sites of cultural production and public signification, dramatic performances emerged as heavily contested realms. As Otavaleños vie for control over these symbolic spaces and their interpretation, academic studies attempt to elucidate what precisely is at stake in this "unending struggle for the possession of the sign" (Comaroff 1985:196).

Scholarly debates reveal varied, and sometimes frustrated, attempts to capture the significance of ritual and communicate its inner workings. For a comprehensive overview of theories of ritual, readers should refer to Rappaport (1999). My position on ritual practices among Otavaleños is that they are reflexive performances through which people represent the world they live in to themselves in an effort to understand it. This interpretation coincides with Barbara Butler's (2006:87) understanding of "mental complexes that people in groups use to help them interpret real changes in a way that preserves a sense of meaning and continuity in a changing society." Butler goes on to situate her perspective in reference to literature on cultural schemas (Ortner 1990), dominant metaphors (Ohnuki-Tierney 1990), and cosmological axioms (Rappaport 1999).

As signifying practices, moreover, rituals demonstrate a capacity for producing culture and not just reflecting it. In the section that follows, I explain the relevance of a theoretical frame that emerges from my ethnographic observations, namely that of festival complexes and ritual seasons. Building on other scholarly literature on the subject, I show the value of this heuristic for understanding ritual in the Otavalo area as layered symbolic experience and sustained reflexive practice.

Ritual Seasons and Festival Complexes

Celebrations throughout the calendar year operate in interconnected and progressive fashion, reinforcing open and expressive communication as a general principle and developing a unique style of interaction among Otavaleños. Rather than representing "time out of time" (Falassi 1987) my observation is that festive rituals in Imbabura constitute prolonged periods of symbolic engagement. This suggestion challenges previously held ideas about indigenous festivals and public ritual—namely the notion that annual rituals are bounded events that punctuate the calendar. In the case of Imbabura the frequency of ritual celebrations, the extended duration of each occasion (ranging from several days to several weeks), the geographical displacement of ritual and festival events, and the overlap of various celebrations within a single context render it more accurate to think of these events in terms of ritual seasons and festival complexes. I designate festival complexes as the broader, multivocal settings wherein ritual practices (often several overlapping within a single festival frame) take place. The term "festive rituals" serves as shorthand for capturing the jovial dimension of the original concept of public feasts and underlining the extended duration and multifaceted organization of the examples I present.

Reference to Michel-Rolph Trouillot's scholarship on historical silencings highlights the significance of this proposed theoretical frame. In an analysis of the Haitian Revolution, Trouillot (1995:83) points out the tendencies of those in power to trivialize manifestations of subordinate groups by treating each historical instance separately and consequently draining it of its political content. His insight lends itself to an observation of similar hegemonic dispositions toward containing ritual expressions by defining them as temporally brief and thematically disconnected (from each other as well as from their social context). Oversimplification of ritual practices silences the political and social weight of the emerging frame of experience and action they represent collectively.

Festivals have historically been thought of as social releases that alleviate the drudgery of daily life and provide a temporary escape from labor and exploitative working conditions. An article published in *El Mercurio,* a daily Ecuadorian newspaper, in 1990 attests to this disposition prevailing today: "Organized dance, parades and costumes are clearly evasions of reality; for three or four days the world of fantasy displaces the world of reality, common workers and laborers feel like princes and princesses . . ." (*El Mercurio* 1990). Several indigenous people I interviewed in 1995, in fact, also conceived of festivals as an opportunity to drown social and personal frustrations in alcohol and dance, and as a day to unwind, as they put it, from the other 364 days of oppression.

The euphoria of the festival, excessive drinking, dizzying round and round dancing, temporary reversal of roles, assumed identities through costume, and the excitement of festival commotion build toward a convincing explanation of Otavalan festivals as "safety release valves" for social tension. From a hegemonic perspective, occasional festivals ensured smoother operation of the system of production and social relations the rest of the year. In fact, as Edgar Patricio Guerrero Arias (1991:73) writes, on numerous occasions in Ecuadorian history the festival was actually encouraged and even funded by large landholders who found it advantageous to inebriate the masses and distract the peasants from the injustices of their social and economic situation. (See also Thurner 2000:362–64.)

Strategic use of festivals for social control clearly operated under the assumption that these cultural practices are self-contained and containable events. Bakhtin's (1984:147) analysis of the festival world as topsy-turvy, however, invites us to consider that because the scope of carnivalesque events makes daily life seem so strange, it "forces one to understand and evaluate ordinary life in a new way (in the light of another glimpsed possibility)." During festivals, indigenous people, who are normally subjected to strict hierarchical divisions, engage in more familiar interaction with each other and with local mestizos. Disguise and alcohol play a central role in breaking down ethnic and class barriers. Indigenous peasants who under normal circumstances may speak barely audibly to a white *patrón,* will voice their opinions and playfully tease someone from a higher economic class under the cover of their festival masks and disguised high-pitched voices. Similarly, alcohol softens social divisions as *copitas* (little drinks) are offered by everyone and to everyone in a gesture of fraternity. The less inhibited, albeit drunk, exchange that results extends the potential for people to transcend, if only momentarily, the bounds of their social spheres. As Barbara Butler (2006:92, 95) eloquently describes, "strong alcohol is favored by humans and spirits for its animating, boundary-erasing, and contractual properties" wherein accepting a drink "creates specially interdependent relationships." Most important, the festival generates an environment that allows "working out, in a concretely sensuous, half-real and half-play-acted form, a new mode of interrelationship between individuals counterposed to the all-powerful socio-hierarchical relationships of non carnival life" (Bakhtin 1984:123).

The danger of this, which colonial authorities eventually began to recognize, is that, as Guerrero Arias (1991:74) observes, indigenous festivals promoted "a critical evaluation of reality . . . that was not satisfied with simply ridiculing the hard life, but instead sought to transform it." The real threat posed by the world turned upside down is not the temporary chaos or reversals it provokes, but the distinct and identifiable alternative to hegemonic order it suggests. Though a revolutionary vector may not be inherent to carnivalesque events (Bakhtin 1984), as Stallybrass and White (1986:14) express, given the presence of sharpened political antagonism, "cyclical ritual with no noticeable politically transformative effects . . . may often act as a catalyst and site of actual and symbolic struggle." This explains, perhaps, why public festivals were violently suppressed at some points in history and ignored at others.

Ecuadorian anthropologist Segundo Moreno Yánez (1996:410) offers historical accounts of increasing prohibitions and censorship of public indigenous festivals in Ecuador throughout the eighteenth and nineteenth centuries. Moreno Yánez argues that colonial authorities eventually recognized that the revitalization of certain festival performances could give way to subversive activity. After an uprising in 1778 in Guano, Chimborazo province, for instance, authorities prohibited "that in the festivals or other indigenous functions, anyone represent the *'Inga'* as a remembrance of a gentile indigenous past or other serious inconveniences that should be avoided."[1] Three years later, as part of the conviction against José Gabriel Tupac Amaru, leader of a millenarian movement that claimed one hundred thousand lives in the southern Andes, Inspector José Antonio de Areche imposed a similar prohibition on all provinces of meridional America that called for a complete suppression of "comedies or other public functions of the type that the Indians use to remember their ancient Incas. . . ." (Moreno Yánez 1996:411).[2]

Ritual and other forms of cultural expression received increasing attention as it became evident they not only constituted sites of social release but battlegrounds of ideology and consciousness. James C. Scott (1985) has defined them as "hidden transcripts" or the "infrapolitics" of subaltern groups—low-profile forms of ideological resistance that work effectively as alternatives to open confrontation. Rumor, gossip, folktales, jokes, songs, rituals, codes, and euphemisms fall under the "subordinate group politics of disguise and anonymity" that take place in public view but are designed to have a double meaning or to shield the identity of the actors (Scott 1990:19). The significance of hidden transcripts, according to Kertzer (1988) and Stallybrass and White (1986), lies in the eventual implications these processes have for what lies *beyond* the ritual sphere.

The extended temporal reference of ritual seasons allows us to ponder the cumulative consequence of ritual performances. In addition, this vantage point accounts for the periodic interruptions of quotidian life. It reveals an oscillating rhythm between ritual and everyday life that evokes a discerning outlook on the relevance of ritual within and beyond the performance sphere. Attentiveness to the layering of events within the frame of festival complexes, moreover, draws attention to the range of interrelated ritual and nonritual activities at play as a thick environment of interpretation and action comes into focus.

Disrupting the Dominant Narrative

Beyond official government bans on public activity, Trouillot's (1995) analysis addresses the discursive strategies of suppression deployed by hegemonic groups. Turning his attention to historiography as the process by which historical narratives are written and legitimated, Trouillot (1995:96) discusses formulas of erasure and formulas of banalization. The first method of silencing deletes historical facts and events simply by omitting them from documentation, while formulas of banalization "tend to empty a number of singular events of their revolutionary content so that the entire string of facts, gnawed from all sides, becomes trivialized." Accounts that consistently depict festivals as chaotic rather than democratic, as dissonant or cacophonous instead of multivocal, fall under these categories of discursive erasure and banalization.

A national obsession with *rescate cultural* (cultural rescue) is one example of how a dynamic of cultural banalization unfolds in the context of Ecuador. Vibrant cultures are reduced to collectable artifacts, and in turn these objects are isolated from their cultural context in a national mission to preserve and protect "cultural products behind glass museum cases from adulterations of the modern world in the name of 'cultural rescue' " (García Canclini 1995:156). Appreciation of indigenous expression is projected as a function of preserving customs unchanged. The experientially rich and symbolically complex realm of ritual is reduced to a handful of repetitive elements. This perspective both minimizes appreciation of indigenous practices and distorts a conceptual understanding of ritual.

Though ritual may be defined by a conservation of form, as Armstrong (1971), Rasnake (1988), Turner (1985), and Whitten (1981) affirm, the production of new cultural meaning based on a generative tension between continuity and change stands in mutual interdependence with it. Dillon and Abercrombie (1988:73) assert that highly structured symbolic forms like myth and ritual are, in fact, anything but conservative forces as people generate new meaning with every ritual production (Tambiah 1985:123–24, Turner 1985). As Bell (1992:123) summarizes, tradition exists "because it is constantly produced and reproduced, pruned for a clear profile, and softened to absorb revitalizing elements."

In spite of these and other analyses that have focused attention on the generative aspects of cultural expression (Botero 1991; Crain 1989; Crespi 1981; Dirks 1994; Guerrero Arias 1991; Kertzer 1988; Mendoza 2000; Scott 1985, 1990; Stallybrass and White 1986; Turner 1974, 1985, 1995 [1969]; Whitten 1981; Whitten and Whitten 1993; Whitten, Whitten, and Chango 1997) tendencies toward a *rescate cultural* of indigenous artifacts, products, and traditions as described by García Canclini (1995) persist in the discourse of both the Ecuadorian general public and the state.[3] Local hegemonic (both indigenous and mestizo) appropriations of cultural performances as means to political ends manifest a similar propensity toward reifying culture. Capitalist market pressures to render native traditions collectable commodities at the level of global marketing and consumption further threaten to trivialize ritual. It is in this context that indigenous attempts toward cultural resignification come to the fore.

Theories and Methods—Discourse, Symbolism, and Semiotics

Acts of satire, parody, imaginative reenactment, symbolic inversion, and rites of historical reversal are effective to varying degrees in defying structural silencings. These practices expose inconsistencies in institutionalized histories and undermine the possibility of deniability in official accounts (Trouillot 1995). As "each performance becomes a record, a means of explanation" (Turner 1985:301), it constitutes a counterassault on hegemonic narratives. The public reflexivity implicit in performance as "social drama" renders it "a kind of collective autobiograph[y] . . . a means by which a group creates its identity by telling itself a story about itself" (Turner and Bruner 1986:40).

Beyond their appeal as alternative representational narratives, the importance of symbolic and semiotic forms lies in their antistructural capacity (Turner 1985). These forms do not simply present a different version of human experience but suggest a different approach to the *production* of knowledge and understanding altogether. The "irreducibly plural" and "inherently paradoxical" (Geertz 1986:378) character of ritual through symbolic and semiotic meaning-making processes challenges the very authority of linear, discursive history as representational narrative. It broadens the parameters of admissible expression and representation, and advances through generalized experience the cultural institutions that allow for the proliferation of alternative expressions. In doing so, it confronts analysts with the task of redefining theories and methods for documenting, understanding, and representing emergent forms of cultural knowledge.

This continual process of theory making is critical, cumulative, and dialogical, involving academics (both past and present) in conversation with one another and with nonacademics. At its best it reflects interdisciplinary

collaboration. Most important, the evolving theoretical and methodological endeavor is productive insofar as it remains grounded in what people
actually do in the contexts we study. Ultimately, theory and methodology
remain heuristic devices. Though they are useful in elucidating some aspects
of culture, favoring one perspective sometimes tends to obscure others. The
chapters in this book render transparent the application of different theoretical approaches, considering the benefits and shortfalls of each. My inquiry
into human and otherworldly dialogical relations in ritual and festival context
reveals three principal analytical strategies: discursive, symbolic, and semiotic.
All three provide distinct insight into the formation of Otavalan collective
identities. One in particular, namely semiotics, the study of the interpretation of signs, emerges from this evaluative process as especially useful for
understanding ritual as embodied experience and action.

In the epilogue to the book *Anthropology of Experience* edited by Edward
Bruner and the late Victor Turner, Clifford Geertz (1986:373) suggests that
the job of the ethnographer is "all a matter of scratching surfaces." He en-
dorses an approach to human experience as legible performance, text, and
narrative. While contributors to this book capture the generative quality of
performance, they also reveal a reluctance to explore questions of emotion
and intuition that lie beyond the discursive and cognitive realm of representation. It seems to me that the thing to consider is not *that* we scratch at the
surface of human experience but *how* we scratch at it. Scholars in the fields of
ethnomusicology and psychology have made important inroads in explicating
experience as experience, not as text or definitional narrative. They have not
only provided a theory that admits the possibility of describing experience
but have actually presented us with powerful methodologies for its analysis.
I draw predominantly on two theorists, ethnomusicologist Thomas Turino
and cognitive psychologist Michael Bamberg.

Ethnomusicologist Thomas Turino follows Charles Peirce's nineteenth-
century theory on the interpretation of signs. Peircian semiotics extends an
understanding of signs beyond verbal language to include images, sounds,
gestures, and objects. As such, it is a useful theory for analyzing richly
layered performances that appeal to all of the senses. For Peirce, the meaning of signs derives from their interpretation by a subsequent thought or
action (Hoopes 1991:7). In other words, signs—including feelings, perceptions, experiences—are not self-evident in and of themselves but rather yield
meaning only through an interpretive process. Signs, moreover, function as
part of semiotic sign-systems and not in isolation (Chandler 2002:2). Also

important for the analysis at hand, Peirce's model equates thought with feeling and action, rendering experience just as "real" (and hence, just as "studiable") as seemingly more tangible aspects of society (Hoopes 1991:9). Semiotics scratches at the surface of affective human capacities and focuses an understanding of symbolic performances, such as rituals, not as reflections *about* or representations *of,* but as actual *processes of* lived experience. Turino (1999:226–29, 234–37) describes the mechanisms behind semiotic chaining processes and shows how they sustain an underlying structure, which is provisional but also progressive. Turino's perspective resonates with my framing of ritual seasons and festival complexes to demonstrate how meaning making unfolds through the cumulative process of Otavalan experience. Semiotic analysis intersects with local emphases on ritual as practice emergent from lived experience and engages ritual as an affective encounter with otherworldly beings.

Michael Bamberg's (1983:138–41) concept of cognitive scaffolding in the development of play frames among small children sheds additional light on sequences of joint signification in ritual interaction. Bamberg observes that participation in social activities requires the spontaneous negotiation of parameters of behavior and action that will allow for coherent communication. With each successive involvement, participants are more likely to develop novel "metaphoric conceptualizations" and increasingly complex interpretive frames. Bamberg (1983:140) writes that this creative and collaborative process is interwoven with the activity of establishing and elaborating interpersonal relationships (intimacy) and with the affective processes of social appraisal (shared understanding).

Combined, Turino's and Bamberg's theories provide essential analytical tools for appreciating both novel and enduring forms of cultural expression, sentiment, and knowledge. Their unique contribution to an evolving understanding of collective performance, experience, and processes of signification unfolds in more detail in the chapters that lie ahead. Immediately following, we remain in Uku Pacha and squarely within a discursive realm of interaction to look at the logistical difficulties behind the production of Otavalan festivals. This example exposes the nature of dialogical interaction in the human realm and reveals the complexity, diversity, and contradiction of the "irreducibly plural" expression and opinion within a community. As a precursor to a discussion on ritual, this section alerts us to the context of broader social circumstances, enduring relations, and politics that frame symbolic and semiotic practices.

Return of the Migrants

In this chapter I consider the complexities involved in planning an annual festival known as Pawkar Raymi, and look at the various types of discourse that emerge in the multivocal spaces that the festival generates. The nature of dialogue among people reveals diversity of opinion, but also creative processes of consensus building necessary for working toward a common objective and living with difference. Here I focus on discursive practices of gossip, rumor, collaborative storytelling, joint conceptualization of ideas, problem solving, small talk, and conflict resolution. In addition to interactions during the Pawkar Raymi, my analysis considers organizing efforts that take place before the festival, and lingering social and political consequences that unfold after the event. A glimpse at the behind-the-scenes production of the Pawkar Raymi reveals how festival events are embedded in broader social circumstances, enduring relations, and politics that span both local and global exchanges.

Myth of the Eternal Return

The Pawkar Raymi, also known as Carnaval Indígena, has a migrating date and takes place either in late February or early March. The festival officially celebrates the tasseling of the maize and coincides with fruit and flower festivals and the extended carnival season of water fights nationwide. Though the festival evokes token elements of traditional agricultural celebrations, it more emphatically signals another event that has become a prominent annual occurrence in the Otavalo and Cotacachi area—the return of the migrants.

The Pawkar Raymi takes place annually as a sports competition and cultural event in the town of Peguche, a community of about five thousand people situated five minutes north of the city of Otavalo by bus. Peguche is characterized by a cosmopolitan atmosphere, which derives, in part, from a regular stream of foreign visitors and that a significant percentage of its population, both male and female, travels seasonally. Community members calculate that as many as 70 percent of the people in Peguche have international experience and that an estimated 25 percent are generally abroad at any given time. Every year, international Pegucheño entrepreneurs return en masse for the Pawkar Raymi. Though the festival is an occasion for welcoming travelers home on the part of relatives and friends who stay behind, it is, in fact, the migrants themselves who often orchestrate this event. Their participation in the production of the Pawkar Raymi adds another dimension to the intricacies of communication across generation gaps and divergent experiences.

Analysis of this festival draws attention to two tendencies, often perceived as paradoxes, that surface persistently in ethnographic examples of contemporary Andean public celebrations. The first refers to the simultaneous celebration of unity and production of diversity in festive rituals. Though organization and production of the Pawkar Raymi require an exercise in consensus building, programming for the event consciously promotes multivocality. Each year, the festival takes on the creation of increasingly diverse and inclusive activities that not only enfold gender, age, and ethnic differences but allow for their reflexive development as actual and conceptual social categories. In the case of this local event with global reach, moreover, partaking in the festival extends to virtual spaces of conversation and involvement through the Internet across an eclectic transnational community. In the example of the Pawkar Raymi, fostering unity and promoting diversity are inherently connected.

The second contrastive relationship addresses continuity and change. Though the Pawkar Raymi is a recent tradition, social networks set in motion for its production are well established. In this chapter, I explore the ways by which existing values, aesthetics, and formulas for social interaction are reconfigured in light of new perspectives, technologies, and financial possibilities brought into play by a generation of Otavaleños with increasing international exposure. As an examination of the festival reveals, compromises are not always seamless. Tensions that arise, nonetheless, often give way to productive conversations about the expectations of traditional practices and the appeal of modern opportunities. Public reflection on continuity and change grapples with implications of the uninterrupted presence of both influences in the everyday lives of Otavaleños. Cultural transformation and social reproduction, as Norman Whitten (1981:23) advocates, must be understood within a unified frame of reference.

The Pawkar Raymi is an apt example for exploring these framing questions given the festival's development against the unique backdrop of local and global processes combined. In this chapter, I begin by describing local social and political circumstances surrounding the Pawkar Raymi and discussing, in this context, some of the challenges of festival production apparent from the onset. I then address the inner workings of event planning and implementation through traditional and expanding social networks. Ethnographic detail in the third part of the chapter illustrates some of the global expectations and local pressures festival organizers face. Finally, I consider how demands from outside of the community, and especially from within, influence a conscious production of moral discourses and egalitarian rhetoric surrounding the festival. The analysis outlines the fragile and inconstant nature of community as process and describes public festivals as contexts for the formation of increasingly complex and emerging social identities.

Brief History of a Recent Tradition

A carnival event centered on an annual soccer competition existed in Peguche in the mid 1960s under the sponsorship of local organizers and enthusiasts. The tournament eventually disappeared, mainly owing to lack of sustainable sponsorship.[1] It resurfaced somewhat transformed in 1995 as Carnaval Indígena and acquired its designation as Pawkar Raymi in 1999. The name of the festival requires some explanation given its allusion to millenarian roots. One festival organizer commented that, "previous to 1999 no one really knew what Pawkar Raymi meant or that, as it turns out, this was a term used throughout Latin America." Today, if one inquires about the meaning of the name, many are likely to contextualize the festival as one of the four Andean *raymis* (ritual feasts)—Inti Raymi, Kulla Raymi, Kapak Raymi, and Pawkar Raymi. This explanation is widely accepted in the region and promoted actively as a historical and cultural interpretive frame for various festivals. Given the extensive travels of the Otavaleños, it is not surprising that certain terms that resonate with local ideals find their way into local discourse. What is clear is that the concept of *raymis* has been borrowed rather unproblematically from Peruvian and Bolivian sources on Inka cultural practices. Notably, this language of *raymis* pertains to the politics of discourse at a particular juncture of intensifying ethnic identity claims in Ecuador. In

Peguche and elsewhere in the Otavalo Valley, Quichua names are used in all sorts of contexts to supplant imposed Spanish designations.

Awareness of this espousal of nonlocal terms alerts us to historical distortions sometimes echoed in the communities regarding the origin of traditional practices. These borrowings, nonetheless, are viable because to some extent they resonate with regional idiosyncrasies. Although the four *raymis* may not be local traditions, observance of the solstices and equinoxes and the agricultural feasts that accompany these occasions is. Tom Zuidema's (1992:18–20) ethnohistorical research provides evidence of this, as does Parsons's (1945:103) investigation. A superimposition of the two sets of events reveals a temporal coincidence of *raymis,* solstices, and equinoxes:

Table of Raymis, Solstices, and Equinoxes

Pawkar Raymi	March 20	Spring Equinox
Inti Raymi	June 21	Summer Solstice
Kulla Raymi	September 22	Fall Equinox
Kapak Raymi	December 21	Winter Solstice

As a modern sports event, Pawkar Raymi explicitly falls into the category of discursive maneuvering toward ethnic self-affirmation. It exhibits few ties to the agricultural and seasonal observations mentioned above, elements of which are more obvious in Inti Raymi and Kulla Raymi celebrations as practiced in Imbabura. Within the broader discursive trend toward valorizing indigenous culture, manipulation of millenarian terms announces a changing social and political tide.

Use of the term Tumay-Pacha (blessing of the earth) in conjunction with Pawkar Raymi, for instance, is recent. *Yachak* and native anthropologist Luis Enrique Cachiguango (2004) asserts in an online article that the practice of reciprocating blessings with flowers and water is an "ancestral tradition" of indigenous communities. The article presents the concurrent celebration of the national Carnaval and the blessing of the earth with flowers and water as a coincidence (not a syncretism). The author, who in this context signs off under his local nickname, "Katsa" Kachiwango, stakes his analysis on a claim of self-interpretation (*autointerpretación*) from the perspective of the protagonists. This self-ascribed authority allows him to imply that the practice of Tumay-Pacha has been recovered from a millenarian past. Cachiguango goes on to commend the mixing of sports with the "profound rituality of the Tumay" in Peguche, taking this as evidence of an "authentic collective expression that affirms the value of ancestral identity alongside modern values and reflects Andean openness to and 'andeanization' of foreign elements, which in turn reveals that native peoples walk at the rhythm of the times . . . while carrying with them elements that characterize them as a community with a unique identity. . . ." (Cachiguango 2004).

Anthropologist Kristine Latta (personal communication, 2/2007) suggests that Tumay-Pacha may correspond to an indigenous intellectual interpretation, while *tumarina* is the term she heard consistently used to refer to the cleansing ceremony.[2] During my research in 2001 the ceremony with flowers and water performed for the opening ceremony was referred to as *ñawi mayllay* (the washing of the face, hands, and feet with water and flowers often performed as a cleansing ceremony at weddings). All three of these terms gesture toward local references. Their insertion into festival rhetoric indicates a conscious correction of the initial appropriation of the Inka designation and a more nuanced assertion of local identity within the politics of discourse. It is significant that in the 2004 publicity materials, reference to the Spanish expletive, "Carnaval Indígena," all but disappeared.

Explanations on the OtavalosOnLine Web site acknowledge that the Pawkar Raymi is, in fact, a recent tradition, but a necessary one nonetheless, and that, as such, it requires conceptual framing compatible with the perspective of its protagonists. Rather than debating the validity of different claims on cultural authenticity, my interest lies in exploring people's impulse to "ritualize" secular activities (Bell 1992) in the context of evolving moral and political identity discourses.

A New Tradition—Overcoming Skepticism

The situation that prompted Pegucheños to revive the festival in 1995 was a confrontation with the neighboring community of Agato. Agato, a longtime rival of Peguche, organized a soccer tournament in March of every year. When the team from Peguche attempted to register for the 1995 competition, the organizing committee in Agato declined their application. Irked by the rejection, a small group of young Pegucheños decided to organize a tournament of their own. Though early emphasis centered on soccer, the festival grew to encompass other sports including men's and women's basketball, Ecuavolley (a unique form of volleyball played throughout Ecuador), and, beginning in 2001, a cross-country downhill bicycle race. In 1998 a cultural night was added to the event, featuring traditional music and dance numbers that celebrated indigenous multicultural expression from all regions of Ecuador. Today the cultural aspect of the Pawkar Raymi includes presentations every night of the weeklong festival spotlighting acclaimed national and international artists.

A number of people I interviewed stated that the organization of the Carnaval Indígena in 1995 was the first time that young Pegucheños had attempted to launch an initiative of their own. They commented that people of the older generation were skeptical that members of the community lacking in social status could convoke public support and produce a successful community event. Typically, individuals gain status in their communities once they are married and can assume, as a couple, a series of ritual obligations and sponsorships known as festival *cargos*. Breaking with traditional expectations of the *cargo* succession meant that the festival organizers would have to overcome doubts from within the community itself. Latta (personal communication, 2/2007) adds that original festival organizers were closely tied to a particular generation of indigenous intellectuals who tended to see cultural and community initiatives as part of a broader political project. This, along with patterns of wealth accumulation distinct from those of previous generations, set them apart as a progressive group within the community.

This challenge to tradition exposed organizers to criticism from outside the community as well. Alternatives pursued for funding the event, in particular, led to significant reproach. Rather than seeking the backing of a single *prioste* (*fiesta* sponsor) under a traditional *fiesta cargo* system, the new organizers went "knocking on doors." In other words, they solicited corporate sponsorship in the city of Otavalo. Roberto Lema, president of the festival organizing committee in 2000, estimated that, thanks to outside sponsorship, less than 5 percent of the festival's cost came from the community's own pockets. That Pegucheños themselves did not carry the burden of the cost was exploited by Agateños as a weakness and used to disparage Peguche's reputation. Agateños qualified this fund-raising initiative as an act of asking for charity and chided Pegucheños for resorting to "begging." In chapter 5 I discuss at greater length the stigma within indigenous communities about begging—an activity considered undignified and generally reserved for impoverished mestizos. Agato's accusation played on traditional expectations that festival organizers overextend themselves financially to the point of substantial debt with kin and fictive kin as part of a social and moral obligation to the community. In addition, the criticism carried racial undertones implying that Pegucheños were somehow acting like mestizos, alerting us to an ethnically inscribed moral discourse on behavior.

External pressures such as these contribute as much to shaping a sense of collective identity in Peguche as internal mechanisms toward building solidarity. Mario Conejo Cotacachi, president of the festival organizing committee in 2002, expressed that while there is division on a regular basis among the eight neighborhoods that conform Peguche, "one of the elements of the Pawkar Raymi has been drawing everyone in. It can be monetary participation, or administrative, or collaboration with *mingas* (work parties). The fact of being Pegucheño means people will say, 'yes, I will participate in this activity.' " The sense of solidarity, according to Mario, comes, at least in part, from the competitive relationship with Agato. "In the presence of an enemy, whomever that may be, Peguche unites. Then there are no boundaries among the neighborhoods; only solidarity," he explained. The sense of enthusiasm, general participation, and local pride surrounding production of the event was palpable when I attended the Pawkar Raymi in 1999 and 2001. Mario's statement, nonetheless, underscores the circumstantial nature of community as it is defined by affiliations in flux and shifting strategic positions among groups, neighborhoods, and individuals subsumed under the encompassing labels of Pegucheño, Otavaleño, or *indígena*.

Criticism from outside the community and from within, at least on these points, eventually faded as the success of the festival, predicated on its progressive organization, financing, and management became apparent. In fact, by 2005, Agato had begun competing with Peguche for corporate sponsorships.

Building Community

Project-centered interaction provides the kernel for the formation of complex group identities. Political philosopher Michael Walzer (1994:189) states that it is "in the context of associational activity [that] individuals learn to deliberate, argue, make decisions, and take responsibility." He goes on to observe that positive planning experiences generate individuals who are stronger, more confident, and more savvy for having participated in a common undertaking, and through it developed a responsibility to and for other people. Michael Bamberg (1983:140) adds that through shared experiences and joint metaphoric conceptualizations (essentially, imagining and organizing an event together) people develop a sense of intimacy. As they frame their interaction in terms of shared understanding, participants generate initiatives and outcomes that can be interpreted as cooperative bids, wherein people become personally invested in a joint proposal. Bamberg (1983:141) sees this dynamic sequence as the necessary underpinning for the development of social identities.

The annual repetition of festival events such as the Pawkar Raymi, in addition, contributes to a "scaffolding process" (Bamberg 1983:155) wherein successive experiences build upon prior understandings, enabling an evolution of joint ideas. The process requires imaginative effort both in expression and understanding as people meet half way in the formulation of a collaborative vision. Pegucheños draw on a variety of resources for talking across difference. Creative use of language including code-switching between Quichua and Spanish and the incorporation of imported terms like "el marketing," "los posters," "la página web," "los cheques travél," "cash," and "el parking," facilitate the process. As Pegucheños work through the challenges of implementing new ideas, communicating artistic and musical concepts, defining aesthetic taste, and incorporating innovative technologies for the festival, they effectively "organize themselves into stable and cohesive groups and find ways of resolving their differences among themselves in a civic manner" (Forment 2003:21). In other words, they begin to imagine themselves as and to act like a community.

The growing popularity of the Pawkar Raymi has come to define this event as a trademark of the community of Peguche. Surrounding communities have, in addition, followed suit with Pawkar events of their own modeled on the programming and organization of the original Pawkar Raymi "Peguche Tio." Roberto Lema remarked that as of 2005 he had seen the development of Pawkar Raymi Agato, Pawkar Raymi Pinsaquí, Pawkar Raymi Ilumán, and Pawkar Raymi San Pablo, among others. The festival itself is not what defines collective identities in any of these places. As I argue here, following Walzer (1994) and Bamberg (1983), it is the process of *organizing* the event that contributes to the development of community.

The Pawkar Raymi Peguche Tio is a product of resourcefulness, innovation, transformation, and openness to new ideas. Its success derives partially from a reconciliation of innovative economic infrastructure and novel aesthetic manifestations with an emphasis on enduring traditional reciprocal obligations. Whether it is on a local or an international level, calling in favors for the Pawkar Raymi commits individuals to long-term entanglement in webs of favor granting and social obligation. In some ways, this is not far removed from the social dynamics involved in passing the *cargo,* revealing the persistence of traditional elements in the context of innovative approaches. Personal ties developed to produce the event ultimately reinforce social networks in the community, thickening an overall relational matrix. The networking means to obtain the festival ends turn out to be important ends in themselves.

Pegucheño Networks—Six Degrees of Separation

Extraordinary human resources operating through carefully maintained formal and informal social networks ultimately drive the Pawkar event. In 2001 the Pawkar Raymi Peguche Tio organizing committee experimented with the use of *organigramas* (planning diagrams), arguing the effectiveness of a bureaucratic-administrative infrastructure for both ensuring a successful event and projecting an image of indigenous managerial aptitude. Most festival business (as is the case with business of any kind in Peguche), nevertheless, continued to take place on the soccer field, in the plaza, and especially around the Ecuavolley courts—a noticeably male-dominated sphere. The shared sentiment among Pegucheños in 2001 was that successful event management is best accomplished by asking friends for favors and soliciting voluntary collaboration.

Immediate ties are the bedrock of all Pegucheño networks. Kin and extended kin connections developed over the course of many generations draw people into long-term reciprocal engagements. These networks are generally extensive in themselves. As information and resources travel efficiently along friendship and kin lines locally and internationally, they reveal that community networking paths among Pegucheños are well worn and reliable. Coordination of the Pawkar Raymi taps into this powerful resource as organizers lean heavily on family, extended kin, and friends in the community to carry out organizational tasks.

Six Degrees of Separation is a 1994 film directed by Fred Schepisi that reflects on the notion that everyone in the world is connected to everyone else through a relational chain of six other people. In the social network analysis lingo of J. Clyde Mitchell (1969) this would be the equivalent of "reachability," a concept that refers to the ability of all people to contact one another through a limited number of steps. Network analyst John Scott (2000 [1991]:32) qualifies the coherence of a relational chain in terms of "how easy is it, for example, for gossip, ideas, or resources to be diffused through the network." Evidence of the strength of networks in Peguche is best exemplified in the fact that festival committee presidents in various years coordinated planning of the Pawkar Raymi from abroad. Committee presidents in 1998, 2000, and 2001 were absent from the community during most of their terms. Several factors contribute to effective networking among Pegucheños and give us insight into how these relational webs unfold, especially across international distances.

Regular long-distance communication by telephone, Internet, or through fellow travelers coming and going from the community facilitates festival logistics. Telephones, which were uncommon in indigenous homes when I first visited in 1995, are now a regular household item. Cellular phones are particularly suited to the lifestyles of indigenous businessmen and businesswomen on the go. The proliferation of telecommunication has certainly made local interactions easier, but in most households landline phones are used for international calls.[3] Word often travels more quickly to the Otavalo Valley from Europe than it does between towns in adjacent Imbaburan cantons. On average, the households I frequented in Peguche, Ilumán, and Otavalo received three or more international calls per week. Relatively affordable calling cards make it feasible for some travelers to phone home on a daily basis. In addition to coordinating the shipment of merchandise one way and electronic money transfers to relatives in the other direction, conversations focus on the details of life abroad and of life at home. Descriptive accounts in these long-distance, day-to-day conversations conform to generalizations regarding the exhaustive nature of Quichua narrative styles. Both the frequency of calls and the detail of accounts provide a richness of information that allows people to maintain a social presence at home by remaining engaged in and informed about community affairs while abroad.

Proliferating Internet use has, in addition, created novel spaces of communication for Otavaleños. The popularity of *correo electrónico* (e-mail) sustains several Internet cafés not only in touristy Otavalo but in rural hamlets throughout the valley. A Web site owned and operated by Otavaleños, www.OtavalosOnLine.com, offers news and information about Otavalan communities both in Ecuador and abroad. The site features photographs of recent events with descriptions of their cultural significance, chat venues (designated "Rimarishun"—Chat Otavalo) in both Quichua and Spanish, directories for finding friends around the world ("Mashikunapak"—Páginas Amigas), social and political commentary, and, of course, links to commercial sites for the purchase of Otavalan goods online. Recently the page has added a blog, a Quichua language tutorial, and an online dating service ("Riksirishun"—Encuentra tu Pareja) with fields for entering search parameters and a button to select "Buscar Tiyu" (find an Otavalan man) or "Buscar Tiya" (find an Otavalan woman) within a given geographical area. Indigenous sports and Otavalan festival celebrations receive ample coverage on the Web site. Announcements concerning Otavalan soccer championships organized abroad appear regularly, along with reports and pictures chronicling the events. For the Pawkar Raymi, migrants who cannot come home for the festival participate as interactive spectators through this medium. The same has become true for New Year's and Inti Raymi, or San Juan, as pictures of these celebrations in places like Madrid, Barcelona, Zurich, Chicago, New York, and Otavalo circulate electronically among "La Comunidad Virtual de los Otavalos" (the virtual community of the Otavalos).

Though frequent communication may have its advantages, regular long-distance exchanges can also involve migrants as unwitting protagonists in reports of illicit love affairs, illegal activities, and unsavory business deals. At the same time that expanding telecommunication services in rural areas have extended the reach of information, they have also internationalized gossip networks. Notably, gossip also functions as a powerful element in the continuance of an individual's social persona in the life of a community, in spite of the person's physical absence. Gossip is by definition based on partial, incomplete, and biased information that, by design or unintentionally, can lead to distortions that result in beneficial consequences for some and damaging action for others. For better or for worse, it keeps travelers embroiled in webs of community conversation in a way that acknowledges their inclusion within the group. In their basic and most critical capacity, social exchanges of gossip and chitchat help to maintain the fluidity of communication patterns (Rosnow and Fine 1976:92). At the same time, gossip carries the implication that people, regardless of whether they are abroad, remain accountable to the community. Rosnow and Fine (1976:91) insist that "gossip is not merely *idle* talk but talk with a social purpose." Though rumors fill an information-spreading role, they also encompass a process of collective interpretation and commentary (Kapferer 1990:8). In other words, they provide a forum for collective critical practices, and for exerting social control, lobbying for consensus, and adapting to change (Rosnow and Fine 1976: 55, 62). These observations ratify the premium Otavaleños place on conversation (*rimarishpa*) as a vital element in the continuation of social networks. Given the growing diaspora within the Otavalan community, the social control extended by transnational gossip networks, moreover, ensures a continuing moral influence emanating from the community across the globe.

The high stakes involved not only tend to compel participation in gossip (Rosnow and Fine 1976:55, 62) but also measure the consequences of using enduring community networks for festival organization in terms of social accountability. Doing a good job for the festival carries personal implications that can define how a person will find himself or herself positioned in future rounds of community activity. Beyond the ability to pull off an event, performance is evaluated in terms of commitment to teamwork, manner of discourse, and attention to group dynamics that will endure beyond the event itself. These collective assessments, which are generally made and proliferated along informal channels of conversation, extend to everyone involved, no matter how minimal their role.

The magnitude of the Pawkar Raymi requires a team of organizers, all of whom are expected to access their social resources. To a great extent, gossip as a means of social control warrants that the involvement of many people in the production of the Pawkar Raymi does not yield a "thin" relational quality to the organizational network—a situation where individual account-ability potentially fizzles in the anonymity of the crowd. At the same time, this arrangement averts a highly centric configuration where the stability of the web of relations hinges entirely on a central coordinator.[4]

The Strength of Weak Ties

Human resources beyond the community are pursued in similar informal and opportunistic ways. Casual conversations often lead to engaging the interest and involvement of outsiders. By way of an example of the typical approach to soliciting support for the event, Mario Conejo explained, "Say one of our friends has worked at a company and mentions, 'I have an acquaintance there.' We integrate him into the commission and go with a proposal to the company with him as our representative. But all of this is based on a sense of personal affinities."

Business networks often afford opportunities for recruiting help in promot-ing and funding community events. Otavalan business transactions generally carry an expectation for developing social connections beyond the immediate exchange of goods, services, or money. Reciprocal social obligations are part of doing business among Otavaleños, who, in some cases, have extended this practice to business dealings with non-*indígenas*. Pegucheño business owners promote the event among their customers and similarly use their influence as patrons at other establishments to raise interest and funds for the Pawkar Raymi. Pegucheños, for instance, constitute a steady and dependable clientele for various Otavalo businesses, including Imbauto, an automobile retailer, and M. M. Jaramillo Arteaga, one of the largest money exchange houses regionally and nationally. Both establishments have become annual contributors to the

Pawkar Raymi. Imbauto, which caters to affluent Pegucheños in the market for the latest model cars, trucks, and sports utility vehicles, donated U.S. $4,000 in 2000 and pledged to renew its funding commitment yearly.

These examples attest to what Mark Granovetter (1973) designates the "strength of weak ties," a concept that underscores the advantage of informal, accidental, and incidental relations in acquiring fresh information or resources beyond one's intimate social circles. Links that start off as incidental have the potential to become more enduring. Eventually, existing members of a network as well as newly integrated members go on to create new contacts, both weak and strong. The overall "density" and scope of a network increases, in this way, through both evolving and expanding relations of obligation. Given the far-reaching personal and business contacts that Pegucheños maintain regionally, nationally, and internationally, mobilizing both immediate and extended networks to achieve an ambitious vision of the festival and funding its production makes sense. This simultaneous dedication to community and openness to outside cooperation, moreover, is compatible with Pegucheños' conception of local development and identity formation, not in spite of but through expanding tendencies.[5]

Attracting resources from outside the community has become indispensable for the continuation of the festival in light of growing expectations and changing social and economic contexts for the production of local events. The costs involved in sponsoring a *fiesta* are increasingly prohibitive and the responsibilities overwhelming for a single *prioste,* even a wealthy *comerciante* (international indigenous businessman). In 2000, for example, the total cost for the Pawkar Raymi was 270 million sucres (approximately U.S. $10,800 based on the average exchange rate for that year). By 2001 that cost had escalated to between U.S. $15,000 and $20,000. And in 2006, Roberto Lema estimated that the price tag for the Pawkar Raymi was close to U.S. $80,000. Skyrocketing *fiesta* expenses account for the dwindling and eventual disappearance of certain traditions in other communities.[6] In Peguche, flexible approaches to fund raising have ensured that the Pawkar Raymi will not suffer a similar fate.

It is clear, however, that outside help must be carefully managed. Experimentation with alternative funding sources in other communities has sometimes had the effect of distorting local practices. I saw, during my stay in Imbabura, instances where nongovernmental organizations (NGOs) and corporate sponsors assumed influential roles in the organization and programming of events. Abbreviated schedules, for instance, were imposed to suit tourist expectations, thwarting the proper fulfillment of ritual ceremonies. In one festival, a sponsoring NGO prohibited alcohol consumption in accordance with an evangelical agenda, and even established a temporary jail to detain both drunkards and alcohol vendors for the duration of the event. At other festivals, corporate sponsors, in contrast, promoted specific commercial alcoholic beverages. Involvement of indigenous political organizations as sponsors, in addition, opened some events to the insertion of political messages (see chapters 3 and 6). In the case of Peguche, exclusive coordination and management of resources by community members ensures that decision making remains in the hands of the community. Outside support and participation within these parameters has become both integrated and integral to local practices, the details of which I turn to next.

El Deporte Une Pueblos

A hot-air balloon floated across the stadium during the inaugural ceremony for Pawkar Raymi 2001 with the message, "Sports unite people. Welcome brothers." The Pawkar Raymi sports championship is a powerful event for fostering solidarity through shared experience, wholesome competition, individual triumph, and team effort. The immediate motivation behind the soccer tournament was to demonstrate that the community of Peguche was capable of organizing a sporting event that could contend with the popular attraction of the match in Agato. Beyond the local display of one-upmanship, the broader idea behind hosting a soccer tournament was to show that *indígenas* were competitive in sports, an area that at a national level has largely ignored indigenous potential. Though Afro-Ecuadorians have managed to break the racial barriers in soccer and come to be recruited actively for regional and national teams, *indígenas* have historically been excluded from consideration. Makeup of the FIFA World Cup Soccer 2006 National Selection illustrated the majority Afro-Ecuadorian ethnic demographics of Ecuadorian soccer. It is worth noting that Otavaleños represented a very different but revealing demographic of the sport as international spectators at the games in Germany. Their presence at the World Cup attests both to the global diaspora of this ethnic community and to their financial prosperity as a consumer group.

"El Mundialito" (The Little World Cup), as the Pawkar Raymi tournament has come to be known, echoes the sentiment and cultural agenda of the international World Cup as "a time to make friends" and overcome ethnic prejudices. Roberto Lema, who has helped with the soccer committee over the years, expressed that the nickname "El Mundialito" is quite apropos because in addition to local teams, communities from beyond Imbabura are invited to participate in an expression of fraternity among Ecuadorian indigenous people of diverse cultural and ethnic backgrounds. Teams invited to participate include Otavalos from across the valley, Saraguros, Kañaris, Tsa chilas, and Salasacas. A team from Napo also participated in a friendly match in 2001. Tournament regulations require that players on teams representative of indigenous nationalities speak Kichwa (or Tsa'fiqui in the case of the Tsa chilas), be descendants of both indigenous mother and father, and have lived in their native area for the last year. In addition, for the Otavalos and the Saraguros there is a requirement that players have braids (Reglamento Campeonato de Futbol, Pawkar Ryami "Peguche Tio" 2004, published online). The tournament is a true world cup with international Otavalan teams like Barcelona, Metro Stars, the Ayllus, and Huaycupungu's team mostly made up of return migrants from Mexico.

Although the festival operates with an understanding of community that extends both geographically and ethnically beyond Peguche, regulations for the soccer tournament reflect an indigenous ethnic agenda and underscore organizers' commitment to creating new spaces for raising the profile of *indígenas* in sports. Tournament rules limit the number of nonindigenous players (national or international, amateur or professional) to three, and the number of players "*de pelo cortado*" or "*sin trenza*" (of cut hair or without a braid) descendants of both indigenous mother and father to two per team. Allowing teams to hire paid professional players, but limiting the number of soccer pros per team, ensures that the competition remains local but also attracts media attention and fuels the enthusiasm of soccer fans. The ability to foot the bill for a professional athlete is also a conspicuous display of indigenous merchant wealth. There is no division for a purely mestizo team, nor is there a division for an exclusively Afro-Ecuadorian team. In the last few years, Ecuavolley tournaments and basketball games with male and female categories have been added in the spirit of broader inclusion along generational and gendered lines. Both the regulations and the discursive framework of the Pawkar Raymi sports tournament are critical public statements about the ways in which Ecuadorian minorities have been excluded from the national project and its social and political vision.

Similar to the FIFA World Cup competition, the "Mundialito" is couched in elaborate opening ceremonies that celebrate indigenous identity in the context of a multiethnic and pluricultural national reality. The inaugural parade features an extraordinary Coraza (ornate traditional festival character that epitomizes extravagance, wealth, and tradition) on horseback surrounded by an entourage of dancers and children. Women of the community carry beautiful arrangements of corn tassels. Other women balance offerings of *medianos* (ceremonial meals) expertly on their heads and carry *chicha* (fermented corn beer) in ceramic jugs. Team *madrinas* and *ñustas* (beauty contestants) escort the players. Organizing committee members and special guests march ceremoniously in their best attire. They carry the trophies for the tournament, one of which is shaped like the FIFA World Cup trophy.

The week of the tournament is filled with cultural activities ranging from musical performances to workshops on Andean cosmovision, popular games of *vacas locas* (carnivalesque costumed cows) and pyrotechnic *castillos* (castles), musical instrument workshops, arts and crafts exhibitions, and community meals. The proliferation of activities generates numerous multivocal spaces creating a layering of simultaneous festival engagements. The festival culminates with a closing ceremony, final acknowledgments, distribution of tournament prizes, and a grand party. The awards ceremony is a popular attraction every year because in addition to trophies, medals, and cash (a recent addition), prizes include live animals.

Popular sports events contain elements conducive to the development of a collective sense of intimacy for both players and spectators (see Geertz 1973 and Manning 1998). As outlined by Janet Harris (1983:32), games are a source of colorful, emotionally exciting entertainment; they offer opportunities for involvement to a wide variety of people with many different interests and capabilities; and, through this, they create in both fans and players a sense of inclusion. The zeal of spectators averaging three thousand per day in 2001 (personal communication, Roberto Lema) for the weeklong Pawkar Raymi soccer tournament; the spirited activity of betting circles; the excitement broadcast by fans through noisemakers and face paints; and the spectacle of inauguration and closing ceremonies in Peguche embody each of Harris's theoretical points. Pegucheños have managed, moreover, to generate this sense of inclusion not just in popular sports but in the realm of exclusive athletic contests such as competitive cycling.

Elite Sports

In 2001 the first Cascada de Peguche Cross-Country Bicycle Race spotlighted Otavaleños as lead contenders in a high-profile, high-cost (each bike ranging from U.S. $3,500 to $5,000), internationally competitive sport. The circuit qualifies as a master-level downhill challenge and a fierce cross-country competition characterized by sixty- to eighty-degree climbs, three- to five-meter downhill drops, and various technical jumps and ramps set against the spectacular background of Peguche's waterfall. Cyclists at all levels (youth, women, elite, and master categories) attempt various segments of the circuit. Even some of the most experienced riders often fail to reach the finish line with either the contender or the bike unscathed. According to Marcos Lema, organizer of the race, with this competition Peguche not only wanted to show the level of sportsmanship in the community but also that an indigenous community could organize and host an elite sporting event.

Initially, the National Cycling Federation turned down a request for help with the event. Marcos, a national-level competitor himself, began asking prominent cycling buddies to support this local initiative by participating in the race. Each of the people contacted was encouraged to bring one or two more participants. Enthusiasm about the event spread quickly through this informal networking approach and the list of registered contestants grew. Soon afterward, Marcos received a phone call from the National Cycling Federation reproaching him for organizing a competition without their prior approval. Marcos says that he recognized that the federation was discreetly covering up for its original underestimation of the event and opening a back door for support. The race in Peguche was integrated into the national circuit, becoming a mandatory National Cycling Federation competition to qualify for international cycling events.

The expectations that the race created made it easier to attract corporate sponsors. Marcos managed to secure more than fifteen promoters, rendering the race the most well-funded event of Pawkar Raymi 2001. The list of sponsors was printed on the back of the official Cascada de Peguche cycling competition T-shirts. The novelty of the cross-country competition generated an impressive turnout. The event catered in particular to mestizos, who came from as far as Tulcán, Quito, Ibarra, and Cayambe with their families to make a day of the event. That mestizos brought their families to an indigenous community was noted as significant, and was seen by Pegucheños as a willingness on the part of *nonindígenas* to develop more positive interethnic relations. In addition to a swarm of outside visitors, locals turned out as participants, spectators, and coordinators. Pegucheños provided logistical support, trail maintenance, live commentating, and radio broadcasting for the race. They also coordinated parking, first aid, security, and refreshments.

These efforts in Peguche created broad-based, cross-class, interethnic, and cross-cultural support for the race. Though the inclusive community defined in popular sports centered on national ethnic minorities, the Cascada de Peguche bicycle race encompassed a much broader demographic in its formulation of community. Although the number of indigenous cyclists is increasing, for this event the majority of competitors are generally nonindigenous, including a few foreigners. An indigenous ethnic agenda persists, nonetheless, to the extent that the race asserts a prominent role for *indígenas* on par with the broader national and international community.

Regional and national newspapers followed the story. Reports on the efficiency with which Pegucheños handled the event contributed to an inversion of the negative stereotypes of indigenous people as impoverished or dependent typically promoted in media representations. Photographs of indigenous professional cyclists and coordinators printed along with the reports perhaps made the most lasting impressions on the national conscience, with inevitable trickling effects toward a reconceptualization of the Ecuadorian hegemonic ethnic and class order. Changes in the external gaze upon the community, I argue, play out against critical transformations in the self-assessment of Pegucheños. The Cascada de Peguche cycling competition rattled national and international prejudices, effectively changing expectations on the part of outsiders (sponsors, collaborators, tourists) of minority groups. *Indígenas* came to be regarded as worthy competitors and competent organizers. Just as people internalize damaging messages of low self-esteem and inadequacy promoted by national hegemonic tendencies (Gramsci 1971), in an inverted application of this process and as a consequence of successful collaborative efforts, Pegucheños are now internalizing notions that underscore their resourcefulness, competitive spirit, ambition, and management abilities.

The Cascada de Peguche race provided, in addition, an exceptional venue for displays of indigenous fashion and idiosyncratic status symbols. Otavaleñas dressed in the finest "seal-skin" *anakus* (wraparound skirts), and donning expensive pink coral and gold jewelry, walked pedigree rottweilers and Dobermans or pit bulls on tight leashes. In the last few years, these aggressive breeds have become the preferred canine varieties in Peguche and other communities. Their thick leather and spiked choke-chain collars accentuate their threatening appearance and cannot be overlooked as status statements in themselves. In addition to the shiny new trucks (invariably exhibiting a dream catcher dangling from the rearview mirror and occasionally a bumper sticker in English), sleek bike racks, presumably used to carry expensive bicycles, were conspicuously displayed. New status symbols allude to acquisition power above and beyond the comfortable (and by national measures, high) standard of living in the community. As for the dream catchers (known in Imbabura as the "Otavalan passport"), they make reference, as do foreign bumper stickers, to overseas travel; and despite being mass-produced in Otavalo itself, they conjure notions of spiritual and cultural intimacy with the highly romanticized North American native tribes. Cellular phones, laptop computers, and digital cameras—projections of affluence, modernity, education, and technology—complete the picture.

Of course, not everyone has access to the symbolic or real capital on display during the event. Organizers avoid using rhetoric that would concede this reality, simply mentioning on the application that appropriate equipment for the practice of cross-country cycling is strongly recommended. Raising the profile of indigenous people in sports and event management visibly boosts indigenous confidence and self-respect more generally as competitors and organizers celebrate their triumphs, and as local spectators identify with the achievement. It is in this vicarious capacity that an elite sport has the ability to become inclusive of a more extended population. The race invites indigenous onlookers to imagine themselves in the light of a different possibility—as future competitors, managers, announcers, sponsors—and raises the bar on self-defined expectations of what *indígenas* can aim to achieve.

Committee members articulated that developing self-esteem among indigenous youths was, in fact, one of the festival's objectives. Each successful event contributes to an affirmation that Pegucheños are good at planning events and effective in managing projects. The aura of confidence among the new generation of Pegucheños seems to be an internalization of the persistent public articulation of this idea. Though these self-impressions and vicarious associations are of utmost importance, they ultimately coalesce into a sense of collective ethnic identity through opportunities to put these skills into practice. Within the community, a system of participatory involvement and rotating responsibility gives novices a chance to emulate and eventually outperform their predecessors. In addition, outreach efforts by the festival committee have involved youths beyond the community. Along with new expectations inspired by the Pegucheño initiative, these individuals potentially take back to their own communities a vision of successful organization and the know-how for project implementation.

Collaborative Imagination—Peguche's Trademark

A stage performance was added to the Pawkar Raymi celebrations in 1998. It contributed in a different way to the promotion of ethnic identity in the context of Ecuadorian multiculturalism. The Pawkar Raymi Peguche Tio extended beyond its community focus to become a multiethnic, pluricultural encounter that brought together different indigenous and Afro-Ecuadorian nationalities and ethnicities. In 2001 music and dance troops from all over the country were invited to participate. Performance groups included Ballet Folklórico Jacchigua, Peguche's own Ñanda Mañachi, a female singer of ballads and *pasillos* (a traditional national Ecuadorian musical genre akin to the Peruvian waltz) from Cayambe, a group called Runa Causai from the Oriente, and an Afro-Ecuadorian group called Oro Negro from the Chota Valley, which was a novelty and a complete hit. The groups performed in their own musical genre and wore outfits representative of their respective regions. Rhythms ranged from melodious ballads to drum-accompanied chanting, danceable *cumbias,* upbeat marimba music, and wailing panpipe tunes, exposing locals and visitors to a variety of musical styles. Funds raised by the festival organizing committee paid for stage, sound, and lighting equipment, professional fees, transportation, and lodging costs for performers. The cultural portion of the Pawkar Raymi festival accounted for more than 50 percent of the total budget that year.

Although a recent development at the time of my visit, expectations for the Noche Cultural, as this part of the festival is called, were already growing. When we talked in March 2001, Mario Conejo was formulating a vision for revolutionizing Noche Cultural during his presidency the following year with an appearance by Charijayac, the internationally acclaimed and locally popular Andean music group. That Charijayac, in effect, provided the main attraction in 2002 attests to Mario's sense of determination and vision and to the festival committee's negotiating power. Mario felt there was no reason the Pawkar Raymi Noche Cultural could not aim to become an internationally renowned event similar to Viña del Mar in Chile. "Why not," he asked, "at least have that vision, that dream that in Peguche we could do it?" Mario explained that with such a high percentage of the young people from Peguche traveling internationally, it seemed feasible to tap into this human capital by asking friends abroad if they would be willing to participate as "foreign ambassadors" for the Pawkar Raymi. This international network would allow Pegucheños to capture new funding sources and court international audiences—an idea very much in consonance with Granovetter's logic of the strength of weak ties. The contagious enthusiasm with which Mario described what he hoped to contribute to this event not only reflects his personal charisma but reveals a more general disposition among Pegucheños toward enveloping increasingly diffuse participants in processes of collaborative imagination.

The Pawkar Raymi is the brainchild of a new generation of Pegucheños, and its growing sophistication is the product of their exposure to political initiatives, novel technologies, and foreign event production standards. David Kyle (1999:439–40) points to Otavaleños' long history of "borrowing" ideas, integrating them into their own conceptions of art, performance, and production, and implementing them as their own. As they do this, Peguche-ños set regional trends in fashion, business, management, and technology. Among locals (both *indígenas* and mestizos) there is a sense of recognition that Peguche might be onto something. The value placed on maintaining involvement on a local level while simultaneously participating in an ever-growing outward demographic expansion (Kyle 1999) is arguably the key to Peguche's achievement.

Envidia: Symbolic Capital Inverted

Pegucheños' locally rooted and internationally developed collective iden-tity generates unique social and symbolic capital (Kyle 1999:440). Symbolic capital refers to certain styles of language and behavior that come to func-tion as a sort of resource for a particular group. As the economic metaphor underscores, not everyone gains access to this standard. Though Peguche's success story may serve as a model to which other communities can aspire, the commercial and social exploits of Pegucheños also result in a widening economic and social gap vis-à-vis other Otavaleños.

Not surprisingly, Peguche's achievements elicit jealousy as much as admira-tion at a regional level. At the same time that Pegucheños combat negative stereotypes of indigenous people perpetuated in nonindigenous national and international circles, they also contend with opposition from within the indigenous ethnic community. *Envidia,* or jealousy, is often the mo-tive behind rumor, slander, and even *brujería* (witchcraft). In the context of pronounced economic differences among Otavaleños, *envidia* propels a powerful mechanism for those without access to economic capital to chal-lenge Pegucheños in the realm of symbolic and social capital. In this sense, *envidia* and its articulation through rumor function as a social leveling device and as a vehicle for potential empowerment among peripheral actors.

Several criticisms circulated after the Pawkar Raymi festival in 2001. There was a buzz about the prizes offered for the soccer championship. People com-mented that for all their effort the players "deserved" more than a bull for first-, second-, and third-place winners, and a pig for the fourth-place winner. The organizing committee's logic in offering live animals rather than cash prizes aimed at reminiscing about a traditional noncash economy. They also conceived of the prizes as an added element of entertainment, which indeed was the case as people walked by to look at the novelty of bulls painted in multicolored advertisements. The unpredictability of the animals, moreover, added to the festive atmosphere, as unwieldy bulls dispersed the crowd every so often, sending everyone screaming and laughing in different directions.

I also heard criticism about the main road to the soccer field. Although the road is admittedly in bad shape, the following statement by a member of a neighboring community captures the thrust of an unfounded expectation aimed at the Pawkar organizing committee: "The committee should have fixed the main road. If they expect so many people to come see *them* play they should fix the road. The president in 2000 offered to fix it, but did not deliver. Since the winnings are of over 50 percent they should really do that."

Several points stand out as we unpack this argument. Most obvious is the exaggeration of the profits made on the event. In 1998 Peguche made enough from the Pawkar Raymi to put a down payment on a lot that could serve as a recreational area for the community. The idea was to use proceeds from future festivals to continue paying for this communal space. Organizers of the event, however, declared that in subsequent years they mostly managed to break even and were lucky if they could leave a small sum in the committee's account to help their successor. Allegations that Peguche made inflated profits from the festival reduced the event to a self-interested, moneymaking scheme that exploited local pockets to benefit a single community. Admission to the Noche Cultural in 2001 was U.S. $1.00—a relatively moderate amount in local terms. The only other fees collected were for parking at the soccer field—a contribution that affected only a small number of people with cars, the majority of whom were Pegucheños themselves. The total cost of the event exceeded U.S. $15,000. Nonetheless, the rumor painted Pegucheños as opportunists out to make a profit and not as culture brokers attempting to promote a paradigm of ethnic collaboration.

The criticism that people from other communities were expected to come see *them* (Pegucheños) play (and that therefore the organizing committee should fix the main road) implied that the crowd was merely instrumental to the event insofar as the festival's success was measured in terms of public attendance. The us/them construction of the comment aggravates the implied split. The expectation that festival attendants should be remunerated communicated both a distancing from the collective effort of the festival and a simultaneous usurping of the credit for the achievement.

People's shift in the allocation of responsibility for road construction and maintenance from the *municipio* to the festival organizing committee signaled a redirected paternalistic dynamic. Kristine Latta (personal communication, 2/2007) asserts that this comment may have also been a veiled criticism that Peguche does not have a *cabildo,* a council that oversees community interests, including community infrastructure. Economic and managerial success demonstrated in the production of the festival was glossed in the popular discourse as political power and obligation. Just as a paternalistic government is expected to care for its citizens, so too Peguche, upon the first sign of independence and initiative, became a new source of remuneration. Both the insider/outsider connotation and the allusion to a paternalistic relation were reinforced by the reference to the president of the committee not "delivering on his promise." This phrase made allusion to the rhetoric of politicians and the unfailing denouncement by *el pueblo* (the people) of some form of deception. The criticism, moreover, implicitly cast Peguche in the role of a new *patrón* and echoed the historical experience of the *hacienda* when, in a display of generosity and due compensation, the *patrón* was expected to extend himself beyond his means. In the context of these assumptions, any of Peguche's initiatives necessarily fell short of the remunerative obligations of local government, a *patrón,* or a traditional *prioste.*

Attempts to discredit Peguche also drew on an incident that took place during a *paro* (national strike) just a few weeks prior to the 2001 Pawkar Raymi celebration. Several cars at Imbauto were allegedly damaged during protest marches in Otavalo. Rumors circulated that Pegucheños were responsible and that this was the reason Imbauto had not contributed as generously to the event that year. Allegations against Pegucheños evoked negative stereotypes of *indios alzados* (unruly Indians), a racist epithet deployed by *nonindígenas* against indigenous activists during the strike (see, for example, Whitten 2003b). The phrase was appropriated and redeployed by indigenous people themselves against Pegucheños in the context of the Pawkar Raymi.[7] Complaints about the festival itself articulated expectations that Pegucheños could not realistically meet. At the same time, discourses emanating from the *paro* reiterated negative stereotypes of *indígenas* that attempted to reinsert Pegucheños in a position at the bottom of the hegemonic racist and classist hierarchy . . . along with all the other Indians.

Discourses such as these are social leveling attempts aimed at checking the social capital of Pegucheños. They are successful to the extent that in the context of the Pawkar Raymi they have heightened Pegucheños' conscious nonmaterialist and egalitarian discourse. Projection of these values during the festival includes conspicuous distribution of wealth in the recent form of cash prizes and the rental of food stalls predominantly to people from outside the community, cited as an effort toward allowing non-Pegucheños to profit from the event.

Pressures from inside and outside the community influence the development of the Pawkar Raymi as a progressive tradition reinvented on an annual basis to meet a variety of expectations. Festival organizers aspire to fulfill growing international demands to modernize, expand, and constantly innovate. They are also susceptible to local social and discursive mechanisms that assert traditional and hegemonic convictions. The variety of discourses emergent in the context of this event contributes in competing ways to definitions of collective identity and negotiations of community as process. The complexities of the discursive realm of human interaction exemplified in the Pawkar Raymi capture more generally the inherent multivocality in Otavalan festival production.

As the bustle of Uku Pacha recedes into the background, the thundering of synchronized dance steps announces entry into the realm of ritual symbolism in the chapter that follows.

3

Encuentros—
Dances of the Inti Raymi

A human wall fifteen men across and dozens of rows deep advances at a slow trot toward the main square of Cotacachi, *La Plaza de la Matriz*. They are the San Juan dancers of the upper and lower moiety coalitions of local indigenous communities who have come to compete with one another in the *toma de la plaza* (taking of the square) during the summer harvest festivals known as Inti Raymi. The sound of boots pounding against the pavement and collective whistling announce the strength and aggression of the *sanjuanes,* as the dancers are known in honor of Saint John the Baptist, whose feast day is celebrated on this occasion—June 24. They have come to test their vigor and their endurance in a ritual battle for the ultimate prize of symbolically winning the town square. The dancers wear goatskin chaps (*zamarros*); tall, broad-rimmed, black, stiff cardboard hats; boots or shoes (instead of *alpargates*); and sunglasses. Many are completely outfitted in camouflage. As they trot to the music of the twin flutes, they wave leather whips (*aciales*) and chant in unison, "*jari, jari, jarikuna . . . churay, churay, carajo*"[1] (men, men, [we are] men . . . put it there, put it there, *carajo*[2]).

Imaginary lines establish precise boundaries among groups, imposing a temporary festival order in the space of the plaza. The *sanjuanes* dominate the street around the central park as they move in a counterclockwise direction around the plaza. Food vendors and game operators set up their stands in the central park.[3] An indigenous public crowds the steps of the church. Local mestizo onlookers view the dancing from the safe distance of second-floor windows and balconies. Mestizo men make toasts over rounds of *trago* (cane alcohol) on the sidewalks that line the plaza, but they stay near a tavern or house for a quick getaway should there be trouble. Military and police stand at every corner. Indigenous women, mostly spouses of the men dancing, carry bundles (*kepis*) and children on their backs, and walk between the San Juan groups on the street as a buffer for the fights.[4] A few foreign tourists weave cumbersomely around the perimeter of the event, maneuvering their cameras above the crowds. Children scurry near their parents.

In this chapter, I examine the dramatic rituals of the Inti Raymi as encounters where Otavaleños reflexively evaluate, perform, and continuously redefine their sense of identity in ethnic relation to urban mestizos, vis-à-vis one another, and as sacred beings within the Andean universe. I focus on the practices and processes that sustain the production of social relations and the transformation of communities, and argue along with Barz (2003:6) that communities perform themselves into being on a regular basis. My interpretation centers on a symbolic analysis of festival dances and costumes in the town of Cotacachi, and addresses three levels of identity construction through performance: 1) At the intersection of the plaza during the symbolic "taking of the square," "transgression" onto urban social spaces constitutes a performed affront to and appropriation of white-mestizo authority. The

The "taking of the square," Plaza de la Matriz, Cotacachi

clash of cultures in this encounter is expressed in the aesthetics of the dance as a sort of counter-conquest and in the bellicose themes of festival costumes as indigenous and mestizo identities are constituted in juxtaposition to one another. 2) The taking of the main square begins with a dancing descent of participants from each community to the city of Cotacachi. The pattern of this dance expresses the mutual dependence between individuals and their communities as they respectively gain strength by way of a forward progression in space and a backward passage in time through memory and historicity. The progressive character of the dance depicts movement, adaptability, change, and regeneration within indigenous communities. 3) In addition to an ethnic assault on urban mestizo domains, the taking of the square constitutes a meeting of different indigenous communities. The dynamics of intercommunity indigenous identity and intraethnic tensions come into relief as dancers confront each other in moiety coalitions in the plaza. Complementary oppositions between local moieties play out in the form of ritual battles. The performance of violence during the dramatizations gives way to actual violence, resulting in injuries and deaths among the dancers. The exertion of the dancers and the blood they spill in the fights are considered to be ritual sacrifices and mark yet another form of encounter with the mythico-religious realm of the sacred (the subject of chapter 4). Through these ritual actions people position themselves as central agents in a cosmic dialogue that asserts their identity as indispensable conduits between Andean time-spaces, or *pachas*.

The various facets of the festival I analyze take place in the context of a series of accompanying rituals: Catholic masses in honor of Saint John, Saint Peter and Saint Paul, and Santa Lucia; costumed dances in household patios; the presentation of traditional offerings (*entrega de la rama*) from the old festival sponsor to the new; an exchange of "castles" (*castillos,* also known as *aumentos*); the preparation of *aswa* or *chicha,* a ceremonial fermented maize beer; communal meals; ritual baths; and pilgrimages to sacred sites in observance of the summer solstice.[5] The timing and style of these activities vary from one community to another. Although I cannot go into detail on all aspects of the festival here, a glimpse at the layering of events underscores the complexity of the Inti Raymi and refers us back to the central concepts of extended ritual seasons and festival complexes discussed in my introduction. This layering of festival activity alerts us, moreover, to varying degrees of religious syncretism and cultural superimposition.

In the last decade or so, the term Inti Raymi, Festival of the Sun, has been introduced by indigenous festival organizers to supplant the Catholic names of San Juan, San Pedro, and San Pablo imposed at the time of Spanish colonization. The politics of discursive inversion have gained particular momentum since 1992, the year that marked the quincentennial of European presence on the continent—which indigenous groups all over the Americas recast as the anniversary of five hundred years of indigenous resistance (Wibbelsman 2004:105–9). Inti Raymi, nonetheless, is also a nonlocal term that makes reference to Inka traditions. Cachiguango (1999:23 and 27) acknowledges the discursive and real transformations this ritual has undergone, but also warns against the superficial interpretation given by non-Andean researchers regarding what is now known as the festival of the sun. "To speak of the Inti Raymi, is not only to speak of a *fiesta* dedicated to the Sun in a gesture of thanksgiving for the harvest, as nonindigenous researchers have defined, but rather to speak of a complex system of life framed by an understanding of the culture of *pacha-vivencia,* of nurturing life throughout the annual agricultural cycle observed by Andean people" (Cachiguango 1999:23). Otavaleños of the newer generations increasingly refer to this festival complex as Inti Raymi. Older folks and people who live in outlying areas generally prefer the term San Juan. Many people only vaguely recognize the name Inti Raymi and speak more readily of the *jatun puncha,* the big day. Cachiguango insists that people continue to affirm the essence of Andean life, thought, and practice regardless of the term they apply. He opts for a combination of the labels Jatun Puncha–Inti Raymi to encompass this broader definition of the ritual. I agree with his interpretation but use the terms variably according to local expression, historical context, and to differentiate between the ensemble of rituals (Inti Raymi), clusters of saints' day celebrations (San Juan and San Pedro y San Pablo), and the big day, or *jatun puncha,* in each community (June 24 and June 29 in the area of Otavalo and Cotacachi).

The Concept of Encuentros

Folklorist Henri Glassie (1982:282) has written that "true communities are built not of dewy affection or ideological purity but of engagement." This eloquent statement encapsulates the concept of *encuentros* (encounters), which appears as a recurring theme in this book and is explicitly performed by Otavaleños in dances of the Inti Raymi. "Engagement" communicates the dialogical nature of communities and the constant negotiation involved in defining individual and group identities. It also conveys an important ambiguity regarding the ways in which people variously come together—friendly encounters, marriages, reunions with family and kin, cultural and social oppositions, conversations, or even violent confrontations. Layering of these experiences adds to the symbolic complexity that characterizes identity formation.

Part I: Interethnic Identity Assertions in the Taking of the Square

Tomas: Acts of Possession

Although the majority of Otavaleños are bilingual in Quichua and Spanish, language differences map onto an ethnic geography of socially constructed racial divisions, with Spanish as the dominant language in town and Quichua spoken increasingly as one travels farther into the rural areas. This social and racial topography sets the stage for the taking of the square. The taking of the square (*toma de la plaza*), referred to sometimes as the taking of the park (*toma del parque*) or of the church (*toma de la iglesia* or *toma de la capilla*), happens over the course of several days. The Feast of San Juan is celebrated from June 24 to June 26. Dancers return to the Cotacachi plaza to continue their dancing from June 29 to July 1 for the San Pedro y San Pablo (Saint Peter and Saint Paul) festivities. There is little variation in form between the two saints' day celebrations, which essentially run as a continuum in Cotacachi. The day of San Pedro on June 29 is considered to be the most important for dancing in this area.

Both the music and the dance that characterize this festival are known as the *sanjuanito*. The rhythm of the *sanjuanito* is binary, with a 2/4 tempo that accentuates the first beat—*1* 2, *1* 2. While the twin flutes (*flautas gemelas* or traverse flutes, also known as *gaitas gemelas*) play a repeating one-part descending pentatonic melody, *conjuntos* (musical groups) featuring guitars, violins, *kenas,* a drum (*bombo*), and sometimes a *melódica*, a *bandolín*, a *charango*, a *rondador,* and a harmonica reveal a two-part musical construction.[6] The guitars and *bandolines* mark the 2/4 tempo accentuated by the *bombo* (bass drum), while the *kenas, rondador,* and violins generally carry the melody. *Conjuntos* periodically trade off with the *flautas gemelas*. The minimalist structure of the festival *sanjuanito* allows for broad variation in musical interpretation. Every year, each community develops a signature composition for the festival. The festival *sanjuanito* effectively captures the sense of ethnic unity (expressed in the minimalist musical criteria of a single genre associated with highland indigenous cultures) that still allows for plurality and variation among communities (see Wibbelsman 2000:19).

An important objective of the Inti Raymi dances is to conquer the plaza and claim the political power it represents. *Tomas* also take place in other areas of Imbabura, most notably in Otavalo, where communities contend for the taking of San Juan Capilla on June 24 and 25. Variations of this performance appear throughout Spanish America. Caillavet (2000:392) points out that the central plaza, whether in Spain or in Spanish America, is, *par excellence,* a political space. The subversive aspect of the *toma* contributes to the labeling of Inti Raymi festivities as acts of political and territorial possession. In the Imbabura area, most of the summer celebrations carry with them both implicit and explicit connotations of a *toma* and celebrate either symbolic or, in many cases, actual displacements of the existing authority.

The very presence of the *sanjuanes* and their public entourage in the city constitutes the principal festival displacement and replacement of the established order. There is an element of collective indignation in the taking of the square as these rituals of reversal today displace and replace downtown, mostly mestizo, Cotacachi residents for the duration of the Inti Raymi. Symbolic inversions enacted by people who have been continuously marginalized reinscribe history with a twist in a gesture of redress for historical injustices and ongoing power asymmetries.[7] Ortiz Crespo (2004:85) describes the ambiguous social context of Cotacachi, where equality among citizens is recognized within a normative framework but practical relations of inequality are sustained for ethnic and cultural reasons. He observes that, in the presence of a state that is either unwilling or unable to guarantee their rights, social actors will take into their own hands collective assertions of citizenship, creating public spaces of dialogue, programs, and projects aimed at gaining access to services and establishing a minimum level of dignity for all. Guss's (2006) analysis of the Fiesta del Gran Poder in La Paz reflects a similar use of public performance as a vehicle for indigenous social and political mobilization.

The concept of *tomas* connected to San Juan dancing extends beyond the ritual taking of central squares in late June. The meaning inherent in the dance has become so publicly recognizable that the *sanjuanito* is performed any time of the year in conjunction with indigenous assertions of ethnic presence and the staking of all sorts of claims. Crespi's (1981:488) assertion that "being Indian traditionally meant celebrating the fiesta of San Juan" underscores the ethnic component of the dance. Just as symbols of authority change over time, so do the sites of power and contestation, and San Juan dancing as an act of possession is accordingly transposed onto new social and political spaces. In addition to regional examples, the indigenous uprising of 1990, also known as the Inti Raymi uprising, announced on a national level the peaceful demonstration of indigenous presence in the capital city (see Moreno Yánez and Figueroa 1992, Selverston-Scher 2001, Alemeida et al. 1992, KIPU 1990). The march on Quito coincided with the summer festivals, which allowed for an easy gloss of the interpretation of *tomas*. The media were quick to pick up on the connotations of San Juan dancing and were soon reporting on the *toma de Quito*. Subsequent indigenous mobilizations have increasingly been referred to as *tomas*. (See Wibbelsman 2004:109–12 for additional examples.) Although sensationalized media representations of indigenous marches often aggravate ethnic stereotypes and fuel political tensions, the impending undertone attributed to the *tomas* is not entirely misguided. The San Juan ritual ultimately enacts the Andean millenarian myth of a periodic renewal of the world through a reversal of the existing order. (See Guss 2006:297, 322 for a similar allusion to millenarian prophecies in the Fiesta del Gran Poder.)

Symbolism of Festival Costumes

The defiant nature of the festival is particularly evident in costume. All improvisations on this festival attire express manhood and authority. Women generally do not dance during the festival, except on the *warmi puncha* (women's day) on July 1, also the feast day of Santa Lucia. Even then, however, the women emulate the men's dance and costumes.[8] Variations on the San Juan costumes among the younger dancers include bandanas, loose hair,[9] open shirts that reveal bare chests, spiked bracelets, sunglasses, and camouflage. Older dancers maintain the white riding pants, white shirts, colorful handkerchiefs tied around the neck, wire mesh masks, broad-rimmed hats, and the whip. Though this attire reflects an aesthetic that corresponds to past sociohistorical contexts, it remains consistent with the interpretation of authority.

Segundo Anrrango, technical director of UNORCAC (Union of Peasant Organizations of Cotacachi) in 2000–2001 and resident of the upper Cotacachi moiety, reflected on the significance of the dancers' attire. He expressed that it quite obviously points to the *hacienda* as a symbol of power. Describing a classic example of ritual reversal, Anrrango said, "It's as if the Indians take this power during the festival days and put themselves in the place of the *hacienda*. Since the *hacienda* no longer exists, the symbolism has passed into our hands. The imagery of the *hacienda* endures in our culture."

Until the agrarian reforms of the 1960s, which divided the lands of the fifty-three *haciendas* in the province of Imbabura, indigenous dancers invaded *hacienda* patios with their music and costumes on the day of San Juan. Groups competed to outdo one another in offering the *rama de gallos*[10] to the *hacienda* masters, who then would distribute food and drink to all of the participants. *Ramas* were also offered to the church priests, engaging them in a relation of asymmetrical, long-term exchange. Groups contended for the attention and approval of the priest, who would reward outstanding performers with food and cloth, in the church plaza (Crespi 1981:489). Throughout the twentieth century, the tradition of presenting the *ramas* was transferred to *hacienda* managers. Crespi (1981:491) writes that when corporate managers rejected the *rama* owing to the burden of having to provide food for hundreds of dancers and because of the loss of labor during these celebrations, indigenous people turned to *compadres* and influential town families. The location of the dancing accordingly shifted to the town center. Through these multiple transpositions, the taking of the *hacienda* patio evolved into the taking of the main town square. In both memory and collective imagination, references to the *hacienda* and the symbols associated with it persist as people celebrate its power and symbolically debunk it time and again. (See also Guerrero 1990.)

San Juan celebrations continued despite curtailment of the *rama* offerings. However, the severing of personal ceremonial exchanges "generated considerable resentment" (Crespi 1981:490). Rejection of the *rama*, Crespi explains, was seen by indigenous people as a rejection of *them* and as a disregard for their welfare as Christians. This enduring perception contributes to a pronounced awareness of ethnic differences along with the social contrasts they imply. Indignant assertions of indigenous inclusiveness in the broader society as equals, performed during the festivals, are to a great extent fueled by these historical aggravations.

Military Costumes and the Theater of Domination

The theme of bellicose confrontation inherent in the festival traces its roots to the development of a "theater of domination" in the European legacy of the San Juan festival, which David Guss (2000:154–55) so eloquently summarizes. He writes that no performance tradition spread as quickly to the New World as the dance of the Moors and the Christians: "The recent victory over Muslim forces, encoded in dramatic dances and pageants, was one of the first evangelical tools used by the Spaniards upon their arrival in the New World" (Guss 2000:155). The reenactment of battles between Muslims and Europeans appeared in Spain in 1150 and was often performed in conjunction with patron saints festivities. The dance, which commemorated the North African invasion of southern Europe in 711, was popularized in 1492 upon the final expulsion of Muslims from Spain. This year, of course, also marks the first European colonial incursions into the New World. Building on the analyses of Bricker (1981) and Carrasco (1976), Guss explains how the dance, which pitted good against evil, was able to accommodate any number of adversaries and soon featured mock battles involving Romans, Jews, blacks, monkeys, and even French grenadiers. Variations of the dance in the New World include the Matachines, Moriscas, Morismas, Seises, Santiaguitos, Tastoanes, Rayados, Concheros, Negritos, Paloteos, Sword Dances, Montezuma Dances, Morris Dancing, and Dances of the Conquest (Guss 2000:202, footnote 21)—evidence of the geographical span of this colonial influence and of the culturally creative adaptations of the original dance.

Max Harris (2003:32) adds that although the official referent of modern versions of these dramatic Iberian Peninsula dances may be twelfth-century religious warfare, there are unspoken references to more recent conflicts. In 2001 the symbols I saw made with thumbtacks (and increasingly drawn with chalk) on the tall black hats of the *sanjuanes* captured enduring historical rivalries and reflected more recent adversarial world events. Among the most prominent symbols were swastikas, skulls and crossbones, ELN (a reference to Colombian guerrilla forces self-designated as the National Liberation Army), the letter R, suns, stars, and *chakanas* (the Andean square cross that stands as a symbol of cosmic intersection and equilibrium).

Segundo Anrrango's observations about present-day festival practices support the remarkable adaptability within the theme of belligerence to changing contexts as noted by Guss (2000). Anrrango commented, "There are changes in the representation of power in the festival. . . . For example, La Calera now dresses in olive camouflage signaling the military as a new symbol of power." During the decade of the 1990s, when camouflage overwhelmed the aesthetic of the festival in Cotacachi, the military indeed had gained national and international renown, first for its performance in the 1995–99 Cenepa Valley border conflict with Peru and later for its mediating role during the constitutional crisis and political turmoil that took place in 1997–98. Finally, on January 21, 2000, high-ranking officers of the military defied executive orders to shoot upon a crowd of protesters and, in an unprecedented historical move, instead joined indigenous and popular demonstrators to oust President Jamil Mahuad Witt from office. These events have redefined indigenous relations with the military and have consequently altered popular perceptions and depictions of the armed forces.

Locally, many young men from La Calera were recruited into the army during the border war with Peru.[11] Those returning from military duties bring their uniforms with them. These items are novelties within the com-

munities, and sheer accessibility to them makes them coveted festival paraphernalia. Along with the camouflage outfits soldiers bring back, people say
that young men from La Calera return from their military service with a
"Rambo" attitude. This observation is often presented as an explanation for
the escalation in festival violence during the San Juan battles. Brian Selmeski (2007:155–78), in his analysis of conscript identity formation within the
Ecuadorian army, describes the rugged paratrooper self-image that recruits
strive to project to those outside the barracks—especially their mothers and
girlfriends—as "Rambo-esque." He argues that martial arts, police, and military films prevalent on television generate a "Rambo factor" in the cultural
undercurrents that often attract young men to military service (Selmeski
2007:155–78). In the context of the Cotacachi area, the San Juan and San
Pedro festival battles arguably constitute an outlet for the performance of
this repressed "Rambo factor."

In addition to these contemporary explanations for the popularity of military regalia in the festival, John Collier and Aníbal Buitrón (1949) state that
in the 1940s the most popular costume for the San Juan festival in Otavalo
was that of the soldier, generally represented simply by a military jacket and/
or helmet. Tannia Mendizábal (1982) similarly reports that in 1978, although
it was not frequently seen, the military costume was present in the dances.
And Hassaurek (1997[1867]:301), writing in 1863, mentions a military coat
among the costumed dancers of San Juan. In Cotacachi the overwhelming
appeal of the military costume in the last decade is linked, at least in part, to
recent experiences. However, Hassaurek's, Collier's, and Buitrón's information demonstrates how certain festival themes and symbols recur within the
context of new interpretations and different world circumstances.

New Symbolism of Authority

Segundo Anrrango drew my attention to a recent manifestation in festival costumes for the Inti Raymi dances worthy of mention and analysis.
He had noticed the emergence of a new symbolism of authority associated
with *comerciantes* (indigenous businessmen). The socioeconomic trend in the
Otavalo-Cotacachi area suggests that representations of indigenous businessmen as new figures of authority may well become increasingly prominent in
the next few years.

This new symbolism of authority is more readily apparent in Otavalo with
UNAIMCO (Indigenous Artisan's Union of Otavalo) at the head of Inti
Raymi preparations and organization, and with wealthy *comerciante* house-
holds in the city as the primary sponsors of the dances. Characteristics of this

San Juan dancer

aesthetic include elegant, expensive costumes and a marked return to traditional festive forms. This can range from a revival of old *sanjuanito* tunes, to
the careful performance of nearly forgotten dance steps, to a reinstitution of
proper offerings of food and drink for festival dancers at each household. My
observations conform to some extent to similar expressions of nostalgia that

Colloredo-Mansfeld (1999) attributes to returning indigenous international migrants in this area.

Displays of wealth, sophistication, and generosity during the festival position indigenous *comerciantes* as the new economic power-holders in the city of Otavalo. In the case of Otavalo, the taking of the city is not altogether a symbolic gesture because wealthy *indígenas* have bought up prime real estate, especially around the commercial center known as the Plaza de Ponchos. What was once a ritual of reversal with indigenous people from outlying communities symbolically assuming power for a day or two has become a celebration of their presence and permanence in Otavalo as business proprietors and homeowners. The fact that in the last decade the festival has transferred a few blocks north from the church square to the commercial Plaza de Ponchos reflects the related shift in conceptions of authority—from religious or political power to economic influence.

This last example of festival costumes and their expression of power elucidates the conceptual leap from the performed appropriation of white-mestizo markers of authority to the actual empowerment of indigenous peoples. Rather than imitating wealth with costume jewelry and improvised caricatures of opulence in carnivalesque style, Otavaleños today embody affluence reflected in indigenous fashion trends and lifestyles well beyond the means of upper-middle-class mestizo families. Otavalan women, for example, wrap long strings of expensive pink coral imported from Europe around their wrists and forearms. The average price of a twelve-inch string of high quality *coralina* in 2001 was U.S. $20. Three to six twelve-inch strings are required for a proper *makiwatana* (bracelet). When multiplied by two arms, the cost comes to between U.S. $120 and U.S. $240. In addition to *makiwatanas,* also called *manillas*, Otavaleñas wear multiple strands of *wallkas* (glass-blown gold bead necklaces), dangling gold or gold-plated earrings embedded with precious stones and pearls, exquisite wraparound skirts made from fine, imported wools, and blouses delicately embroidered with local flower designs. A single everyday outfit can cost more than U.S. $1,000. On special occasions, their husbands don well-made wool hats and heavy ponchos. European and American fashion-label collared shirts and Italian leather shoes complete the outfit with an inclusive price tag of more than U.S. $700.[12]

The growing economic power of indigenous households is not only reflected in substantial material possessions but also in the gendered nature of acquisition and ownership, and the privileging of education in investment decisions. Otavaleñas sit behind the driver's wheel of their own Chevrolet trucks and sport utility vehicles. They park these latest-model cars in front of their neoclassical Italian villas and drive their children to private schools. Education is a critical marker of economic and social status. Youths from wealthy and aspiring indigenous families often go to universities in Quito or abroad. There is a great emphasis on the schooling of girls, reflected in the increasing number of indigenous female professionals and community leaders. Emphasis on the social and professional development of women reflects less prejudicial division of gender roles among *indígenas*. It is also an indicator of the upward mobility of a society and its attempts to redistribute resources in a socially inclusive manner.

Politically, *indígenas* in Imbabura have ascended to power, with indigenous mayors in the cities of both Otavalo (Mario Hernán Conejo Maldonado 2000–2004, reelected for a second term) and Cotacachi (Auki Tituaña Males 1996–2000, currently fulfilling his third elected term), and other prominent leaders as detailed in my introduction. The appropriation of symbols of authority and the empowerment of indigenous people in historically white/mestizo-dominated realms, nonetheless, continues to underline cultural contrast rather than assimilation. Satirical emulation of the hegemonic culture in the context of the festival constitutes a way by which people reflexively think through their own cultural essence and reaffirm their ethnic uniqueness in antithetical terms.

Part II: Community Identities in Formation

Performances of Unity, Community, and Diversity

The taking of the square is clearly a displacement of white-mestizo society. This challenge to the hegemonic culture, however, is neither simple nor entirely unified. Simultaneous to the indigenous identities defined in juxtaposition to an urban-mestizo referent is a process of intraethnic identity differentiation among and within indigenous communities. The complex performance of the ritual enacts the simultaneity of identities defined variously vis-à-vis one another and emergent in different contexts, flexibly emphasized from one moment to the next as people respond to the thick environment of the festival. Here, I focus on the dancing descent to the plaza, and analyze community solidarity and individual reflexivity that prevail during this part of the ritual.

La largada de los sanjuanes (the departure of the San Juan dancers), which marks what could be described as a dancing pilgrimage from each community to the town center, embodies both unity and individual difference.

The morning of each festival day, dancers gather in their respective communities. They drink together in a ritual pattern of offering and accepting drinks from a communal cup, and pouring libations to the Earth. Drinking during festivals as well as in quotidian contexts among Runakuna is ritualized. *Chicha, trago,* and beer are consumed from a communal cup in rounds of offerings. Generally, one approaches people in order, offering drinks in a clockwise direction among a group gathered in a circle by saying *upyashunchik* (let's drink together). At each serving, participants pour libations to the Earth. Some people feel it is proper to pour an offering to the Pacha Mama before drinking, and others fling the remnants on the Earth after they have consumed the contents, with the dual purpose of cleaning the cup for the next participant. Ritualized consumption of alcohol is inherently dialogical. Offering a drink is an invitation to engage in dialogue; accepting a drink constitutes a willingness to enter into conversation. No one drinks alone or in silence (see also Butler 2006:89–98, Salz 1955:99).

Sanjuanes begin by dancing in their own communities in a rotating circle to the music of twin flutes, stomping on the ground on the descending first beat of the rhythm, *levantando polvo* (lifting a cloud of dust around them) to awaken the Earth. Depending on the distance from the community to the town plaza, they will depart mid to late morning to arrive in Cotacachi at noon, the hour at which the sun's rays are perpendicular to the Earth's equator.

The zigzag movement of a single line of dancers descending from each community periodically develops into a revolving spiral and then repeats all the way down to the central plaza. This dance pattern was referred to by some people as *serpenteado.* This dance sequence characterizes the *largada* in the Cotacachi area. Nine communities dominate the *toma* in Cotacachi—Turuku, Topo Grande, Topo Chico, and Santa Barbara from the *hanan,* or upper, moiety; La Calera, San Martín, Cumbas Conde, San Ignacio, and Quitugo from the *uray,* or lower, moiety. Seventeen other communities participate in various *tomas* around the canton. Once they reach the plaza, dancers of upper and lower moiety communities join their respective coalitions and dance in formation around the plaza.

Taita Alfonso Maygua, a resident of La Calera, initially called my attention to the importance of the *serpenteado.* During a presentation for the community of La Calera of video footage I had taken of ritual dancing in their community, Taita Alfonso took it upon himself, as educator and cultural broker under the title of community *yachak,* to explain the significance of certain events captured on film. At one point, he stopped the video and scolded the younger generation for dancing in a way he characterized as *"totalmente desorganizada; aculturizada"* (totally disorganized; acculturated). In a single top to bottom motion, he drew on the chalkboard the following design, and stated:

> Before, we used to dance like this, *quingueado* or *serpenteado,* which means curved or turning corners. Why did we dance like this? *Serpenteado* is the path of the water that upon reaching its destiny accumulates as a whirlpool and swells in order to begin a new river. These teachings were good. Now, there is not any order in the dancing. There are no longer people to teach this or people who even know what it means.

Taita Alfonso reminded people of the importance of the original interpretation and the purpose of the enacted pattern, and highlighted that every aspect of ritual performance has a specific meaning. His emphasis on origins and the differentiation of ritual performance from everyday dancing warrants particular attention. Taita Alfonso's criticism of the disorganized dancing warns against an unchecked acceptance of an outlook that favors creative interpretation over structured practice. People often concluded, in light of the prevalence of discourses on multiculturality in the area, that they must

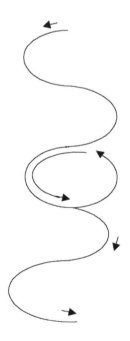

Serpenteado Dance Pattern

embrace, or at the very least tolerate, alternative interpretations, tastes, preferences, choices, and lifestyles in an eclectic reconfiguration of community and traditional practices. For Taita Alfonso, there is a correct and an incorrect way of performing the dance. The form itself allows for, and in fact encourages, creative variation. Nonetheless, alternative interpretations and renditions of the dance are limited by the indispensable conservation of the ritual's original meaning. As Mircea Eliade (1963:14) writes, this is because ritual not only contains the secret of how things came into existence but also, as is the case with myth, "where to find them and how to make them reappear when they disappear." The *serpenteado* pattern specifically depicts individuals traveling along a similar winding path and eventually coming together as a community. It is as a collectivity that they gain strength, Taita Alfonso Maygua stated, by remembering who they are. This shared experience subsequently impels individuals with renewed energy to continue along a new meandering path, which Taita Alfonso depicted as the birth of a new river.

Barbara Butler (2006:81–82) offers a diagram similar to the one drawn by Taita Alfonso Maygua to capture the to and fro, up and down, back and forth movement that so preoccupies people in their quotidian exchanges. She argues that this concept reveals more than a customary pattern. Butler understands it as a "basic cosmological principle that is acted out in ritual and observed in such diverse things as the alternation of generations, the back and forth movement of the shuttle in weaving, and the obligatory reciprocity of people, communities, ecological zones, and spirits."[13]

The reflexivity and regeneration enacted in the *serpenteado* dance, in addition, resonate with the concept of "chthonic power" or "inner qualities" that Norman Whitten (1988:283) describes in the context of Amazonian Ecuador. *Serpenteado,* from the Spanish *serpiente,* means serpentlike; but among bilingual Quichua-Spanish speakers undoubtedly refers to a boa constrictor (*amarun*). Norman Whitten (1988) describes Amazonian Canelos Quichua practices wherein the *amarun* is a central symbolic concept. Upon slaying an anaconda or other boa, Canelos Quichua people typically sever the constrictor's head from the body and bury it separately on land, away from its lair in the water. Mythically, the body eventually grows toward the head, engendering a more powerful resurrection of the constrictor. This phenomenon is known as *tupaj amarun* (Whitten 1988:295). The meeting of the body with the head, derived from the Quichua verb to meet or encounter (*tuparina*),[14] symbolizes the inherent abilities of Andean communities to reconstitute and reproduce themselves (Whitten 1988:283). The emphasis on community, process, continuation, rebirth, and transformation in Taita

Alfonso's memory of the dance resonates with these concepts. The hydraulic metaphor in Taita Alfonso's explication, moreover, confirms a worldview that spans both Andean and eastern Amazonian cosmovision wherein people are thought to be contained by their own essence in the same way water is contained by and simultaneously contains the world. The pervasiveness of both water symbolism and serpent images as vehicles for the movement of ancestors is documented by Jeannette E. Sherbondy (1992:46–67) in the context of pre-Inka Andean practices, and confirmed by Norman Whitten (1988:283) in contemporary indigenous interpretations of water as a medium for transformation and transposition.

The notion of *tupaj amarun* alludes to the Inkarrí myth, which prophesied the return of the last Inka to restore world order. It became prevalent in the Andes in the modern era mainly in reference to the leader of the eighteenth-century millenarian movement, and also to Tupak Amaru I, who was beheaded in the main plaza of Cuzco in 1572. The name Tupak Amaru draws its force from the prediction of the inevitable upheaval anticipated to occur when the body of the anaconda successfully meets up with the head.

Aya Uma wrapped in an anaconda skin during Inti Raymi celebrations in the highland community of Urcuciqui, Cantón Cotacachi

It also points to the looming danger of the liminal time between death and rebirth during which the *amarun* lies underground harnessing its strength (Whitten 1988:295). The symbolism of the *serpenteado* dance pertains explicitly to the concept of *pachakutik,* understood generally as an overturning of time and space. Michael Uzendoski (2005:23, 165) describes this powerful phenomenon as an embodied subjectivity of transformation that inhabits each person and is expressed in the poetics of "destroying, recuperating, and transforming society and history" for the production of a better life (see also N. Whitten 2003:x). Regeneration through symbolic (or real) eschatological overturning described in the concept of *tomas* and developed more explicitly in the analysis of ritual fighting (chapter 4), which Ariruma Kowii (1999a) describes as "the encounter of opposites from which something new transpires," emerges as a continuing motif in the *serpenteado* dance. Before turning to the ritual fights of the *tinkuy* or *makanakuy* in chapter 4, in the section that follows I elucidate the necessary and accompanying cosmogony of the process underlying the *pachakutik.*

Tuparina

In certain communities, the *serpenteado* is performed as a double helix. This rendition of the dance probably best captures the concept of *encuentros* as a dialogical interlacing often referred to as *tuparina.* This variation of the dance shows progression through binary complementarity, which lies at the heart of indigenous values. The performance of this interlacing also captures Linda D'Amico's (1993:17) observation that, "rather than progressing only ahead, time and space are interwoven in zigzag-like patterns which (re)act in a complementary manner." The prominence of the double helix also strikes a resonance with Macas, Belote, and Belote's (2003:218–20) use of the signature herringbone braid (*jimba*) of the Saraguros of southern Ecuador as a metaphor for understanding how indigenous peoples "maintain their autonomy and identity through a process of ethnogenesis in which they combine and recombine their learning about life."

I observed this interpretation of the dance in the community of Peguche, Cantón Otavalo, for the San Pedro festival. In Peguche, the dance is not part of a descent of individual groups to the main plaza, but is instead performed within the community itself by costumed participants who dance in the central plaza inside a demarcated festival space. *Banda* music played by a brass band in 4/4 meter, with an emphasis on the first beat, accompanies the dance. Dancers progress forward in two parallel, interlacing lines with a simple, shuffled walk. Each step falls on the beat of the music. *1*, 2, 3, 4 -

1, 2, 3, 4. The rhythm is marked by a conservative swaying of the arms and the body for four beats in one direction and then in the other.

The significance of the dance is underscored by the antagonistic presence of the Aya Uma (literally, spirit head). The Aya Uma wears a double-sided, hoodlike mask with "horns" on top.[15] Kowii (1999b:21) suggests that the two faces of the Aya Uma symbolize the *ñawpa* and *kipa*, the past and future of Quichua cosmovision, gazing respectively toward the *hanan* and the *uray*. Although his performance hinges on innovation and improvisation, the costume of the trickster spirit head remains relatively unchanged from year to year. In contrast, the costumes of the line dancers reflect contemporary themes and depict corrupt politicians, popular television and movie characters, and international political figures, or reveal local social dynamics such as the presence of evangelicals, regional vendors, hippies, tourists, reporters, and researchers in the Otavalo area. Though the costumes change in response to social and historical contexts, the dance pattern of the *serpenteado* remains consistent.

It is significant that this trickster spirit head, who enacts both order and chaos, dances in the main plaza separate from the winding lines of dancers, trying to interrupt the intertwining double helix. The Aya Uma lies down in front of the dance troupes, blocking their passage. He mimics the troupe leader and tries to lead the dancers in the wrong direction. And much to the amusement of the crowd, the dancers wind around and over him without missing a beat. They ignore his leadership and remain indifferent to his efforts to sabotage the choreography. The Aya Uma often performs backward, and shifting roles unexpectedly he tries to impose order, waving this *acial* and making dancers dance just so. Dancers also ignore these impositions of order. My interpretation is that the inevitable progression of the *serpenteado* is an enactment of the moral fabric of society that the Aya Uma unsuccessfully tries to disrupt. The motion of the *serpenteado* is flexible and adaptable, and always returns fluidly to the double helix or interweaving metaphorical serpents.

Amarushina Tuparin—The Traveling Festival[16]

The progressive character of the *serpenteado* in both renditions of the dance underscores the importance of movement, adaptability, and change. Perhaps the most important and most overlooked dimension of the San Juan festival is its tendency to travel. In addition to the displacement of dancers from their respective communities to the town centers on the day of San Juan, on the evening of June 22 people gather at various sacred water sources for the Armay Chisi, or ritual bath, to prepare for the dancing. Then, on the eve of San Juan (*la víspera*), June 23, dancers and musicians go from one household to the next, visiting friends and kin over the course of the entire night. *Sanjuanes* traveling on foot generally stay within their own communities. Groups of young men might venture to neighboring towns. People with transportation will travel from Otavalo to Cotacachi and sometimes as far as Ibarra, stopping in smaller communities along their dance circuit. What is more, the Inti Raymi festival itself transfers from one town to another.

The migratory sequence of the festival in Imbabura and northern Pichincha provinces roughly conforms to the following pattern: Dancers mentally and spiritually prepare for the ritual days in advance, and on June 22 they gather at sacred water sources. In the Otavalo and Cotacachi area, La Cascada de Peguche is the most prominent site for ritual bathing. People from different communities attend the ritual inaugurations of San Juan at the sacred spring of San Juan Pukyu in the community of Ilumán. Ilumán reserves this privilege both because of its reputable shamans and because of the victory over water rights against the provincial government, which added political significance to the celebration.[17] Dancing and fighting begin in Otavalo and Cotacachi simultaneously on June 24 for three days. Generally people attend the festivities in Otavalo for San Juan and flock to Cotacachi for San Pedro, on June 29, when the heavy fighting breaks out. Inti Raymi in Cayambe, located in the neighboring province of Pichincha to the south, is next, with parades and a different style of music and dance in the tradition of *coplas*. *Coplas* are humorous couplets repeated twice to music in 2/4 rhythm that invite creative lyrical variation from other members of the group. Notably, the celebrations in Cayambe include much more female participation. San Pedro in Peguche and Agato has taken place as late as August some years, and is one of the area's most popular costumed dances. Although the Inti Raymi offers the clearest illustration of the traveling nature of ritual celebrations in the Imbabura area, other festive rituals follow a similar pattern. Among the most notable are Coya Raymi, Tarpuy Raymi, Fiestas del Yamor (Otavalo), and Fiestas de la Jora (Cotacachi) in September; Pawkar Raymi and Carnaval in February and March; and Semana Santa (Holy Week and Easter) celebrations in April.

La Víspera

The *serpenteado* in its various forms captures the nature of the traveling festival as processions of dancers and musicians meander along *chakiñanes* (footpaths) from community to community, competing with other groups in musical encounters, renewing connections among kin, growing across the landscape like the giant regenerative *amarun*. The reunions that take place in each household and the collective experience of traveling together reenact the concepts of dialogical interlacing, *encuentros,* and the continual renewal of individuals and community illustrated in the festival dance patterns.

On the eve of San Juan, June 23, 2001, I was invited to join a festival group from the community of Peguche. Friends and relatives gathered with their costumes and musical instruments. Although dancing on the *víspera* remains predominantly a male activity, women and children do join in for the earlier part of the evening. Popular costumes included men dressed as women, scary *ñustas* (horrific indigenous beauty queens), monster masks, obscene Catholic priests[18] and pregnant nuns, vampire politicians, camera-laden *gringo* tourists, Mexicans, Arabs, North American Indians, Ninja Turtles, and women dressed as Zuletas (indigenous women from a neighboring region with a distinct ethnic costume featuring embroidered blouses, petticoat skirts, and bowler hats). Worthy of particular mention was a *"Reina de la Iglesia Evangélica"* (Queen of the evangelical church) with wild, flowing hair. I participated as a Texas *ñusta*—half *indígena,* half cowgirl beauty queen. We proceeded from one house to the next, entering the patio or main room of each house and dancing in a revolving circle, first in one direction, then in the other—much like the dancing that occurs in the taking of the square, but also like the spiral of the *serpenteado* that swells and eventually spills over into a continuing path.

Musical battles, which during the eve take the place of actual fighting in the plaza, ensued as more groups flooded the courtyards of local residences with distinctive styles of *sanjuanito* music and dancing. Younger, upper-class Otavaleños who, from the perspective of a group of dancers from Cotacachi, danced "in a sophisticated manner," got edged out of the courtyard by older generation musicians from Topo, who danced *con fuerza* (vigorously), revealing both regional and generational differences. Individuals expressed their musical likes and dislikes, and asserted their affiliation to particular groups based on these criteria.

Hosts brought out food and drink for the *sanjuanes.* The generosity of the hosts depended on the level of acquaintance, the quality of the performance of the dancers and musicians, and the creativity of their costumes. Other groups dancing in the courtyard joined our entourage. Our group swelled in size. Eventually, when it became too large, the original members skillfully lost the unwanted company and proceeded to another household. Inclusion in and exclusion from any given group were continuously negotiated throughout the night.

The chill of the highland summer nights and the darkness along the wind-ing *chakiñanes* provided a unique space for conversation. Joke telling lightened the tone of more intimate dialogue along the paths. The disguised falsetto voice in which people spoke and sang for the duration of the festival lent itself to light-hearted teasing. People say that the falsetto voices imitate the manner of speech of the souls to make them feel welcome as they return to the community to join the living in a celebration of San Juan. People talked together, recognizing the landscape, telling stories about the secrecy of these *chakiñanes* in the *hacienda* days, and remembering local folk stories about the *chusalongo,* a mischievous creature with an enormous penis that seduces young women who venture to the mountain alone. Familiar landmarks and the historical and social changes inscribed on the landscape seemed to affirm the dancers' individual and collective association with this place. Recogni-tion of the surroundings and knowledge of the stories told in connection to the land helped the *sanjuanes* regain orientation in their drunken state, and generated a sense of reassurance not only of where people were, but of *who* they were.

As the evening progressed, reunions with relatives, friends, and former love interests jogged old memories. Nostalgia often set in as people lament-ed missed opportunities for love or remembered deceased *compañeros* (col-leagues) and reminisced about dancing with them during San Juan. The pas-sage through geographical terrain was also a journey through memory, both collective and personal. The Andean concept of *Ñawpa,* which simultaneously designates forward in space and backward in time, captures this progression. *Ñawpa Yachaykuna* refers to the deep knowledge that derives from the past in all its dimension, conceived of as lying right in front of a person as he or she progresses along a life path. It is an element of both anchoring and continu-ity. The future, on the other hand, lies behind us in the Andean time-space because we cannot see it. Passage through the liminal time and space of the *víspera* effectively enacted the processes of unity, community, and diversity shaped through both memory and collective experience.

A Moveable Feast

During the period of the Inti Raymi, people prolong the festival experience by traveling to different communities as the celebrations displace themselves. The moveable character of the Inti Raymi allows for individuals to participate in markedly different capacities throughout the course of the festival season. People serve as organizers at one event, dancers and musicians in a different place, hosts in one town, guests in another, and audience someplace else. This type of rotation requires a broader and more flexible understanding of the lived experience of individual identities. Changing roles allows individuals to court social relations from different vantage points. Dancers exert themselves, demonstrating their stamina and strength; musicians flaunt their rhythmic skills; hosts attempt to outdo one another in their generosity. Each gains respect for performing his or her respective role to the best of her ability and to the limit of his resources.

In addition, the displacement of the festival allows for comparative assessment at the level of households and communities, providing a vocabulary that more clearly nuances the criteria for ethnic inclusion. The reputations of individuals and entire towns often ride on the quality of reception offered to the *sanjuanes*. Greeting the *sanjuanes* properly responds to a code of local social commentary and has implications for local politics and social relations. José Manuel Quimbo, president of UNAIMCO in 2001, for example, centered the event in Otavalo on the generous reception of the San Juan dancers. In an effort to dispel the negative image that people in Otavalo offer meager portions of food and drink during the festivals and only spend money on improving their own situations, UNAIMCO bought 180 guinea pigs and 120 chickens to feed the *sanjuanes*.

During Inti Raymi 2001, UNAIMCO staged a symbolic taking of an abandoned restaurant to assert their claim on a highly contested piece of real estate in central Otavalo. At the time, Quimbo explained to colleagues involved in the logistics of the plan that the *toma* of the Allimikuy restaurant was just like the *toma de la plaza*. Possession of the structure allowed UNAIMCO to receive the dance groups properly, in a house, in accordance with tradition. After hosting the *sanjuanes,* another coordinator for the festivities expressed great concern that the chickens sent from a supplier in Quito were rather small and that this was a source of embarrassment that potentially compromised the image of generosity they were trying to project.

UNAIMCO's goals for the near future are to gain regional, national, and international recognition not only for its role in promoting artisan guilds but for its influence in defining a new identity in Otavalo and serving as a representative institution for the city and the canton. The taking of the Allimikuy house positioned UNAIMCO as a political actor of consequence in the context of a performed and actual *toma*. The abundance of food and drink offered during the Inti Raymi ranked the artisans' union as an important economic force in the city. And, that UNAIMCO did all of this with attention to cultural detail and festival protocol legitimated the organization as a cultural broker. Nothing short of this was at stake in the slight weight difference of the San Juan chickens.

The etiquette of festival hosting, along with its social implications, has become increasingly important as Otavaleños cast their political and economic nets more broadly. Especially during the summer months, Otavaleños traveling abroad will smuggle cooked guinea pigs, hominy, and *tostado* (roasted corn—the essential accompaniment for any indigenous meal) past foreign customs officers. Tucked in their personal items, one might find an Aya Uma mask, as people make efforts to replicate some aspects of the festival back home. The tradition of the Inti Raymi practiced abroad brings migrant communities of Otavaleños together in celebration of their ethnic identity. The emphasis on celebrating the Inti Raymi wherever Otavaleños reside underscores the importance not just of meeting socially but also of recognizing one another and themselves as Otavaleños. It is significant that in the Spanish usage, *encontrarse* (to meet) captures both a reciprocal and a reflexive connotation conveying the notion of "finding each other," but also of "finding oneself."

So far we have seen the taking of the square in an interpretation of ethnic contrast and the *serpenteado* dance as a process of individual reflection and community formation. In the following chapter, I explore two other types of dancing practiced during the Inti Raymi: (1) the spiral as a form that circumscribes the individual within the whole, wherein membership in communities and moieties becomes the overriding reference point for identity; and (2) stomping on the ground as a dialogue with the Earth and as a form of ritual sacrifice. These dance forms become prominent once the San Juan dancers descending from their respective communities reach the main plaza in Cotacachi, where they confront each other violently in ritual battles.

Mythico-Religious Encounters—
The Clash of Aciales

Once the San Juan dancers reach the main plaza in Cotacachi, small groups gradually join larger upper- and lower-moiety coalitions in preparation for a competition among moieties to win the church square. This chapter centers on the performance of violence in intercommunity dynamics and on human sacrifice as a conduit for mythico-religious encounters. By mythico-religious encounters I mean contexts wherein people exist alongside and interact with beings from other time-spaces. It is when the passage to other realms of experience is opened that the collectivity is fully conjured into being as a community in holistic terms. As practical circumstances lead to variations on the socially defined ideal of ritual death, I examine the poetics of violence and the socially and morally encoded discourses on meaningful death. These elements combined reveal the ways by which symbolic violence emerges as a constitutive element of both intraethnic integration and interethnic differentiation.

Centripetal Force

Groups move around the main plaza in Cotacachi in a counterclockwise direction to the birdlike tune of the twin flutes. A man occasionally blows a *churu* (conch shell). At each corner of the plaza, musicians play the more upbeat 2/4 rhythm of the *sanjuanito,* traditionally led by the *rondín* (harmonica). It bears mentioning that male children as young as four or five years also dance alongside their fathers, imitating the movements of the grownups.[1] Dancers alternate their rotation, moving first in one direction then in the other when someone calls "*vuelta! vuelta!*" (turn). Calling the *vuelta* or *tikray* (half turn) is not done randomly. The person that calls the turn indicates by shouting "*vuelta! vuelta!*" that he is undergoing or intending to undergo a personal transformation. The group acknowledges this and follows. As the circle turns, the spiraling, centripetal motion draws more dancers into the rotating mass. "It's all about the collective," says Segundo Anrrango, "the moment of the dance and of the fights, one disappears as an individual. One forgets one's own name. The only thing one knows is that one is part of the group."

I heard similar descriptions from several dancers who said that transported by the repetitive rhythm of the music, the shouting, the whistling, the alcohol, and the revolving form of the dance, they lose themselves as individuals in the identity of the group, of the *ayllu*, the larger community. Magdalena Fueres, director of Jambi Mascaric, the healing center associated with UNORCAC, confirmed during an interview that the aesthetic of the dance underscores participation as a collectivity. She stated that, in fact, people believe there is the danger of hearing a different tune if one ventures too far from the group. That is when people become susceptible "*a que le coja el aya*" (to being overcome by a spirit). The intimacy achieved through collective dancing and ritual violence illustrates the affective and physical bond at the heart of group identities that ethnomusicologist Thomas Turino (2004:18) describes:

> as activities that involve and coordinate the sound and motion of relatively large groups of people, singing, chanting, dancing, and marching can create the actual sense of collective unity through sounding and moving together. Sonic and kinesic synchrony comprise signs of similarity often experienced below the level of focal awareness. The subtle signs involved (detailed ways of moving, sonic attack, articulation, pitch coordination, rhythm) are not perceived as explicit propositions *about* identity but rather are the very experience *of* similarity, *of* identity, each participant responding to and coordinating with the sounds and movements of others. Group performance experiences tend to have very powerful somatic and emotional affects precisely because they are the experience of a special kind of physical bond with others. (See also Mendoza 2000:33)

Tinkuy

Segundo Anrrango describes the *tinkuy*, the ritual battle.[2] "The fight is like a war." He stops. "No, it *is* a war." Anrrango's reformulation of his statement blurs the boundary between symbolic representation and metaphoric enactment as lived experience. Potential and, in the case of the Inti Raymi, very real fights overflow from the realm of symbolism to that of experience. This is what fuels popular attraction to this event. In Cotacachi, performed combat unexpectedly gives way to actual violence.

The ominous mood in the town center is set hours in advance of the *sanjuanes'* arrival, with the presence of police and military armed with tear gas canisters and launchers, and army trucks stationed at each corner of the plaza. In 2001 there were between sixty and seventy police and military guards assigned to the festival.[3] Parsons (1945:111) documents police presence in Otavalo during the fights as early as 1940, attesting to the sustained presence of violence in this tradition. And Hassaurek (1997[1867]:307–8) writes about fights and great rural battles among the Indians on the second day of San Juan during his 1863 travels in Imbabura.[4] Concern builds weeks before the festival as indigenous representatives, police, municipal authorities, and religious leaders meet and discuss strategies for controlling the fight. In the communities, speculation about the disputes to be settled begins brewing, because the Inti Raymi fights are considered an opportunity for leveling accounts and resolving conflict accumulated throughout the year. In anticipation of the festival, Cotacachi residents leave town.[5] On the day of San Juan (June 24) and especially San Pedro (June 29), business establishments around the Plaza de la Matriz, the main town square, draw their heavy metal window and door shutters down low or close for business altogether.

A blood sacrifice is expected during the ritual. Blood is associated with fertility, and during the summer harvest festivals, it must be spilled to revitalize the Earth for the next planting season. Luis Enrique Cachiguango (2001) explains that this act is part of the cycle of mutual nurturing wherein "the Runa nurtures the Pachamama and allows himself to be nurtured by her." In Cantón Otavalo, the sacrifice is generally performed with what is known as the *gallo fiti*. The offering involves tearing off the head of a rooster while the animal is still alive, and splashing the blood on the ground as well as on people standing close by. The *gallo fiti* signals the passing of the *fiesta cargo*. By tearing off the rooster's head, an individual publicly indicates his acceptance of responsibility for sponsoring the *fiesta* the following year. In Cantón Cotacachi, the sacrificial animal blood to nurture the Earth Mother is replaced with the human blood of the dancers themselves.

Fear and anticipation are quite justified. The male energy of the *pukyus* (springs) is particularly strong at this time of year. Cachiguango (2001:21) states that springs and waterfalls become acutely energized from 11:00 A.M. to 1:00 P.M. during the day, and from 11:00 P.M. to 1:00 A.M. at night on June

Tinkuy

22. At this moment the doors of communication with other *pachas* (time-spaces or universes) open. Male forces are unleashed and brim over, causing a universal imbalance that then calls for resolution. Reimposing equilibrium requires violent confrontation. "This is why," Cachiguango maintains, "Runakuna have to confront each other; except it is actually the *ayas* who are fighting."

Participants in the ritual bath are considered to be in a delicate liminal state; in a trancelike possession that allows them to be conduits for otherworldly communication. When dancers from *el bajo*, the lower moiety led by the community of La Calera, bathe ritually before the fight to gain strength through temporary possession of an *aya*, or spirit, people consider them half crazed (*medio enloquecidos*). They elicit caution in this condition because as extremely powerful and morally ambiguous beings, *ayas* have unpredictable effects on different individuals. Similarly, people from La Calera consider dancers from Topo, the leading community of *el alto*, or the upper moiety, to become *medio salvajes* (wild or savage) during the San Juan and San Pedro season.

Dancers from Topo do not even bathe ritually. They believe that if they did, they would acquire excessive strength. Socially, they have a responsibility not to exceed the limits of festival violence. Once blood is spilled and the ritual obligation is fulfilled, there is no purpose in continuing the fight. The act of not bathing for the fight strategically boosts the reputation of Topo as the more powerful of the two moieties, as well. For emphasis, one dancer added, "They say that the ones from Topo are like the 'terminator' from the movies." He pronounces the word in English: "*el terminator*," and explains, "Even when his eye is hanging out or his ear falls off, somehow he goes on fighting."

In 2001 I witnessed a ritual fight in the center of the plaza. Whistling announced the impending clash. As the aggressors advanced counterclockwise around the plaza toward a new corner, the group occupying the corner acknowledged their desire to fight by delaying their retreat, thus prompting the confrontation. Rocks began to fly, sending vendors, onlookers, musicians, children, and dogs scurrying in all directions. I ducked into a store just as rocks pounded against the door being closed behind me. Police immediately fired tear gas to control the fight, creating a battleground effect of lingering haze. The clash of *aciales* against human bodies and stray rocks ricocheting off the shieldlike cardboard hats, also designed to hide the identity of the *sanjuanes,* lasted only a few minutes before the fighting moved into the side streets. People slowly emerged from their temporary refuges, retaking their positions on the street, behind their food stands, and at the foosball tables. Those who had access to cigarettes, including children and elderly women, puffed on them to fend off the effects of the tear gas. Victims had been quickly enveloped by their entourage and hidden from both the competing side and the police. The only evidence left behind was the blood-stained sidewalks and loose rocks around which people gathered in speculation.

Pain, Endurance, and Religious Transcendence

Vigor and endurance characterize the dance. Anrrango showed me several scars, proud mementos of injuries from San Juan fights in his younger years, many of which sent him to the hospital emergency room. Aside from the strength demonstrated in the fights, the dancing itself demands vigorous effort. The dancers move in a circle, stomping on the ground, lifting a cloud of dust around them, shouting "*Churay! Churay!*" (Put it there!) and "*Kashnamari! Kashnamari!*" (This is how we are!). They are able to dance almost continuously like this for days, taking only short breaks to eat and drink. The stomping, according to the many participants with whom I spoke, is a way of communicating with the Earth, of letting the Earth feel their presence and of waking up the Pachamama. It is also a form of self-inflicted pain and a trial of endurance offered in sacrifice. The high-impact style of the dance causes significant damage to joints, especially knees and ankles. Dancers, moreover, often borrow boots, which do not form part of their regular attire. In addition to the lack of habit in wearing this footwear, borrowed boots often fit too loosely or too tightly, and are generally worn without socks, causing painful blistering.

When at one of the festivals I commented on the impressive stamina of the *sanjuanes,* a Quichua friend of mine responded, "That's the difference with the Indians." We return to Crespi's (1981:488) observation that in the mid twentieth century, "being Indian traditionally meant celebrating the fiesta of San Juan." Her comment indicates the widespread popularity of the festival among Imbabura- and Cayambe-area communities. Beyond the avid participation of Otavaleños in honoring San Juan (who eventually came to be known as the "Indian saint"), my friend's response refocuses our attention on certain qualities that capture the essence of being Indian and that serve as reference points for ethnic differentiation. "Being Indian" is not only defined by participation in the celebrations of San Juan but by the capacity to *endure* the dance.

Physical strength, endurance, exertion, and survival characterize the everyday experiences of indigenous people in the Imbabura area. They constitute what Turino (2004:9) describes as "the subtle signs of social identity that are the result of deeply embedded habit." Collective recognition of an ability to endure is the foundation of the self-assurance indigenous people demonstrate in facing their problems and engaging in physically and morally trying experiences, whether it is the dance of San Juan, intense agricultural labor, international travel, *levantamientos* (uprisings), or protest marches to the capital.[6] In contrast, in the communities it is considered common knowledge that white people do not have the same capacity for work. Countless times I heard "*mamitica, no ha de poder*" (poor thing, she will not be able to do it), said in a tone of compassion toward me and other white people in reference to our supposed inability to lift heavy things, do physical labor, or stay awake.[7]

Endurance and especially not sleeping, according to Mircea Eliade (1963), are not merely about conquering physical fatigue but are, above all, proof of spiritual strength. He states, "remaining 'awake' means being fully conscious, being present in the world of the spirit" (Eliade 1963:131). From an Andean perspective, Cachiguango (2001:22) explains that the victims of the San Juan fights are considered to be privileged, because they have been selected by the Pachamama as the link between humans and beings from other worlds. Through insomnia, the agony of the dance, and the blood ritual, they become human *chakanas* (cosmic intersections) upon which the realms of Andean time-space converge momentarily.

The Poetics of Violence: Discourses on Meaningful Death

The death of one or two dancers each year is considered necessary for the ritual. These deaths, however, are not indiscriminate. Human sacrifice must conform to certain criteria in order to fulfill the ritual obligation. Neil Whitehead (2002:192–93) encourages us to think beyond statistical incidences or the medical features in our search for meaning and to focus instead on how violence is performed and collectively understood—in his words, on "the poetics of violence and the discourse and discursive practice to which it gives rise." In this section, I turn to reflexive community discussion surrounding a San Juan death in 2001 to draw attention to varying interpretations and justifications of violence and death within the context of the Inti Raymi festival complex.

Reports in the media stated simply that a death had occurred during the San Juan festival in accordance with the ritual tradition in Cotacachi, offering little detail about the circumstances surrounding the fatality. These reports reflect a tendency on the part of town officials and mestizo residents to dismiss festival deaths as results of reckless violence and to subsume "any act of violence as a manifestation of a return to barbarism" (Sorel 1999:175). In tourism pamphlets published by the *municipio*, reference to the poignant social critique performed in Inti Raymi dances is omitted and the "mimetic interplay between colonial violence and the violent representation of indigenous people" (Taussig 1987 quoted in Whitehead 2002:191, see also Quiroga 2003, Whitehead 2002:8, and Guss 2006) is ignored altogether. In spite of the presence of an indigenous mayor, municipal advertising promotes the Inti Raymi as a tourist event. Packaging of the festival in these terms minimizes public appreciation of the profound meaning of the dance. It leads, moreover, to an underestimation of the intensity of the fights because of a conflation of tourist event and ritual—the first being a dramatic presentation with no ensuing consequence; the second, a powerful socially and cosmically generative act. Tolerance of the fights goes only so far as townspeople are able to profit from the tourism it attracts. Beyond any concern for the lives of the indigenous dancers themselves, apprehension on the part of business owners centers on how unruly fighting might turn tourists away and affect business around the main plaza.

In the communities of both upper and lower moieties, conversation about the occurrence in 2001 lingered. Though community members affirmed that violence was a necessary component of the ritual dancing, there was an uneasy sense that this particular death was problematic. Two members of an upper moiety community had inflicted repeated blows upon a twenty-nine-year-old man from a lower moiety village, crushing his skull against a sidewalk. The manner of the killing was deemed particularly brutal. The two men from Turuku had attacked the young man from San Martín with a heavy *acial* made of *madera de monte* (wood from the uncultivated foothills) and a *churu* (conch shell). The detail of the dense wood used for the *acial* in many conversations indicated disapproval of the deliberate choice of a potentially lethal material. Nonetheless, people explained that this type of improvisation in the construction of weapons was understandable given the increasingly violent nature of the fights. The circumstances of the death, on the other hand, were highly questionable.

On the second day of San Juan in the afternoon, the upper moiety dancers were returning to their community through El Ejido (the arboretum near Turuku). Dancers from San Martín had followed to provoke them. The Topo Grande coalition reacted violently to this affront in their own territory and San Martín was forced to withdraw. Segundo Anrrango commented that it is generally in the heat and disorganization of the retreat that victims fall. Usually people who are less integrated in the "game of violence" are those who are most vulnerable. In this case, the misfortune befell a young man who had only recently joined the dance. He was inebriated according to some, but most importantly, he had just gotten off work from one of the flower plantations in the area and had not had time to incorporate into the collective rhythm of the dance. I thought of Magdalena Fueres's remark about the danger of dancing to a tempo different from that of the group. The young man was caught off guard, and then it had been too late for him to run as he fell victim to the attack.

In *el alto* (the upper moiety) there was silence regarding the killing and a general sense of lack of fulfillment, according to people I interviewed. "It's not as if they are happy about it because the next day they are no longer drunk and they are reflecting on what happened," stated one person with whom I spoke. Colleagues at UNORCAC who are residents of Turuku reported that the two responsible for the death *"están silenciosos"* (are silent), an expression that carries the subtext of being ashamed. I inquired further as to why this particular death elicited such remorse. Anrrango explained that among the criteria for selecting the captains of the dance troupes was good judgment:

The one occupying this position must be a judicious man who does not arrive at death only for the sake of violence. Instead, he has to control that this does not happen. This is the condition for being a captain. The other condition is that if the confrontation is inevitable, the captain must not flee the conflict. He must confront the fight. I imagine that it is based on this profile that the actions of all dancers are evaluated.

According to residents of the upper moiety, the manner of the death in question reflected none of these attributes. This had been an opportunistic killing, unnecessarily violent in nature, in which, it was said, neither victim nor attackers achieved transcendence.

Liability for the death, nonetheless, was absorbed by the group as a whole. Festival injuries and deaths are conceived to be part of a collective action and responsibility. Individual culprits are unlikely to be singled out, and generally no one seeks legal reprisals for misfortunes that occur as part of the annual ritual. In this case, the sense of generalized responsibility was further substantiated by the involvement of UNORCAC in attempting to curb the fights. UNORCAC principals had decided to incarcerate the captains of upper- and lower-moiety dance troupes in an effort to control the violence. It was while the troupe leaders were in detention that the death occurred. Subsequent criticism revolved around the fact that this death might have been avoided had the captains been directing the fight. To make matters worse, UNORCAC's idea that keeping troupe leaders in jail for four days would appease violent behavior backfired. After the incident, captains were released early. They returned to their respective communities to dance with renewed aggression in the days that followed, causing furious clashes during San Pedro.

UNORCAC offered the widow financial compensation to help with funeral expenses. Representatives of the organization supported her by attending the funeral, explaining that they did so "because in truth, there are no personal offenders."[8] Although violent encounters retrace territorial and cultural moiety limits annually, it is the very performance of interlacing moiety distinctions that reconstitutes ethnic unity on a periodic basis. The shared experience of the fighting tradition in itself affirms an ethnic affinity. The statement offered by UNORCAC refocused accountability for the violence on the collective— upper and lower moieties combined. Financial remuneration, however, also insinuated acknowledgment of a wrongful death.

Shortly after the incident, UNORCAC declared the tragic loss of the young man's life a "sacred death." By elevating "death only for the sake of violence" to "religious sacrifice," the organization secured some honor for the family of the deceased, and bestowed social value upon what would otherwise constitute a meaningless death. Whitehead (2002:207) writes that in the case of ritual murder in the Patamuna and Makushi traditions in Guyana and Venezuela, some claims to *kanaimà* (ritual violence) are similarly used to supply meaning to an otherwise purposeless death. "This means," he explains, "that the broad cultural acceptance of the poetic of [ritual violence] works to obscure which cases are a reflection of the ritual action of kanaimà and which are part of a thanatology that uses kanaimà to create meaning in death" (Whitehead 2002:207). Variations on the ideal ritual death accommodate a range of mythico-religious experiences. Discourses on ritual violence, however, also allow for consideration of different social motivations that in some situations, as was the case with the fights in Cotacachi in 2001, allow for personal and collective reconciliation with a wrongful death. In this sense, the ritual realm provides an alternative space for justification and collective judgment separate from both the official legal apparatus of the state and from the influence of indigenous justice (a self-ruling system of sentencing within communities).

Conceptions of Violence

The distinction between ritual sacrifice and nonritual violence has implications for the ways in which societies understand and regulate expressions of violence and death. Since 1995 I have engaged Segundo Anrrango in an ongoing conversation about the difficulty of reconciling indigenous and mestizo perspectives on violence during the Inti Raymi fights. Though indigenous community members and mestizo town dwellers share concern over the escalation of violence during the fights and the consequent rising death toll associated with the festival, their motivations for controlling the violence and their proposed solutions are at odds.

Initially the confrontation between moiety coalitions involved fistfights that were halted the moment blood was drawn.[9] People from the upper moiety claim that because they were agriculturists and the folks from the lower moiety were artisans, the coalition led by Topo Grande was physically stronger and tended to win the fights. To compensate for the disparity in bodily build, dancers from La Calera, the lower moiety, introduced weapons. This triggered the escalation of violence during the San Juan dances. The story told by members of La Calera accuses the upper moiety of aggravating the fights. In either case, traditional *aciales* gave way to heavier whips laced with wire (later telephone cable) and with grips made out of *madera de monte*. The wives of the dancers began hiding a *doble acial,* a backup whip, in their *kepis* or backpacks in the event their husbands suddenly found themselves defenseless. Rocks became especially popular in the early 1990s when cobblestone was being laid in the streets near the plaza. That year numerous injuries and eight deaths resulted from pelting attacks. Two years prior to my arrival, there were knife injuries, and in the summer of 2000 three dancers from Topo suffered gunshot wounds. Although they all recovered, the incident anticipated that for the next festival season, dancers from the upper moiety might turn out with firearms to avenge the attacks.

This set of circumstances focused particular attention on security for the 2001 festival. Municipal authorities defaulted to recommendations that fights should be transferred outside the town center or suppressed altogether. Indigenous mayor Auki Tituaña tried to strike a compromise by encouraging dancers to congregate in the newly inaugurated Plaza del Sol, located a safe distance away from the town. Because this was the festival of the sun, Tituaña reasoned, it would make more sense for the groups to dance around the enormous, abstract metal sculpture of the sun erected on the outskirts of town. Predictably, this simplistic transposition of symbols was rejected by the communities. The point of the fights was to take the church. Some people alluded to the significance of taking the church in reference to an ancient *tola* (burial mound) that lay beneath it. Others said it was just tradition to dance in the church plaza. The mayor was dismissed as an "*indio urbano*" (urban Indian) who understood nothing of local practices. (For more on tensions between the *municipio* and the UNORCAC, see Ortiz Crespo 2004, Ramón Valarezo 2002, Pallares 2002).

Ideas by festival committee board members (mostly mestizos) for maintaining order included creating a civil patrol made up of high school students. The untroubled tone of the discussion signaled indifference to and possibly ignorance of the severe consequences of Inti Raymi festival encounters. Indigenous representatives found themselves obligated to spell out the gravity of the situation and underscore the need for combined indigenous, military, and ecclesiastical intervention. In contrast to the municipal board's downplaying of the situation, UNORCAC committed one of its most respected *dirigentes* to coordinate the effort. Alfonso Morales had gained public visibility and respect in the region based on his work on regional sustainable development projects (see Rhoades 2006). He was, in addition, perceived to have an unbiased disposition because he was a resident of neither moiety. As a member of the evangelical church, moreover, his participation was considered more objective. The permanent escort of women from both moieties who had monitored his role in mediating the conflict the previous year were satisfied with his evenhandedness and approved of his appointment for the job in 2001.[10] UNORCAC insisted that an *indígena* had to be at the head of the violence-monitoring forces in order to educate military and police about when and how to break up fights, with some sensitivity to the ritual dimension of the event.[11]

Emphasis was placed on confiscating deadly weapons in order to avoid unnecessary deaths, but not on stopping the fights. In a series of meetings prior to the festival, traditionally antagonistic groups were identified and "hot spots" or common sites of conflict beyond the plaza were mapped out.[12] In collaboration with police and military, an indigenous team would communicate via cellular phones to monitor situations likely to spill over into a larger territory. Father Gonzalo Flores from the Church of La Matriz represented a critical link both owing to his authority as Catholic priest and his experience as chaplain for the police forces for more than twenty years. Jambi Mascaric organized transportation for victims to the hospital for expedient treatment. Their role served two purposes—ensuring that participants received adequate medical attention and providing a legitimate alternative to police arrests for dancers who, crippled by the fights, would be unable to dodge the authorities.

Fellow workers at UNORCAC expressed vexation that the very mestizo people who criticize the violence of this indigenous ritual were unwilling to address it seriously, except to mandate suppression of the tradition in an undiscerning manner. These were the same people who would climb to their second-story windows to watch the fights from a distance and later complain that the festival was no good this year because there was not enough violence. Assertions that mestizos sometimes incited San Juan dancers to fight, but slipped away from the conflict simply to watch the bloody skirmish once the battle began, were laced with criticism. (See Tannia Mendizábal 1982 for a historical perspective on this interaction based on her 1978 study of the San Juan dances in Cotacachi.) From an indigenous perspective, morbid fascination with the death of others (specifically, indigenous others) characterized mestizos as "socially perverted," and by doing so, implicitly traced a moral difference between *indígenas* and mestizos.

Violent Rituals and Conflict Management

Discussion of ethnic difference in the perception of violence and indigenous attempts to grapple with escalation of ritual and nonritual violence within their communities continued in a series of workshops organized by

UNORCAC. These sessions began shortly before the festival in 2001 and continued throughout the year. Objectives outlined for the workshops included diagnosing the problem of festival violence, collecting grassroots suggestions regarding how to improve the festival, and reminding people of the original significance and intention of the confrontations. At the meetings I attended, people indicated that there were multiple factors that accounted for the increasing violence of the festival. The participation of mestizos and the influence of Western culture were cited as catalysts for unwarranted acts of violence. In conjunction with suggestions for curbing extreme violence so that people could dance *tranquilamente* (in peace), community members commented on the value of the Inti Raymi fights that remained within ritual parameters as a mechanism of conflict management. One of the main reasons put forth in favor of the continuance of the San Juan tradition was the importance of the festival as a venue for settling disputes accumulated throughout the year. Hassaurek (1997 [1867]:329) records the same motive for the fights in the nineteenth century. Thomas Turino's (1993:23) description of conflict avoidance during the year among Conimeños in southern Peru reflects a similar attitude among Otavaleños:

> People do not typically confront or criticize others publicly, or call attention to them within group interactions. Obviously tensions exist, and people are certainly criticized in private, among family or trusted friends. This difference between public and private behavior, however, underlines the fact that community solidarity is an ideal, part of an ideology that, precisely because of its constant public articulation, becomes deeply internalized.

As the fighting tradition disappears (or is suppressed by local authorities) in communities throughout Otavalo and Cotacachi, this cultural means of managing conflict is truncated from the realm of options for regulating intraethnic tensions. Several workshop attendants implied a correlation between the loss of the San Juan tradition and rising day-to-day conflict in their communities.

Although conflict management within communities is an important issue, this functional explanation for the continuing violence of the festival seemed somewhat unfulfilling. It came across as an attempt to formulate a rational argument, in the context of a solution-oriented meeting, about something that lies beyond the bounds of rational explanation. People do not dance San Juan for the sake of conflict management in their communities; they dance during the festival because they "feel" the need to do so. They say they feel "lighter" after dancing. Others say they feel an "obligation" to dance. A number of people get called upon in dreams to dance San Juan. People find it difficult to articulate clearly their reasons for participating in the festival, and many conclude that one simply has to experience the dance to really understand it. More than anything, the group's attempt to justify the festival communicates people's desire to continue their traditions and to defend their right to their own manner of cultural expression.

Short of actually experiencing the fight, my sense is that to gain a deeper understanding of ongoing festival violence we must shift away from rational argumentation and enter the realm of ritual interpretation. Emilia Ferraro (2000), in her excellent analysis of the San Juan festival in Pesillo, provides a point of entry. She conceives of the festival of San Juan as part of the cycle of production and reproduction of the cosmic order. This order, she argues, revolves not around reciprocal relations, as so many of us have affirmed, but around the concept of perpetual debt vis-à-vis the sacred (Ferraro 2000:181, 193). Ferraro (2000:172–77, 186–90) describes the *rama de gallos* and the *castillo* as *rituales de aumento* (rituals of increase or interest). For the *rama de gallos,* an individual who accepts one chicken during San Juan must return twelve chickens for the festival the following year. The *castillo,* also known as *aumento,* involves people taking money, fruit, bread, or alcohol attached to a reed carousel that hangs from the ceiling of private indigenous homes during San Juan. Those who have taken these goods return the following year to pay back double the amount of the loan. Though among commoners these rituals constitute acts of acceptance that ratify social dynamics along horizontal relations as equals, Ferraro (2000:190–91) writes that it is actually Saint John who makes the money grow and the chickens multiply. The ritual "payments" and ongoing debt are therefore obligations toward the saint. Human interaction with the sacred is vertical in nature, states Ferraro, and implies a relationship of debt, not reciprocity. This debt, moreover, can never be fully repaid (Ferraro 2000:192). Ferraro explains that, in fact, it would not be advantageous to resolve the obligation of debt because the "increase" it implies is necessary for the prosperity of social and material life. "If the cycle of debt were to end, life itself would end, since this debt represents the 'cost' of life, the price one must pay for it" (Ferraro 2000:192).

We return to a discussion of the escalation of festival violence. Chacon, Chacon, and Guandinango (2002:21) reported that after the 2001 incident in Cotacachi, allies of the man from the lower moiety who was killed during the Inti Raymi publicly stated that they would avenge the death by killing two *hanan* men the following year. It is possible that they were simply referring to the fact that two men from the upper moiety had attacked their comrade. This observation merits further consideration, however. First, it confirms that revenge is due to take place within the frame of the ritual. Second, taking into account Ferraro's (2000) analysis, it potentially alludes to a form of *aumento* similar to the one practiced with the *castillos,* where repayment for anything taken one year doubles in the next ritual cycle. Within this interpretation, the escalation of festival violence may very well reflect a requirement of the ritual itself as a form of payment toward a mounting debt vis-à-vis the sacred.

Historical Contentions, Community Introspection, and Moral Assertions

In spite of the fact that the Inti Raymi celebrations take place in the public domain, the festival retains an aura of ethnic exclusivity and cultural intimacy that shields the dancers' interactions from the critical gaze of the broader society. In addition to the spiral of moiety coalitions at each corner of the plaza, a bird's-eye view of the counterclockwise rotation of dance troupes around the plaza reveals a larger spiral defined in ethnic terms. The density of the crowd and the centripetal motion of the dancers capture not only the figurative allusion to introspection but also the physically and socially hermetic performance of the groups. As this larger rotation draws increasing numbers of indigenous people into the dance, it projects an ethnic force that by the same revolving action drives nonindigenous people to the peripheries of the square in centrifugal fashion.

The performed counter-conquest of the historically racialized space of the plaza as political arena comments on ethnic differences in terms of historical injustices, power inequalities, and social exclusions. This aspect of the dance posits identities in mutually exclusive terms. The fact that, aside from taking possession of the main square, the Inti Raymi dances also aim at a *toma de la iglesia* (taking of the church) adds to this interpretation an ethnically inscribed stake in a moral claim. While the emphatic step of the festival *sanjuanito* asserts indigenous ethnic presence in the city, it also affirms a spiritual wakefulness among indigenous communities. The taking of the church represents not only an appropriation of Catholic religious authority but a consummation of that authority through indigenous transcendental experiences. By way of mythic performances, moreover, people engage the contradictions of imposed cultural values, and transform foreign power, as Reeve (1988:33) suggests, into an indigenous form of power. Varese (1996:67) similarly describes this process as a form of social "allomorphism" wherein "the same substance after adoption is perceived and socially imagined as having a different form from the original one, as having an ethnic/indigenous form and value." Dismissal by nonindigenous Ecuadorians of the tradition of the San Juan battles as savagery bred by inebriation or as the inexplicable practices of *los indios* further distances white-mestizos, through negative stereotyping, from understanding the powerful numinous dimension of the dances. These dynamics contribute to a continuing contrastive formation of indigenous and white-mestizo identities in historical, social, experiential, and ultimately moral-religious terms.

As the spiraling motion of the *sanjuanito* and the stomping of the dancers' footsteps reverberate through these chapters, they remind us, nonetheless, of the fluidity of inclusiveness and exclusiveness of identities defined in intricate relation to one another. The dances of the Inti Raymi are lived experiences of community introspection and reflections about the dialogical nature of identities. As communities periodically perform themselves into being through a sequence of encounters during the annual Inti Raymi festivities, the progressive character of the dances ultimately underscores the generative and regenerative outcome of these engagements.

In the following chapter, I turn from a discussion on socially negotiated meanings of ritual death to the ongoing dialogue the living maintain *with* the dead. Chapter 5 illustrates the moral obligations implicit in Otavalan conceptions of the contiguity of *pachas*.

5

Conversations with the Dead

Major holidays are opportunities for people to assemble. They are also occasions for the congregation of souls. *Las almas,* the souls, are said to return to the communities several times during the year. San Juan and San Pedro in late June are one such season in Otavalo and Cotacachi. One of the local researchers I worked with at Jambi Mascaric explained that people purchase new clothing in anticipation of the arrival of *las almas* and then, on June 29, don their best outfits to greet the returning souls during a ritual visit to the cemetery. On the eves of San Juan and San Pedro (June 23 and June 28, respectively), men and boys dress in costume and speak in falsetto tones as they dance along the moonlit *chakiñanes*. Dancers say that they are imitating the souls to make them feel welcome. The returning souls, like the returning migrants for the *fiestas,* are said to reenter from the north, through Colombia, after traveling the world over.[1]

The intimacy people maintain with the souls of the deceased stems as much from a belief in parallel worlds of existence as it does from day-to-day experiences with sickness and death in the communities. In addition to the annual festival deaths I described in the previous chapter, incidence of severe and fatal illness, whether attributed to witchcraft or poor medical care, accounts for highly developed everyday discourses on death. In this chapter, I show how the collective sense of empathy that results from personal experiences of sickness and loss sustains charitable acts among the living. Extension of this social obligation to the dead affirms their inclusion as part of the broader Runa community. I explore the implications this has for Otavalo Runa conceptions of community, morality, ritual, and memory.

Conversations with the dead are mediated through food. The practice of feeding the souls appears as a recurring component of festival complexes. In the context of the summer festivals, an analysis of the practice of feeding the dead allows us to explore a female set of values manifest in the kitchen and the cemetery centered on empathy and sharing. These aesthetics complement male performances of aggression and force in the public space of the festival plazas.

Days of the Dead

Most literature on commemorative ceremonies for the dead focuses on the Day of the Dead generally celebrated throughout Latin America on November 1 or November 2. In the Otavalo and Cotacachi area, the obligation to the dead coincides with major festivals throughout the year. In addition to Finados (November 2), the offering to the dead is made on New Year's Day (January 1), Holy Thursday or Good Friday (in April), and San Pedro (June 29). Feeding the souls marks the transition between ritual seasons.

In her study of the Bolivian Laymi, Olivia Harris (1982:45) describes ceremonies for the dead similar to the ones I analyze in this chapter. Laymi temporal arrangement divides the year in two halves—one for sorrow and hard work, the other for feasting, pleasure, and rest. Among the Laymi these agricultural and ritual seasons are marked by a feast for the dead. Harris (1982:57) understands the Laymi practice of feasting with the dead as an extended celebration that begins with the arrival of the souls on the eve of All Saints and concludes with a proclamation of community and a celebration of the end of the rains at Carnaval in February or March. This assessment of extended ritual seasons in which the dead play a central role resonates with my observations in Imbabura.

More recently, Juanita Garciagodoy (1998) and Peter Wogan (2003:98) have challenged understandings of commemorative ceremonies for the dead as occasions confined to a single day in the annual ritual cycle by indicating that the practice and the preparations actually extend for days and even weeks. They have accordingly shifted their designation of this cultural practice to the plural—Días de Muertos. Their analyses, nonetheless, continue to revolve around the November 2 nationally recognized holiday in most of Latin America. This leads Garciagodoy (1998:51) to conclude that this celebration is "a focal point for the construction of a [Mexican] national identity." The case that Wogan (2003) describes in Salasaca, Ecuador, and my own analysis, which emphasize differences with the national holiday, favor an interpretation of this tradition as an expression of ethnic and moral identities.

In addition to their correlation with the four major holidays, ritual visits to the cemetery in Otavalo and Cotacachi take place on Mondays and Thursdays of every week. The importance among Runakuna of sustaining contact with the ancestors is underscored by the frequency of these visits. They challenge the assumption of a clearly delimited holiday, revealing instead a familiar day-to-day interaction among the living and the dead.[2]

Gendered Spaces

San Juan dancing during the eve of the festival and in the public space of the plaza constitutes a male-dominated activity, as seen in chapters 3 and 4. In contrast, the obligation to the dead is primarily fulfilled by women. Just as the plaza, the soccer fields, the Ecuavolley courts, and the bars are recognizably male domains, the spaces of the cemetery and of the kitchen correspond to women. The separation, of course, is not complete. Men often accompany their families to the cemetery, although they do not cook and distribute their own food offerings unless they are widowers. Similarly, women participate in the Inti Raymi activities that unfold in the plaza.

Gender symbolism is evident throughout the Inti Raymi festival complex, beginning with a basic division of upper and lower moieties into the masculinized *hanan* and the feminized *uray*. This gendered division of time and space is enacted variously throughout the celebration and underscores a contrast to Western conceptions of gendered spaces inscribed in terms of public and private social spheres. On the third day of San Pedro, which coincides with the celebration of Santa Lucia and is known as *warmi puncha* (the women's day), for instance, Runa *warmi* dance aggressively around the plaza, dressed in chaps and sunglasses, wearing tall cardboard hats and carrying whips, pounding their boots against the pavement and whistling as the men do. Their dancing contrasts radically with the minimalist movement of women's dance steps on all other occasions. The women sometimes fight. More often they parody the male fights of the previous days by throwing oranges instead of rocks. On the women's day, men assume the peripheral role of bringing lunch, carrying the children, and taking care of their inebriated wives, much as the women did for them the first two days. The men who want to keep dancing on the third day return to the plaza dressed as women. In spite of the gendered division of tasks and obligations, however, the public dance of the Inti Raymi clearly remains a celebration of masculine aesthetics.

The performance of an explicitly female aesthetic in the spaces of the kitchen and cemetery defines a set of social values that stand as counterparts to the masculine rituals of the Inti Raymi. Moreover, as Mary Weismantel (1998 [1988]:26) observes, it is in these domains that indigenous women assert a specifically feminine sort of political power. The offering to the dead, known as Wakcha Karay, refocuses social values of reciprocity on expressions of empathy and charity. While the men sleep off the all-night dancing of the *víspera* or congregate with other men to dance in the square on June 29, women get up early to cook for the dead.

Pantheon of Souls

Wakcha Karay literally means the offering to the orphaned or to the poor. In ritual context, it extends the obligation of charitable giving to the dead. In some parts of Ecuador, for example in Salasaca and Tigua, *pobre* (poor) can mean soul. Cachiguango (2000:304) clarifies the etymology of the name as he explains the contemporary meaning and practice of the Wakcha Karay. *Wakcha,* he writes, referred to orphans, widowers, or people without family in the Inka Empire. The root *kara* means to extend or offer, generally with reference to food. Cachiguango interprets Wakcha Karay in the framework of an Andean cosmovision wherein the dead and deities embodied in the land-

Wawas de pan *(bread dolls) offerings for the dead*

scape are included among those without family or resources. He traces four variants of this ritual: Pampa Wakcha Karai (the offering to the fields), Llaki Wakcha Karai (the offering of sorrows and natural disasters—performed only as needed to avert natural disasters and to ask for rain), Urcu Wakcha Karai (the offering to the mountains), and Wañu Wakcha Karai (the offering to the dead) (Cachiguango 2000:304–6). This chapter focuses on the latter.

I refer to the Wañu Wakcha Karay hereafter simply as Wakcha Karay. It is significant that many people in the communities simply use the quotidian expression *ir al panteón* (to go to the cemetery), indicating a less formal and ongoing communication with the dead. Sustained interaction with *las almas* and parallelisms between the worlds of the living and the dead come into relief in the context of everyday Runa life, especially in experiences related to illness and death. These experiences provide a necessary backdrop for understanding Runa cultural practices regarding the dead.

Otavalan Conceptions of Illness and Death

I walk up the steep dirt road from the Pan-American Highway to my home in Ilumán Bajo, arriving a little out of breath at the edge of the abandoned railroad tracks. My *comadre* sits on the ground, shelling dried maize in the patio. Her fingers move quickly along the cob as she chats with our neighbor from across the street. They have been talking about Tocary, the neighbor's youngest of nine children, who constantly entertains us with her good nature and her cleverness. Tocary is a sickly toddler. They say that every month or so Tocary becomes *como muertita,* as if she were dead. She has seizures, her eyes roll back, and she stops breathing—possible symptoms of epilepsy, the presence of which Bernhard Wörrle (1999:144–48) has documented in the region as the disease of "*la pérdida del alma*" (the loss of the soul).[3]

Cursory tests at the local hospital have yielded conflicting prognoses for stomach infections and possible heart problems. Although doctors' visits are free, prescription medicines totaling $7 per week at the government-subsidized pharmacy are too expensive for the family. Sporadic use of Western medicines has proven ineffective. Tocary's mother believes that baptism and pilgrimages to the city of Baños to pray to the revered Virgin for the child's health have alleviated some of the symptoms. Tocary also showed improvement after eating a stew made of black puppies, recommended by a local *yachak*.[4]

At three years old, Tocary is not only keenly aware of her precarious health but is already socialized into local discourses on death. Her most recent pun has kept people laughing the entire afternoon as the anecdote is repeated in typical Quichua storytelling fashion. When I arrive, our neighbor relates the episode once again, now with the interruptions of others already familiar with the story, including Tocary herself:

Earlier that day our neighbor had been talking with other women in the square, with Tocary tied to her back in a carrying sheet. At eye level with the rest of the adults from the vantage point of her mother's back, the toddler dabbled in the conversation in broken Quichua and Spanish. Runa children learn through relatively unmediated observation and participation, receiving conversation from their mother's perspective, seeing what she sees, ingesting bits of what she smells and eats, observing what she does from the ubiquitous position of their carrying sheet. As children grow older, their arms are released from the sheet, allowing mobility and some degree of self-sufficiency, and they are included in conversations. They speak for themselves and are addressed directly. On this occasion, when one of the ladies asked about the child's health, Tocary herself responded, "*kawsashachá . . . wañushachá . . .*" (Who knows, maybe I will live . . . maybe I will die . . .).

Not only had Tocary emulated something she had probably heard her mother say on numerous occasions, but the exaggerated high pitch of her tone at the end of each phrase revealed a hint of mockery. Our neighbor said that everyone burst into laughter upon unexpectedly hearing such a grim statement from the tiny voice coming from behind the women's circle. Adults derive enjoyment from watching children gradually develop social skills by imitating grownup behavior. The retelling of the anecdote, in which Tocary was actively included, celebrated the child's socializing efforts as a member of the community. Beyond this, however, I wondered if Tocary's comment might have triggered nervous laughter because it pointed to the precarious balance between life and death in Runa communities.

Kawsashachá . . . Wañushachá . . .

People in the communities constantly speculate about their death and that of others. It was always difficult for me to assess, when asking folks about their health, whether someone was deathly ill or merely had a cold. "*Quién sabe, Michellecita, ya mismo he de morir*" (Who knows, Michellecita, I will probably die soon), was a common response to my question. After living in Ilumán for several months, it dawned on me that a common respiratory infection could, in fact, kill someone in the countryside. Several factors conspire to produce this reality.

During three field visits I made to the area in summer of 1995, summer of 1999, and 2000 to 2001, staff at the Hospital San Luis de Otavalo were constantly on strike. Lack of medical attention owing to strikes and poor treatment extended to *indígenas* when the hospitals are operational redefine the gravity of any illness. People in Ilumán and Peguche complained that they often felt discriminated against as *indígenas* at the Otavalo hospital. A couple of friends at advanced stages of pregnancy risked the longer trip to Ibarra, saying that they felt more comfortable delivering their babies at the hospital there.

Insensitivity to culturally different conceptions of the body on the part of doctors trained in Western medicine further deters *indígenas* from using hospital resources, especially indigenous women. Young Runa women are reluctant to be examined physically and will delay submitting to Western-style poking and prodding, generally by male doctors, until their pain is unbearable. Gerardo Fernández Juárez (2000:351), a European scholar conducting research in Bolivia, explains that reluctance to visit the hospital among many Aymara stems from conceptions regarding the hermetic nature of indigenous bodies. Conventional medical practices are predicated upon opening the body to rid it of sickness. In contrast, *yatiris* (healers) insist on keeping the body closed and thus protected against outside agents responsible for inflicting disease. Open bodies, in addition, expose intimacies that should remain private, concealed from indiscreet gazes (Fernández Juárez 2000:354).

Needles, transfusions, vaccines, and surgical instruments violate the principles of the hermetic body. Fernández Juárez (2000:351, 354–55) notes, moreover, that these "little machines" and the extraction of fluids for laboratory exams conjure associations with the dreaded *kharisiri*, a fat-sucking monster known in other parts of the Andes as *pishtaku* and *ñakaq*.[5] Nathan Wachtel (1994:73) describes the *kharisiri* as a white man or a mestizo. Weismantel (2001:xxi) adds that the *pishtaco*, "creature of the night: a white man with a knife, pale and terrifying . . . waits alone in the shadows along isolated country roads, searching for victims to eviscerate." What is more, this fiend is also known as "*el operador*," the surgeon. Stories about the *ñakak* abound in Imbabura, spreading distrust of white doctors. In immediate historical context, proximity to Colombia and an awareness of the profitable traffic in human organs from this country—consequence of the ongoing guerrilla conflict and the availability of body parts that result from the violence—fuel stories of the *pishtaku* in the Imbabura area. (For other interpretations, see Meisch 1997:290, Whitehead 2002, and Orta 2004:232.)

Bad experiences at hospitals substantiate apprehension about inadequate treatment and propagate impressions of conventional medical practices as ineffective, dangerously neglectful, and potentially lethal. One day as I was writing my notes, my *comadre,* Carmen, came upstairs to talk. She had just returned from visiting a *comadre* who was very sick. "So young," she said with tears in her eyes. "She is swollen all over, lying in bed. She can no longer walk. Her feet swollen, her stomach swollen. She can no longer eat anything. She does not want anything." She had just had an operation at the hospital to prevent future pregnancies, and it is from the hospital that she returned like this. "*Mal operada ha de ser*"— an operation gone bad. They told her at the hospital that there was no cure; that there was nothing more for them to do; that it was best for her not to return there and simply go home to die. Mamita Carmen dried her tears and started back toward the kitchen, saying that she would make egg whites to take to her *comadre.* She had heard this was good for curing fatigue.

Language problems add to the anxiety of visiting the hospital. Not only do Quichua speakers worry they will not understand, but the impersonal tone in professional registers of spoken Spanish, compounded by racist/racial condescension communicated in both language and gesture, deters people from asking questions. Fernández Juárez (2000:354) states that the patients he interviewed were surprised by the brevity of their appointments with doctors and complained about the "lack of dialogue." I was often asked to accompany people to the hospital in order to do the talking for them—"*para darme hablando,*" they would say. My job was to extend the conversation and prevent the doctor from dismissing indigenous, and often illiterate, patients with a hastily scribbled prescription. As a foreigner and a *mestiza,* people knew that I could command this attention, and they banked on this social capital when they were able.

The lack of proper dialogue is seen by *indígenas* as deficient treatment. Health is understood in holistic terms. The idea of treating the illness as opposed to caring for the person physically, spiritually, psychologically, and socially is foreign to many indigenous people. Home remedies in the communities combine medicinal herb teas, prayer, candle burning, incense burning, and human touch—namely *frotadas* (massages) with an egg. Rituals become more elaborate with the level of expertise of the healer. A number of people cure illness entirely through prayer. Xavier Perugachi, who self-identifies as a *sabio* (one who knows), is a healer at an alternative medicine center in Otavalo called Jambi Huasi (Medicine House). He describes the role of *sabio* or *yachak* as a sort of psychologist and educator whose purpose it is to give moral force and develop strength of character. Although he alleviates people's physical ailments, his focus is on "waking people up." By talking with people about their past, he helps them to become "awake, free from stupor and shyness, so that they feel courageous . . . and so their spirit will feel like dancing" (*despierto, sin bobería ni recelo, para que se ponga valiente . . . y que el espíritu tenga ganas de bailar*). His counterpart, Dr. Miriam Conejo, M.D., who trained in Cuba and is director of the clinic, explains, "The *yachak* treats what we could call cultural illnesses in addition to problems that fall within the realm of Western medicine."

Jambi Huasi employs three doctors in conventional medicine and three in traditional medicine, or *medicina indígena* (a *yachak*, a *partera* [midwife], and a *frotador* [massage expert]), allowing patients to choose the type of attention they prefer. The number of patients treated using Western methods in 1999 was approximately two hundred per month, while more than four hundred per month visited the *yachak* (although some of these were repeat visits). While Dr. Conejo works with a stethoscope, X-ray machine, sonogram, and laboratory, Sabio Perugachi diagnoses illness with guinea pigs, candles, and crystals. The waiting area of the clinic replicates the courtyard of most indigenous homes, with cement benches built along the outer wall of the structure. The environment at the clinic is both familiar and conducive to conversation among patients. Women embroider while they chat with each other; their children play together in the patio. Unlike hospitals, these centers charge a fee for diagnosis and treatment. In spite of this, patients noisily fill the patio, often brimming over into the street. The popularity of the clinic suggests that indigenous access to health resources is not entirely a matter of cash flow, but to a great extent a strategic investment of household means in an economy of cultural reassurance.

In addition to practical obstacles to conventional health care, mysterious connotations that surround illness and death render diagnoses elusive. The term used in Quichua for describing death is *wañuchiy*, to make someone die. The suffix "chi" indicates indirect or third-party involvement in an action, implying, in the case of death, that external forces are at work. Exposure to malevolent spirits that appear as dust devils, contact with dangerous sites where *supay* are known to linger, walking under rainbows (*kuichiks*) or rainbow-shaped natural and manmade structures, or receiving *preparados* (mixtures of cologne and flowers left in people's patios as curses) are causes of illness or death in Runa communities. In Tocary's case, her deathlike episodes are attributed by people in the community to the *diablos* that live in the ravine adjacent to her house. Ravines are frequent repositories of evil and are linked to *mal aire* and *espanto*,[6] conditions that generally affect children who have come into contact with dangerous places and have had an encounter with an evil spirit (see also Corr 2000, Parsons 1945).

The ravine in our neighborhood serves as a garbage dump and is an unhygienic place conducive to sickness in conventional terms. There is a clear recognition of the ravine's general contamination and the diseases it breeds, but this understanding is most often articulated in terms of bad energy or an evil presence. Tocary's lapses are also attributed to *brujerías* or *suciedades,* witchcraft and "dirty doings." Maledictions in the form of letters, sprinkled cologne and flower mixes, broken raw eggs, or buried needles are occasionally left outside people's homes. Although these "dirty doings" may be directed at neighbors or other people in Tocary's household, because she is the youngest, she is more susceptible to their pernicious effects. Women and children are considered especially vulnerable to *brujerías* as well as to *mal aire* and *espanto.* This is why Runa men customarily walk several feet in front of their wives and children. This practice does not reflect *machismo* or gendered hierarchy, as is commonly assumed, but rather a responsibility on the part of the men to protect their families from evil spirits by essentially acting as a human shield and absorbing the negative energy.

Infant mortality in Imbabura province ranks among the highest in Ecuador, 90.9 per 1,000 among the indigenous population, and only half as many among nonindigenous infants (Océano Grupo Editorial 2000:175, 176). The combination of rudimentary health care and obscure influences surrounding illness render death difficult to anticipate and to prevent. This unpredictability affects the ways in which people talk about death and fosters compassion among community members. It carries the notion that no one is exempt from misfortune, which resonates more broadly with mores of commiseration based on the menace of a generalized experience with market ups and downs, economic crises, rampant theft, illness, and unforeseen accidents that can abruptly reverse social and economic standings. In the context of a tight-knit community, individual misfortune, moreover, is not anonymous, but necessarily falls upon a relative, extended kin, or, at the very least, an acquaintance. This social intimacy drives the experience of adversity closer to home even when it does not occur in one's immediate family. This ability to imagine oneself in the predicament of a less fortunate person is best rendered as Christian empathy, and is, perhaps, the basis for the collective sense of obligation in communities to care for the poor, the orphaned, and the old.

Giving to the Orphaned and the Poor in Everyday Context

People in Imbabura communities collectively practice what James C. Scott (1976) has described as the minimal subsistence ethic of the moral economy of the peasant. A variety of redistributive mechanisms ensure that no one in the community falls beneath minimum subsistence requirements. Occasionally this takes the form of offering food or unused clothing to destitute passersby, often elderly or disabled people. Most of the time, however, goodwill operates within the frame of enduring relations of mutual obligation.

Poorer neighbors, widows, or the wives of emigrant husbands with limited access to agricultural work implements and technical know-how sometimes came to beg my *compadre* for help in their fields. He would agree to plow their fields with his team of oxen or spray their crops using his portable pesticide tank. He expressed pity for their situations. Although most of the time a *"dius si lu pagui"* (may God repay you, thank you) was all he could expect, help was given and accepted under the implication of a reciprocal favor in the future.

People without their own land to farm are also pitied. Landlessness implies inability to ensure a livelihood. Even wealthy migrants without land fall into this category. Those who have the means to buy land and neglect to do so are reprimanded by their families and, through gossip networks, by the community as a whole. When my *compadres* called a *minga* (work party) to plant a potato field in July 2001, a landless mestizo couple came to ask for work. The term used without exception for asking favors is *rogar* (to implore or beseech). Beyond the gesture of urgent supplication, *rogar* recognizes a hierarchical difference among the parties involved (or discursively conjures deferential behavior as if there were one). The practice of imploring acknowledges that people have a choice in extending goodwill and casts a semblance of kindness rather than calculation on mutually beneficial work arrangements. My *compadres* agreed to allow the couple to work in exchange for a small portion of the harvest. The couple would receive some dry maize and fava beans, and when the potatoes and sweet peas were ready for harvest, they would collect some of that too. The couple was assigned two *wachus* (rows) to plant and care for periodically until the harvest. Giving them "ownership" of the potato *wachus* somehow seemed like an attempt to offset their landlessness. Furthermore, the extended involvement of caring for the field implied an ongoing, if only provisional, relationship modeled on *compadrazgo*. The insinuation of *compadre*-like ties lent social legitimacy to the couple's presence in the community as outsiders and justified in the eyes of others the benevolence on my *compadres'* part.[7] Even though my *compadres* did not really need it, accepting the assistance of this couple corresponded to a broader rural indigenous institution of moral economy that allows people to receive subsistence help through sanctioned cultural channels structured to avoid compromising the dignity of all parties involved.

Other households I visited often had *apegados*—literally, people who have become attached to the household, many times living in an adjacent structure the family has outgrown. As people build cement houses, they abandon their original adobe homes or sometimes use them as guinea pig and chicken pens. If the adobe structures are not in too much disrepair, people in need of a home might ask to live in them. Sometimes these people are poorer relatives, and even when they are not, they are treated with affection as if they were distant kin. *Hacer apegar* carries the connotation of fondness as well as inclusion. In many cases, these relations are eventually formalized through actual *compadrazgo* commitments. Entire families, either in transition or impoverished to the point of homelessness, can become *apegados*. Other times, children (mostly males from the age of ten or twelve) will become *apegados* to work in a family workshop. They often retain this position for many years, working, living, and eating with the family and becoming, for all practical purposes, permanent members of the household, much like a foster child. Orphaned children and, sometimes, abused children in the community are quickly taken in by neighbors without necessary regard to kin connections. All forms of *apegados* correspond to the definition of *wakchu,* which Cachiguango (2000) associates with orphans and widowers, and other dictionaries define as "individuals who for lack of parents or work lean on another for subsistence" (Cordero 1989:38).

Feeding the Souls: Charity in Ritual Context

Charitable dispositions in everyday interactions are reflexively enacted in ritual, and through their performance sanctioned as collective values. Ritual charity operates within an encompassing system of reciprocity and complementarity. Inti Raymi fights, for example, reestablish the balance of cosmic energy and impose equilibrium among local moieties. Similarly, the redistributive dimension of the Wakcha Karay upholds the principle of egalitarianism among the living, and, as Cachiguango (2000:310) asserts, it also effects parity and interdependency with other worlds. The dead depend upon the living for nourishment, conversation, and creativity that will literally keep them alive. Herein lies the explanation for the extension of social and ritual obligations to the dead not as relics from the past to be remembered, but as contemporary kin in a parallel realm to be reckoned with.

I visited the cemetery in Ilumán on three of the major holidays—New Year's, San Pedro, and Finados, in addition to going twice on a regular Monday and Thursday. During Semana Santa I attended the Wakcha Karay in Cotacachi. The following is a description of a typical visit to the cemetery in Ilumán:

By 4:30 A.M. our wood fire outside was lit and the enormous pot of sweet peas and beans was coming to a boil. Inside, *tostado* (roasted corn) was popping loudly over the gas stove. Enough rice to feed several dozen people simmered on the back burner. Mamita Carmen moved agitatedly from the stove to the wood fire supervising the cooking. Whereas for the family's daily meals we generally improvised if we did not have certain ingredients, on this occasion she was fastidious about adding generous amounts of salt and onion to enhance the flavor. This deliberate preparation corresponds to the slow cooking that Camacho (2006:167) describes as integral to indigenous conceptions of carefully prepared food as nourishing and strength giving. As Camacho (2006:158) and Seremetakis (1994, cited in Camacho 2006), point out, moreover, memory, knowledge, and experience are considered to be stored in specific foods and crops "whose tastes, aromas and textures are part of people's shared sensory landscapes and local histories."

At 9:00 A.M. we packed up the food, a couple of serving dishes, and some plastic bags. On our way out, my *compadre,* catching a whiff of the delicious meal, told us in jest not to share the food at the cemetery, but to bring it back for him to eat instead. Carmen answered with a reprimanding look and a chuckle. With these items tied to our backs in carrying cloths, my *comadre,* her two youngest children, and I began our uphill trek to the cemetery in Ilumán. We were careful to avoid the path traveled by a funeral procession the previous week, so as not to inadvertently follow the soul on its journey. Foot traffic intensified as we neared the cemetery. People passed us in a hurry, greeting us hastily and complaining that they were running late. The entrance of the cemetery was crawling with candle saleswomen, flower vendors, visitors, food vendors selling treats for both the dead (*rosquitas* and fruit) and the living (fried fish, watermelon, and lupin beans), and an ice cream salesman. Carmen borrowed two dollars from me to buy bananas and two dozen *rosquitas* (dense, unleavened bread in the shape of a small wreath).

The cemetery was brimming with activity. We had to step around people and over food bundles to arrive at the three tiny crosses of the graves we had come to visit. Two small mounds marked the resting places of children Carmen had lost, Oscar and Martha Cecilia. A third cross without a corresponding mound bore no name and represented a child she had miscarried. As soon as we sat on the ground next to the graves, a little girl arrived with a bowl filled with *tostado,* sweet peas, rice, beans, and collard greens. Carmen accepted the plate with the customary *dius si lu pagui* and emptied its contents into one of the plastic bags we had packed. She then refilled the bowl with the food we had brought, topping off the heap of *tostado,* beans, and rice with a *rosquita.* Carmen politely gestured to the mother of the little girl sitting several plots away in acknowledgment of the exchange.

Food and *chicha* arrived faster than we could distribute our own; up to four people approaching at one time. Carmen skillfully fielded the offerings, measuring out what she gave in return depending on the relation she maintained with each person. Relatives and close friends received larger portions and a bonus *rosquita* or banana. At the same time, she sent the children off with bowls of food to present to others. As we received food, Carmen instructed us to put it into different bags. She commented that some people cooked badly, without salt, and that she would take this food home to feed the pigs. She was discreet, however, about sorting the food. After the initial rush of

Food offerings and exchange at the cemetery

exchanges, she opened one of the bags of tasty food, placed it on top of the grave, and invited us to eat. We only ate what others brought us, reserving the food from our own batch for distribution. Other friends with whom I visited the cemetery on another occasion preferred to mix all the offerings together. They called this *chapukamlla,* and explained that it was a common practice both at the cemetery and at weddings. The food tasted so much better this way, they assured me.

Eventually, Carmen called over three *rezadoras* (prayer experts). For each prayer they said, she deposited a small bowlful of food into their plastic bags, alternating occasionally with a couple of bananas or *rosquitas.* Carmen would recite the name and relation of the person for whom she wished to pray. The *rezadoras* would begin their prayer "Martha Cecilia, *angelito . . .* (little angel)" for children who had passed away and " *. . . alma difunta*" for deceased adult souls. Carmen also asked them to pray for her older children who were abroad in Switzerland. In this case, the prayer began with the name of the person, followed by " *. . . alma viviente . . .* (living soul)." The *rezadoras* prayed in a cacophonous mixture of Spanish and Quichua. Their voices came together in unison only upon reciting, "Our Father," "Hail Mary," and "Glory Be . . ." in Spanish. This individualized style of participation in collective prayer also characterized regular prayer sessions I attended. Finally, Carmen sent two of the *rezadoras* away and retained the one she considered recited best.

There was a lack of solemnity in all of these proceedings. The oration of the *rezadora* receded to the background as Mamita Carmen chatted with me about the babies who had died, and as the children played in unrestrained voices with their collectible Pokemon game pieces (*tasos*). The result was a dissonant mix of *"virgen santísima, madre de Dios . . .,"* clashing Pokemon battle noises, and the children's laughter. The *rezadora* interrupted her monotone recitation to hack and spit. Later, she snatched a fly in midair and crushed it with a stone against the dirt of the burial mound. All the while, she continued to pray. *Difuntos* are said to enjoy partaking in the laughter and conversation of the living.

On our way out of the cemetery, two and a half hours later, Carmen stopped by the grave of her father to tell him that although we had not sat with him, we had been nearby. She spoke to him in ordinary terms, reassuring him that she had paid a *rezadora* to pray for him.

Runa Afterlife: Parallel Worlds

The concept of an embodied soul with needs and wants similar to those of the living requires Runakuna to care for their deceased relatives in a way that is both familiar and personable. Similar inclinations toward anthropomorphizing natural features in the landscape and humanizing religious saints lay bare the contiguity and, moreover, the permeability of realms of existence.

One evening over coffee, my *compadre* talked about the three ponchos he was having made for himself in Atuntaqui, a community just north of Ilumán Bajo. The family joked, saying that with the purchase of these items he would be ready for his funeral. Segundo protested that when he dies, they should not send him off with all of that. Had they not learned during Holy Week that Jesus was buried *"con un trapito no más"* (with only a loincloth)? As the children's laughter subsided at the thought of their father in a loincloth, the conversation segued into a discussion of burial practices among *indígenas*.

Segundo explained, "First you have to put a little plate and a little wooden spoon." Food must also be included—an orange, an egg, and bread. Carmen added that one must send two or three changes of clothes, and needle and thread so that the deceased will be able to mend their garments. Sewn into the shirt, so that the *difunto* does not lose it, should be some change. "The old coins" (which have now come to mean simply the recently retired *sucres*), Carmen explained, *"para el pasaje"* (for the fare). I did not ask about the mode of transportation that would require a fare. In his analysis of funerary rituals in southern Peru, Gose (1994:123–24), however, mentions that the souls must travel west toward the mountain of the dead, and overcome several obstacles along the way, one of which is the crossing of a river. In addition, women are often sent with their cooking implements, and men with agricultural tools so that they will be prepared for the work that awaits them in a parallel realm of existence.

I asked Carmen if this is how they sent off her mother, who had died only fifteen days previously. She said yes, *"completito se le mandó"* (we sent her with everything). With this, she confirmed that rather than reflecting nostalgia about times long gone, providing for the journey of the dead is a contemporary practice in the Otavalo area. During the first year of her mother's death, Carmen would visit the cemetery every week and bring food. One has to go, she said, otherwise the *difuntos* get hungry and come to complain. Though Segundo did not seem convinced one way or the other about these beliefs, he expressed a desire to at least have a set of new clothes, neatly ironed and ready for when he dies.

"Embedded" Economies: Food as Mediator of Social Relations

Karl Polanyi's (1957 [1944]) concept of embedded economies captures the notion that economy stands in various relationships to society and that it need not appear "economic," by conventional standards, in order to function as an organizer of production, distribution, and consumption (Halperin 1984:252). The "embeddedness of economies in noneconomic formations" can encompass reciprocity in the context of kinship systems and redistribution in the context of politico-religious systems. Although among Otavalo Runa the food is said to be for the dead, it serves as an equally powerful mediator for relations among the living. Sharing food at the cemetery is a sign of trust and acceptance. Parsons (1945:123) records in her notes her primary informant's strong position on sharing food: "'If you eat [proffered food], we are friends,' once said Rosita; 'if you do not eat, we are not friends.'" Underneath the symbolic gesture, nonetheless, is an acknowledgment of differences in access to resources and quality of life, evident in Carmen's careful separation of the food from different households into distinct containers. As a *gringuita,* I was often warned to be selective about the food I ate and discriminating about the households in which I ate. This caution, to a great extent, addresses a national reality (both rural and urban) of poor water treatment and other unsanitary conditions that lead to contamination and diseases such as typhoid, cholera, worm infestations, and amoebic dysentery. Spoken by nonindigenous family and friends in Quito, however, this admonition carried the tone of ethnic prejudice based on the conception of *indígenas* as dirty and unhealthy—a disposition that Colloredo-Mansfeld (1999:29) labels "hygienic racism" and that draws more broadly on literature about ethnic contamination (see, for example, Colloredo-Mansfeld 1998, Orlove 1998, and Quiroga 1999).

This generalization contrasts with the cleanliness I observed in many indigenous homes. Parsons (1945:10) makes a similar observation in her ethnography and states that it was, on the contrary, mestiza households that were unkempt. Defying the generalization, too, is variability within any given community. Colloredo-Mansfeld (1999:208–9) notes that commercial success among some *indígenas* evokes metaphors of dirtiness that aggravate class differences "as some of the wealthy reject poor *indígenas* with caustic remarks about their soiled appearance." Class prejudices aside, people are aware for pragmatic reasons of the lack of potable water in certain households, informed about cholera outbreaks in different communities, and observant of the cleaning habits of neighbors. Criticism of lack of cleanliness more often implied poor upbringing than low income. Activities like sweeping the street-side courtyard of the house and washing clothes are conspicuously public. They project an image of household cleanliness, respectability, and status. Many indigenous homes have dirt floors in the courtyard and inside the house. Nonetheless, they are kept meticulously swept. These routines expose differences among households, informing people's decisions to accept or politely reject food in ordinary circumstances, and choices regarding how to sort offerings at the cemetery.

Issues of trust, moreover, are central in a community that boasts twenty-four official *yachaks* (in 2001 the number of members in the Asociación de Yachaqs de Ilumán), and three times as many unofficial practitioners, designated by some as *brujos* (witchdoctors) or *piratas* (pirates). Witchcraft and maledictions are daily concerns, and accepting food or drink indiscriminately exposes one to the risk of poisoning by enemies. Several *yachaks* I interviewed make it a habit to drink or eat first anything they offer to guests, patients, or researchers in order to dispel fears of poisoning, especially because it is well known that they derive their power from an ability both to heal and to kill. Given the seriousness of witchcraft-related illness, accepting food in this community is unmistakably a gesture either of trust or of complete naïveté. At the cemetery, a sense of solidarity emerges from the relative anonymity implicit in the mixing of food from different households.

To share food is to flirt with possibilities of contamination and sickness. As such, it conforms to a moral economy of both subsistence and commiseration that allocates bounty as well as symbolic and potential death throughout the community. Peter Wogan (2003:106) writes that the consumption of food at the cemetery represents partaking in a spiritual rebirth. He suggests that the pairing of symbolic foods for Finados, specifically the anthropomorphic *wawas de pan* (bread babies) and the *colada morada* or *yana api* (a thick, deep-red beverage made of berries), evokes parallels to the Eucharist of the Catholic mass (see also, for example, Weismantel 1991, Abercrombie 1998, and Bastien 1978). Gose (1994:119), on the other hand, points to a symbolic redistribution of death, as well as the ideal of community solidarity in life and death, underscored in historical practices such as the "mixing and remixing of bones as successive graves are dug on the same spot."

Food mediates other types of social relations as well. Elderly men and women, widowed and destitute, frequent the cemeteries on a weekly basis, asking for charity. One of the regulars is my godchildren's paternal grandmother. Widowed and with their children married and tending to their own households, elderly people often lack the help necessary to keep up with regular household activities—tending properly to fields, caring for animals, meeting community obligations, paying social visits. Eventually they come to depend on others for charity. This social trajectory seems to be expected and corresponds to the gloss in meaning between old and poor, both expressed as *wakcha*.

Carmen has told me about the poor treatment she received at her mother-in-law's house as a newlywed. *"Hasta la comida mezquinaba"* (she was even miserly and mean-spirited about the food), says Carmen, tears of resentment streaming down her face. Food, in fact, plays a particularly important role in the relationships among wives and mothers-in-law in the realms of the kitchen and the cemetery, where, as Weismantel (1998 [1988]:177) signals, relations among women are unmediated by men. When Carmen sees her husband's mother at the cemetery, she nonetheless places some bananas and a bowl of food in the old woman's collection pot. Charity overrides resentment as food offerings facilitate reconciliation. Carmen's charitable gesture, however, is not without a critical edge because her own generosity publicly contrasts with her mother-in-law's past mistreatment. As Weismantel (1998 [1988]:179, 182) writes, the etiquette of food exchange allows for "culturally impeccable behavior" that nonetheless carries an arsenal of symbolic weapons for personal reproach. Carmen's attitude also resonates with Parsons's (1945:152) observation about her primary informant: "Rosita's method of feeling superior is to run herself and her family up rather than to run others down." Indeed, as Garciagodoy (1998:45) notes, "the process of giving is empowering because whether rooted in excess or in deprivation, it grants the giver a position of high status."

Socializing and Status in the Public Space of El Panteón

There is a preoccupation among cemetery goers with projecting the best impression of their household's status. Competitive social positioning revolves around cooking an exceptionally tasty meal for the cemetery. Each household shows its generosity, and its ability to fulfill the ritual obligation, through the abundance and quality of food prepared. Though public display of culinary skills is presented as an effort to please the souls, it functions as a veiled social commentary on differences among households. In the context of a general social disposition toward avoidance of direct confrontation, deflecting attention to food preparation and the dead functions as a mechanism for contentions over status.

Status is determined in relative terms that take into account the unique circumstances of each household. For instance, lack of salt or sugar in the food is seen as an indicator of poverty in the case of one household and a sign of negligence in another. If the shortcoming is thought to result from poverty, the insipid food will be gracefully accepted (even if it is placed in a separate bag for the pigs) and the family offering will be praised in private and through gossip networks for continuing to fulfill their ritual obligation in spite of their difficult circumstances. Participation in the Wakcha Karay, therefore, enables some families to maintain a respectable social status despite their lower economic standing. In contrast, a family with means that has not prepared the food with care will be reproached (again, through the indirect channels of community gossip) for superficial fulfillment of their duty to the dead, underscoring that their well-to-do condition does not translate into social status.

Elements such as timeliness, frequency of visits, and length of stay inform social assessments as well. It is in this context that I came to understand the rush to arrive at the cemetery early. On one occasion, when a woman and her daughters picked up their bundles to leave the cemetery shortly after we had arrived, my godchild was quick to state, "*tan poquito se quedan . . .*" (they stay for such a short while). The comment was disguised as an off-hand observation. It revealed, however, that violations of ritual etiquette and social expectations become opportunities for criticism, negative evaluation, and one-upmanship.

The busyness of the cemetery scene reflects a sense of agitated competition also shared among the younger generation. Young people occupy the cemetery as a space of conversation, fashion displays, and courtship. Young men in high platform shoes and denim bell-bottom pants, a number of them sporting the latest style in shimmering lycra shirts, stroll along the margins of the cemetery in groups. This imported fashion distinguishes the young men of Ilumán from those of other communities in the region. Young girls, dressed in their best *anakus* (wraparound skirts) and *fachalinas* (shawls), giggle and crowd together as they walk past the boys, pretending to ignore them. As with other public celebrations, the Wakcha Karay offers a culturally sanctioned opportunity for attracting a mate.

Young men compete for the attention of the girls by flaunting material possessions. In addition to fashionable, clean, and well-pressed clothing, vehicles are important markers of status. Those who have trucks will drive to the cemetery at the top of the hill rather than undertaking the customary pilgrimagelike walk. Arriving at the cemetery in a private car conveys a personal association with modernity. It is effective as a claim to status, however, precisely because it continues to operate within the frame of local tradition. Young women, by contrast, perform to more traditional expectations. In addition to non-Western clothing, the social reputation of girls is determined by knowledge of proper etiquette in helping to carry and distribute the food. Girls are expected to behave conservatively and to keep their interaction with teenage boys limited to an averted glance, a muffled giggle, or the exchange of a few polite phrases. Otherwise, people will say that they have been "talking," or worse, "walking" with a boy. Both teenage boys and young women respond to two sets of social expectations. At the same time that they try to make an impression on one another, they also appeal to each other's families because all activity at the cemetery takes place under the watchful eye of their female kin.

The Segregated Space of the Cemetery

"The dead are those who have lost their memories"
—Eliade 1963:121

The jovial atmosphere on the Runa side of the cemetery contrasts sharply with forlorn tombs on the mestizo side. In the segregated cemeteries of the area, mestizo gravesites are unkempt, weeds overwhelming the headstones— telltale signs of rare visits. I ask Mamita Carmen about this and she tells me that the *mishus* only visit on Finados.[8] Although mestizo families may keep up the tradition of the bread dolls and the *colada morada,* they do not bring food to the cemetery to share. They do not exchange food with other mestizo families, and certainly not with *indígenas,* a gesture that confirms that separation in the cemetery carries over to segregation among the living. Carmen's voice carries a disapproving tone. Beyond the type of food one makes and eats, the very sharing of food is central to indigenous identities. Sharing food with beings from other realms of existence, moreover, carries the assertion of a moral responsibility. Carmen explains that one has to visit and talk to the *difuntos.* It is through conversation and interaction with the living that souls are kept alive. Lack of acknowledgment of the dependency of the dead upon the living by mestizos is considered neglectful, and *indígenas* regard *mishu* souls to be *"muertos de a de veras"* (really dead).[9]

Cement tombstones and statuettes on the mestizo side, engraved with names and dates, assert a permanence that the wooden crosses displaying names written in black magic marker on the Runa side lack. This physical impermanence underlies indigenous practices to sustain the memory of the dead. Drawing on Pierre Nora's 1997 (1984–92) *Les lieux de mémoire,* María Todorova (2003:3) traces a distinction between *milieux de mémoire* as "sites of living or lived memory, or rather sites that provide direct access to living traditions" and the fixed or externalized locations of memory embodied in official monuments and commemorative markers (*lieux de mémoire*). Her analysis bears upon the ethnically segregated cemetery in Ilumán.

When we purchased new crosses during Finados at one of the many seasonal stalls of the Otavalo market selling crepe paper flower wreaths, multicolored crosses, and other cemetery accessories, Carmen slowly pronounced the names of her deceased children for the saleswoman to write down. Because Carmen is illiterate, she did not worry about the spelling of the names. She instructed the woman, however, not to inscribe any dates. I later asked her why there were no dates on many of the Runa crosses. She said it was better this way *"porque sino han de quitar el puesto"* (because otherwise they would

Wooden crosses for sale at the market

take away the plot). "This is why people come to visit, because if they do not, they will take away the plot and bury someone else there," she explained.

In addition to food, *chicha,* and flowers, visitors bring work implements. They pull the weeds around the grave and till the earth to make the burial look recent. Though this is done for aesthetic purposes and to express caring for the dead, the more practical reason is to deter others from taking over an occupied burial site. Even in death people must guard their sliver of land. In an area where *indígenas* have defended their land rights for generations, the premium placed on having *un pisito* (a little plot of land) in life carries over to territorial practices in the cemetery. This observation strikes similarities with Wogan's (2003:103) assertion that inscribing the names of the deceased functions as an archive that legitimates a legal claim. People, in spite of their illiteracy, indeed guard the names on the crosses at the tombs of their relatives as claims to the small parcels. Anxiety over losing the cemetery plots translates into a vigilance in safeguarding indigenous contexts of memory where generations to come can commune with their ancestors.

Indigenous emphasis on practice contrasts with mestizos' reliance on the permanence of the tombstones for commemoration of the dead in lieu of carrying out rituals with due diligence. Observation and veiled judgment by

Impermanent crosses in the indigenous side of the cemetery in Ilumán

indigenous people regarding differences in how the dead are remembered underlie ethnically inscribed claims to their moral identity as conscientious and charitable human beings. Ultimately, *indígenas* see themselves as true Catholics and practicing Christians in implied juxtaposition to mestizos. Wogan (2003:108) writes that, in the case of Salasacans, *indígenas* "wrestle control of Christianity from the whites" by appropriating church symbols such as "archival" lists of names and holy water (see also Corr 2002:19). In similar form, on Finados, Otavaleños legitimate their claims as true Catholics by monopolizing the presence of the parish priest in their area of the cemetery. Indigenous initiatives to hijack Christianity are perhaps best illustrated by the appearance of Jesus himself at the cemetery in Cotacachi on Good Friday to deliver a mass in Quichua for Wakcha Karay. Dressed as Jesus, the president of CICUJ (Indigenous Catholic Communities United with Christ) not only assumed the authority of the priest by giving a sermon, but did so in the exclusive physical and ritual space of *indígenas* and in their native language. Moreover, he impersonated Christ and accepted offerings of food and money as a returning ancestral soul and as a fellow *indígena*.

On occasions when mestizos do visit the cemetery, their behavior is solemn. Among mestizos, ritual contexts seem to elicit comportment that noticeably differs from their usual disposition. They speak in hushed tones, move about self-consciously, and stand over the graves with hands clasped, heads bowed. They pray, weep, and hastily depart. That *indígenas* conduct themselves at the cemetery as they would anywhere else speaks to the informal, quotidian air about Runa rituals. It also suggests the relative constancy of Runa identities in shifting contexts.

Differences in behavior at the cemetery can be attributed not only to distinct beliefs about the dead, but more profoundly to conceptual differences regarding memory. Among mestizos, remembering the dead involves rousing disembodied recollections through the mnemonic triggers of dates and names inscribed on headstones. Among *indígenas,* the dead are not considered shadows of people from the past but contemporaries. Visits to the cemetery are less acts of commemoration than they are rituals of communion and family gathering.

Kitchen Philosophy

Death is a frequent topic of discussion and collective reflection, perhaps because of the mystery that surrounds it or because of the conceptual challenge it poses as a major existential transition. Talking at the dinner table after our day at the cemetery, my *compadre* made light of the practice of going to the *panteón*. "Everyone knows the dead cannot eat," he said in a tone that seemed to imply that feeding the dead amounted to superstition. My guess about the direction of his argument was misguided, though. He resumed by saying that though they obviously cannot eat, the dead can smell the food. This is why the dead are always hungry. Then the conversation took another unexpected turn. Segundo said that people know this, but that they leave food on the graves anyway for stray dogs and poor mestizo children to eat later. Embedded in the gesture of charity, once again indirectly mediated through the act of feeding the souls, was the assertion of an inverted racial-economic hierarchy wherein mestizos are pitied for their misfortune and *indígenas* emerge as charitable. As in the case of Carmen and her mother-in-law, this charity retains a critical edge.

I was privy to a similar contemplation during roadblocks staged in support of the national indigenous strike in October and November 2000. One of my godchildren asked her father what would happen if the trucks were not able to circulate. My *compadre* responded that people in the cities would go hungry. They both thought for a moment about the poor people in the cities with nothing to eat. In that reflection there was an awareness of the empowerment of the countryside. Was this an example of the awakening of consciousness that grassroots politicians hope for (and state politicians dread)? It is interesting that the term *pobrecito* (poor person, diminutive added for affection) is ambiguous. In the context of the conversation it expressed pity. However, calling the city folk *pobrecitos* also reverses the urban-rural hierarchy of wealth and power distribution through a discursive inversion. In the wake of the latest national economic crisis, Otavalan wealth in land, agricultural and craft know-how, and migrant revenues add to rich cultural practices that infuse Runa identities with self-assurance. Landless and tied to pitiful wage earnings, divorced from their ethnic heritage through an obsession with *blanqueamiento* (ethnic whitening), disconnected from their ancestors, and lax in their ritual traditions, mestizos indeed seem comparatively impoverished. It is worth pointing out that *pobre* can also be synonymous with *alma* in Runa conceptions, and that the dead are those who have lost their memory.

Chapter Postscript

Mass Otavaleño migration has put a new twist on the importance of place, as graves and homes are abandoned by those who travel abroad. This raises a question as to whether the practice of visiting the cemetery as context of memory will eventually fade, leaving only the nostalgia associated with ghostly spaces devoid of living traditions.[10] The trade diaspora has also spawned class dynamics that influence cultural habits in the region, although this seems to be modifying rather than superseding ritual practices of feeding the souls. Conversion to Protestantism presents a more serious threat to the tradition. My *comadre* was particularly distressed when her daughter, who had converted to the evangelical church, began pressuring her parents to do the same. One night Carmen came up to my room seeking refuge from the unrelenting arguments of her oldest daughter. She told me that she was afraid to change churches; that she wanted to die in the Catholic Church. When I asked her for an explanation, she said, "in the evangelical [church] they say that the priest does not go to the cemetery. People do not go to the cemetery the way that we do in our church." Carmen's concern was aimed at the thought of severing ties with the living upon dying. Visits by the Catholic priest to the cemetery offset the dead's inability to attend church. In popular perception, this allows Runa souls to continue practicing their religion even after death.

Burial plots and crosses at the cemetery in Ilumán

Misgivings about evangelical churches derive, moreover, from rumors that they cremate their dead.

Finados was the last ritual celebration I shared with my family in Ilumán. As I prepared to return to the United States, Mamita Carmen reflected on the fact that three of her five children had both left for Europe and converted to the evangelical church. Now I was leaving, too. She wondered, "*¿quien ha de venir a traer comidita? Toditos han ido*" (Who will come to bring me food? They have all left). She was, of course, referring to the food she would depend on the living to bring to her when she died.

In October 2003 I learned that my *compadres* had converted to the evangelical church. Mamita Carmen has stopped going to the cemetery as often. She still participates on occasion in the exchange of food with neighbors for Wakcha Karay, but no longer pays *rezadoras* to pray over the souls of the dead.

Stations of the Cross:
The Eternal Return to Existence
and Hence to Suffering

Festivals of Memory

"The eternal return to existence and hence to suffering" refers to a phenomenon known as *transmigration,* which Mircea Eliade (1963:85–144) describes
as the joining of the beginning to the end in a process that through memory
constitutes a gradual return to the origin. For Eliade (1963:107) religious
ceremonies are "festivals of memory." He is careful to signal a difference,
however, between memory (*mnemne*) and recollection (*anamnesis*), wherein
"recollecting implies having forgotten" ("and . . . forgetting is equivalent
to ignorance, slavery, and death") (Eliade 1963:119). In chapter 5 I traced an
analogous distinction in the ethnically inscribed practices of remembering
the dead, contrasting nonindigenous commemorative approaches and Runa
traditions of communing with the dead. In an application of Pierre Nora's
(1997) distinction between *lieux* and *milieux de mémoire* (sites and contexts of
memory), I showed how mestizos rely on permanent tombstones to preserve
the memory of their ancestors. In contrast, the impermanence of Runa grave
markers underscores indigenous cultural emphasis on *practice*. While mestizos
visit the inscribed headstones as anamnetic (versus mnemonic) prompts that
elicit tenuous recollections, Runakuna approach the cemetery as a living
context of encounter with their ancestors, as a festival of memory.

Ancestors are brought into festive participation as embodied souls with
material needs and tangible influences. Beyond the detailed remembrance
of people who have passed away—their personalities, their favorite foods,
anecdotes about their lives—the symbolic enactment of parity between the

worlds of the living and the dead through the sharing of food and conversation during the Wakcha Karay affirms the relation between the living and the dead as contemporaries. Eliade (1963:120) writes that it is memory that confers the possibility of contact with the world of the dead. I build on this assertion and suggest that among Runakuna it is more specifically empathetic memory rooted in experience and cosuffering that sustains this connection.

We have seen how memory and empathy work in tandem to render ritual encounters occasions for communion and commiseration across generations—both living and deceased (chapter 5). Here I argue that indigenous rituals do not just elicit a remembrance of the past; they effectively resurrect it. In previous chapters, I discussed festivals as contexts of dynamic and dialogical encounter. Following the outline of the *chakana,* I traced the horizontal human and vertical otherworldly dimensions of ritual encounters, drawing on ethnographic examples that detail the celebration of collaborative organization for the Pawkar Raymi (chapter 2), the assertion of ethnic community during the taking of the square (chapter 3), the connection to natural and spiritual realms through the ritual sacrifice of the Inti Raymi (chapter 4), and the conversations with the dead for Wakcha Karay (chapter 5). This chapter adds a dimension of timelessness to the concept of ritual encounters as experiences wherein the past and the present (and more elusively, the future) converge.

I now turn to chapter 6, which focuses on an exploration of Runa notions of an extended moral and political community inclusive of the dead from a past defined in mythic and historical time. Runakuna reconstitute this understanding of an all-embracing community annually through their observance of the Catholic ritual of the Stations of the Cross. I describe two separate renditions of this ritual, also known as the Via Dolorosa—the Way of Sorrows, focusing on the competing moral discourses that emerge against the backdrop of the politics of popular culture. As the drama of the Stations of the Cross unfolds, an analysis of the aesthetics of performance informs the ways by which these discourses develop in ethnically encoded terms, and how they both reflect and influence divergent systems of interpretation and experience. The resulting moral claims ultimately center on suffering as eminently political.

Ritual performances, as I argue throughout the book, constitute deeply contested social terrain—arenas of ongoing cultural and political contention, moral posturing, and economic contingency. My final ethnographic example returns us to an inquiry into the stakes involved in the "unending struggle for the possession of the sign" (Comaroff 1985), bringing to bear a powerful return to origins in moral-religious and political terms. The politics of performance reveal an intrinsic relation between ritual and the political mobilization of a community. Millennial identities come into focus in the enactment of the Stations of the Cross as indigenous groups sustain control over both the interpretation and the style of production of ritual practices. The community as a whole achieves empowerment, as Gramsci (1971) points out, once collective expression gives rise to culturally institutionalized forms of alternative moral articulation and political action.

Semana Santa: Politics as Usual

In March 2001 quarreling erupted at a municipal meeting in the town of Cotacachi among members of the festival organizing committee for Holy Week. The argument revolved around the production of the Stations of the Cross, the Catholic dramatization that depicts Jesus' ascent to Golgotha to be crucified on Good Friday. Municipal interests focused on the Stations of the Cross as a major urban tourist event. Mestizo actors had traditionally performed the representation as part of the procession on Good Friday. In 2001, however, the director of the troupe of actors was sick and unable to assume the responsibility. This opened a window of opportunity for indigenous catechists to propose a Quichua-language performance of the *cuadros vivos*, the "living portraits" of the Via Dolorosa, for the general public. In response to municipal misgivings that this rendition would not appeal to tourist expectations, the catechists asserted that for them this was an act of faith and not tourist production. Catholic priests were caught off guard by this moral conviction on the part of the indigenous cathechists. Perhaps sensing a challenge to the Church's moral leadership, one priest went so far as to characterize the insertion of indigenous elements in the Catholic tradition as irreverent, and threatened to report the other priest to the archdiocese if he supported the catechists. The discussion came to an impasse. In the weeks that followed, the director of the actor's group worsened and passed away. His widow petitioned the *municipio* to allow the troupe to perform the Stations of the Cross one last time as a tribute to her recently deceased husband. The *municipio* acceded to the request, and the result was the performance of two different renditions of the Stations of the Cross—one staged by the mestizo actors in the city of Cotacachi as a dramatic presentation sanctioned by the *municipio* and the Church; and the other undertaken as a religious procession by indigenous devotees in the community of Arrayanes on the periphery of the canton.

Given the racialized and racializing segregation of space in the context of Cotacachi, it is tempting to conclude that the indigenous performance was *relegated* to the outskirts of town. That the catechists opted not to compromise on their understanding of ritual by relocating the performance was, in fact, a concerted decision that supported a steadfast moral-political statement. The account that follows contrasts the two events, both of which I was able to attend in their entirety.[1] Analysis of the two renditions reveals an approach to ritual as representation in the tourist production in Cotacachi city, and a pursuit of ritual as religious experience in the indigenous fulfillment of the living portraits of Christ in Arrayanes. I argue that the aesthetics of expediency in a performance style insistent on narrative abbreviation, aural and visual editing, and dramatic impressionism in the production of the Stations of the Cross as tourist event in the city of Cotacachi circumscribed the religious drama both as a professional performance and as entertainment. In contrast, the rendition in Arrayanes featured semiotic multivocality, overflowing detail, generalized participation, and sensual experience. An aesthetic of pronounced repetition, extended temporal duration, and spatial range framed the indigenous ritual as shared community experience. My analysis centers on the ways by which these performance aesthetics come to sustain competing moral, and ultimately political, discourses.

Expediency and Performance in Urban Context

The performance in the city of Cotacachi was well rehearsed. The actors were trained to project their voices and exaggerate their gestures for dramatic effect. Roman soldiers escorting Jesus doubled as experts in crowd control for the rowdy urban audience, delimiting the performance area with a brightly colored rope. The troupe was photogenic, exhibiting well-crafted, matching costumes. Each scene, performed at street intersections or in doorways that served as improvised stages along the main avenue, was brief, lasting no more than five to ten minutes. The crowd would then move on for one block, stopping for the next dramatic frame. Prayers (Our Father, Hail Mary, Glory Be . . .) were only inserted during scenes where they complemented the dramatic narrative, at which points devotees among the crowd would chime in. The performance relied on its visual impact and on its adherence to a minimalist version of the Bible story.

Jesus, the sizable cross he was carrying, and the torrent of people, actors, vendors, and raucous teenagers finally poured forth in chaotic fashion onto the main square. The crucifixion was to take place in front of the Church

Professional actors' rendition of the Stations of the Cross in Cotacachi City

of La Matriz in the central plaza. This was to be the last portrait, abbreviating the stations to twelve instead of fourteen for dramatic effect.[2] The actor portraying Jesus was hastily stripped of his garments and tied to the cross. There were no accompanying thieves and no playing dice for Jesus' clothes—perhaps considered to be peripheral narrative threads that would detract from the main story. To my disbelief, when Jesus dropped his head, indicating his death and the end of the performance, people applauded.

Walking with Jesus

The all-indigenous troupe of performers in the rural community of Arrayanes was clearly amateur. A number of them had to be reminded of their lines; others mumbled shyly into the microphone. The soldiers guarding Jesus surrounded him so tightly that it was difficult for the audience to see what was happening. Costumes were simple—mostly improvised except for the matching Roman capes and spray-painted cardboard helmets. The Roman soldiers wore high-top sneakers or shoes with socks to represent military boots. The most striking aspect of the rendition was its duration. The in-

Living portraits of Christ in Arrayanes

digenous depiction of the Stations of the Cross resisted abbreviation. Each stage of the procession was extended, fraught with repetition of gestures to convey the idea of temporal and spatial transition.

After a lengthy enactment of the first few stations at the schoolhouse, the procession got underway. Participants, the majority of them indigenous, walked down a rugged dirt road, slowing down to chat with people they knew from other communities. An ice cream vendor wove through the crowd advertising multicolored popsicles and adding a festive element. The congregation, however, was by no means rowdy. Once we got to the highway, weekend traffic quickly backed up behind the procession—buses, cars, jeeps, tour vans headed to the Cotacachi-Cayapas reserve and the crater lake, Cuicocha. We would advance about a quarter of a mile and stop for each new station. In addition to the detailed enactment of the scenes, at each stop, everyone kneeled on the asphalt and prayed an Our Father, Hail Mary, and Glory Be. Not a single car honked or tried to bypass the procession.

Upon reaching the place where the crucifixion was to take place, the Roman soldiers spent half an hour digging the holes needed to erect the three crosses. Jesus, who had been prematurely tied to his cross, just lay there uncomfortably until they finished digging. Once the crosses were up, Jesus and the two thieves hung painfully from their arms. Coordinators rushed to borrow materials at a nearby house and eventually improvised a foot rung for the actors to stand on. No one seemed to mind these delays as performance and the practicalities of daily life intertwined in a single experience.

While the twelfth station in Cotacachi was brief and highlighted an expeditious and dramatic death, here the soldiers rolled dice for Jesus' clothes and taunted his thirst with vinegar in an extended scene. Jesus died almost unnoticed while the soldiers gambled. The performance continued after his death, with one of the soldiers thrusting a lance into his side. Jesus was finally taken down from the cross and the body carried off by the women. There was no climactic finale and certainly no applause.

Whereas in Cotacachi the crowd simply dispersed, in Arrayanes, a respected community leader, former president of UNORCAC Alberto Anrango, approached the microphone upon the conclusion of the religious procession. Jesus reemerged in full costume to walk and listen among the audience—a seamless transition between performance and real life in a sort of resurrection that was entirely befitting of a fulfillment of the fourteenth station. Anrango congratulated the community in Quichua for taking on the responsibility of the performance and for enacting the *cuadros vivos* in accordance with indigenous traditions and in a language and interpretation of their own. He then reflected on the experience they had just been through:

> In the same way that Jesus fought against the Romans, we too, the poor of today, have to fight against the tyrants who harm us. They are the corrupt ones. The poor, not just indigenous but also nonindigenous, white-mestizos, blacks, have to fight against those who have dominated this country for all times . . .

This reflexive turn, along with Jesus' reemergence as part of the crowd, confirmed the shared nature of the procession and shifted the focus from Jesus per se to the poor who, like Jesus, had suffered unjustly.[3] This final confluence of events effectively transposed the biblical story into contemporary social context and political relevance.

Two Crucifixions in Juxtaposition

From its inception, the performance in town was planned as a tourist attraction. Eye-catching costumes and visual impressions achieved through snapshot-quality poses functioned as external anamnetic referents for recollecting the story of Christ's crucifixion. Dialogue was minimized, highlighting only the most recognizable phrases to carry the story. Suffering and sacrifice, central themes of the Stations of the Cross, were reduced to visual cues focusing on Christ's bloodstained clothes and face. The short distance traveled and the relative brevity of the event omitted any real, if only trivial, suffering either on the part of the performers or the accompanying public.

The final expression of applause upon the symbolic death of Jesus, aside from striking me as ironic, confirmed the spectaclelike aspect of the performance. Clapping created a schism between audience and performers. Although the audience was able to recognize and appreciate the performance aesthetically, this applause signaled an emotional dissociation from Christ's suffering and from the numinous experience of the ritual. As the crowd dispersed immediately following the performance, it was clear that the event had not brought onlookers together in contemplative dialogue as a community having passed through the intensity of a ritual process.

The event in Arrayanes constituted a different experience. Attention to detail manifested itself primarily in terms of practice and less as a factor of costume. Enacted segments marking transition were long, and spoken dialogue in Quichua by the actors was lengthy, requiring the narrator to assist them with their lines. The distance covered by the procession was substantial—about five kilometers—demanding exertion on the part of the public. The length of the walk and acts of talking casually along the way, sharing food, offering help, and praying together imbued the experience with pilgrimage-like overtones. It also blended everyday dispositions into the performance script. Among the cast of performers the physical sacrifice was quite real. Either by design or owing to oversight by coordinators, the actors suffered through the performance.

As a basic human experience that bridges sensation as well as emotional and evaluative registers, pain and discourses about suffering are pivotal in the recognition of a common humanity. Such emotional and visceral responses to a performance appeal to theories of embodiment and experience. Signs *of* feeling, namely semiotic icons and indices, can contribute significant depth to an analysis of performance as felt experience (Turino 1999:223–24). Semiotic indices and icons work at the level of emotion and are experienced as real or natural connections. Often operating in tandem, icons are based on resemblance, and indices derive from signifying relations that draw on co-occurrence in actual experience and on personal experience. The progressive nature of semiotic sign-object chains, moreover, builds on cumulative and collective experience.

A third level of semiotic sign relations involves *rheme* and *dicent*. These add a qualitative dimension to the relation between sign and object, signaling whether a representation simply falls within the realm of the possible (in the case of *rheme*) or whether the representation carries a true/false judgment (as in the case of *dicent*). Body language such as facial expression, body position, and gesture are *dicent* signs interpreted as being the direct result of a person's actual attitude, and grasped as actually being affected by it. They are often bundled with indices to achieve more complex semiotic combinations.

As the sequence of signification progresses, we may see in an application of these definitions to the description at hand that the cross, for instance, can symbolize Christianity or Christian redemption. At the level of iconicity, the cross evokes the crucified Christ. Similarly, based on the criterion of resemblance, the suffering Christ may be perceived as iconic of human suffering. An analysis of *dicent*-indices establishes a connection between the performance of agonized facial expressions and pain. An indexical relation elicits a correspondence between suffering and injustice, experienced as co-occurring phenomena both in historical perspective in the Christian story and in the personal experience of contemporary indigenous people. Indexicality renders these relations naturalized, casting them as inextricable causal dynamics in a way that one immediately calls forth the other. From a Catholic outlook, suffering and redemption may also work in the same way.

This semiotic process, which draws on personal experience, is what enables individual suffering to find resonance with Christ's suffering, and, through the equivalence, to become transformative, religious pain (Glucklich 2001:29). This intimate identification with Christ through empathy and now through cosuffering supports indigenous ethnic claims as brothers with Christ, and not just in suffering but, through suffering, in the redemptive cleansing of the world's sins. Beyond the assertion of a common humanity of shared pain, the transcendental character of religious pain acts as a socially and spiritually integrative force that defines a moral community (Glucklich (2001:34). Ultimately, the achievement of this moral community through the experience of transformative pain encircles the sufferers from both the past and the present in an all-embracing condition of interrelatedness—*communitas*—which Turner (1974:238) describes as "almost always thought of or portrayed by actors as a timeless condition, an eternal now." (See Orta 1990:81 for a similar interpretation.)

Shinallata Kawsanchik: Embodied Memory and Performance as Lived Experience

Empathy, once again, emerges as a key element in this collapsing of time. In everyday life, the personal and vicarious experience of pain in its many forms—suffering, distress, sickness, grief, sorrow, hunger, agony—contributes to a moral community of charitable obligation among the living. Empathy in ritual context encircles people from the past (as well as animated landscapes and otherworldly beings) into this moral community. Empathetic memory sustained through ritual holds this inclusive community together in an eternal present. It is essentially the linchpin at the center of the *chakana*.

The performance of detail constitutes the foundation for embodied memory and understanding. Indigenous performances I saw during the year centered on dramatizations of indigenous day-to-day life, namely the planting, harvesting, and processing of maize and other crops, and the celebrations that accompany these activities. Presentations were often accompanied by statements like, "*shinallata tarpunchik . . .,*" "*shinallata llankanchik . . .,*" or "*shinallata kawsanchik. . . .*" These phrases—"this is how we plant," "this is how we work," "this is how we live"—defined an overall theme and aesthetic of indigenous renditions. Representations were, without exception, drawn-out, and illustrated every detail of the processes they portrayed. Repetition of motion was the principal technique for reminiscing about the past and for depicting for the audience any given traditional activity. As I filmed these events I was coached not to abbreviate the recordings and told that the repetitions were, in fact, especially important to document.

Indigenous performances in general aim to emulate life, not just reference it. In a rendition of the preparation of the soil for planting, for instance, performers walked away from their symbolic *wachus* (planted rows) with callused palms and muddy feet—some semblance of real experience encrusted under their toenails and splintered into their skin; the line between experience and representation suddenly less discernible.

Magdalena Fueres, director of Jambi Mascaric, explained that the best performances were those that accurately depicted *all* of the process of the annual cycle—planting, harvesting, the *minga,* the *uyansa* (celebration of joy after the harvest), the preparation of food by the women, the communal lunch—everything the way it really used to be done. She pointed out the minutiae of men rolling up their pants legs and symbolically working in the mud, pulling the weeds, and cutting corn stalks for the cattle; the subtlety of women removing their jewelry before their performance of traditional cooking; and the nuance of performers stumbling around acting drunk after the celebration of the harvest. These details, in her assessment, illustrated that the best performances captured "something real, not invented." Such realistic renditions of the way things used to be done bring the past into the present in the context of performance, and, in a moment of suspended disbelief, render the present and the past concurrent rather than contiguous.

It bears mentioning that invoking the extended community through this type of embodied ritual remembrance ultimately tempts Andean millenarian myths—specifically, the Inkarrí myth and the religious revival of Taki Unquy—with moral-political implications. The myth of Inkarrí (or Inka Rey, spelled variously *incari, incarrí, inkari*) recounts a prophecy, which gained popularity in the eighteenth century, of the return of the last Inka (see chapter 3). Jan Szemiński (1987:179) writes that the Inka's return was associated with moral cleansing and the restoration of the world to its proper order. It called for the destruction of Spaniards and sinners in order to achieve this goal. Guaman Poma (1980 [1615]) illustrates the decapitation of Atahualpa, the last Inka emperor, in *El Primer Nueva Corónica y Buen Gobierno*. Atahualpa's body was dismembered and the various body parts buried in different places throughout the empire. The Inkarrí legend relates that when the far-flung body parts of the Inka emperor come together as one again, the Inka will be resurrected and return to power against the oppressive system of the Spaniards, bringing colonial reign to an end. In her analysis of Guaman Poma's writings, Rolena Adorno (1986) asserts that Guaman Poma clearly saw the effects of colonialism as "*el mundo al revés*" (the world turned upside down), a time of chaos. Szemiński outlines the relation of the Inkarrí myth to the indigenous rebellions of Tupac Amaru and Tupac Katari in the eighteenth century, and documents the ongoing appeal of this prophecy in twentieth-century indigenous insurrections.

Taki Unquy (also spelled Taki Onqoy, literally "dancing sickness") similarly calls for the return of the *wakas* (*huacas,* Andean ancestor gods) along with upheaval and renewal through the elimination of Spaniards (Stern 1993[1982]:51–55). "The great truth of Taki Onqoy, native-white conflict," writes Stern (1993[1982]:56), "was embodied in two moral principles: resistance against the Hispanic world, solidarity within the Andean world." Frank Salomon (1999:33) writes that Taki Unquy constitutes a "revolution in the uses of memory" that not only required followers to hark back to pre-Inka deities, but importantly, caused them to begin thinking of the *wakas* as "emblems of a new macro-category—the indigenous—as opposed to the global domain of the foreign" (see also Spalding 1999:955). In their analyses of both myths, these authors underscore the powerful political implications of a moral rhetoric articulated in ethnically exclusive terms.

The Moral Community

Resurrection of the mythical and historical dead, embodied in Jesus and those like Jesus, as part of an extended moral-political community was achieved through empathetic memory and performance as embodied experience in the indigenous rendition of the Stations of the Cross. In the urban performance, lack of any real suffering either on the part of the actors or of the public precluded emotional and visceral connections to the performance. The distance established between audience and performers, and between participants in general and the suffering Christ, prevented the event in Cotacachi from operating as a context of empathetic memory.

The dramatization in Cotacachi, however, does not necessarily reflect a failed ritual. The structuring of events as secularized performances in the city suggests a reluctance on the part of local political entities, church authorities, and the relatively comfortable Cotacachi middle-class urbanites to engage in a potentially transformative dramatic dialogue. Turner (1995[1969]:200) points out that ritual liminality, a phase of indeterminacy, for the strong represents weakness because, as antistructure or condition of reversal, it requires them to abandon the structured hierarchies they enjoy. This explanation would, in fact, account for the institutionalized approach in Cotacachi to the Stations of the Cross as an event of fixed interpretation as opposed to a dynamic context of experience. Performance aesthetics in the city expose a positioned discourse of urban empowerment that is predominantly political and economic, not moral or religious. This emphasis is reflected in the *Plan de Desarrollo del Cantón Cotacachi,* published by the *municipio* (no date:25, 33–36), wherein important religious festivals consistently appear with affixed labels and descriptions under systematized economic development policies for the promotion of tourism (see also Ortiz Crespo 2004:131). In other words, framing of the Christian drama in secular terms is a premeditated component of the broader urban project of local political and economic self-affirmation in Cotacachi.

The indigenous catechists responded to this assertion with a corresponding moral argument and a statement of faith. From this perspective, the only way the "strong," in hegemonic terms, enter the human community is through the forgiveness of their sins via the sacrifice of others. Suffering, whether it is in the form of endurance, individual and collective transformation toward a moral agency and a sense of *communitas,* or transcendence in the form of religious sacrifice, is empowering. The collective self-determination derived from suffering for the expiation of society's sins can easily be harnessed as impetus for other agendas. Rituals of status reversal and symbolic inversion that project the poor as the redeemers of the world echo back to my *compadre*'s reflection (chapter 5) about the city folk who would go hungry without the support of the countryside. A generalized epiphany regarding the power of the "weak" resonates, moreover, with the call to action articulated by Alberto Anrango.

Asserting that the poor have paid long enough for the tyranny of the corrupt bankers who have oppressed the country since the beginning of time, Anrango calls for people to rise up and fight against the modern tyrants the way Christ "fought" against the Romans. Although the concept of Christ rising up against his assailants is nowhere to be found in the representation of the Stations of the Cross, the semiotic chain reaction that enabled the original indexical connection between suffering and injustice, and between suffering and redemption, overflows the delimitations of the performance script, and in a creative indexical reshuffling establishes a correspondence between suffering and retribution.

The ease of Anrango's transition from Christlike to modern poor, and from Romans to tyrants to corrupt bankers, is predicated on the semiotic work already underway prior to his political intervention.[4] His political spin, in addition, coincides with the relation Turner (1995[1969]:128) signals between *communitas,* poverty, marginality, and structural inferiority. Anrango's speech reformulates inclusion in the brotherhood of Christ more specifically as comprising the poor—an ethnically "open society" of *indígenas,* non-*indígenas,* white-mestizos, and blacks. Turner's (1974:165) clarification that liminal poverty need not be confused with real poverty (although they may overlap) recenters an awareness of material differences on moral conviction. He writes that "liminal poverty, whether it is a process or a state, is both an expression and instrumentality of *communitas*" (Turner 1974:165). *Communitas* as conceived by Turner is a voluntarily egalitarian and nonmaterialist community. In other words, it is not a factor of circumstance but of choice in conformance with a moral economy of reciprocity that circumscribes a leveling process that may impoverish economically, but empowers politically (Varese 1996:63). Anrango's carefully chosen words reflect a similar awareness, juxtaposing not poor and rich but poor and corrupt in a contrastive conceptual pair that does not condemn financial achievement per se (and therefore does not preclude subaltern people from moving up the economic and social ladder—an important distinction to make in an area and an era of economic success for groups that have been historically marginalized).

Although there were no explicit references to liberation theology in Anrango's speech, both his rhetoric and his message are pregnant with overtones of "a movement engaged in the overturning of 'institutional structures of sin,' " as Orta (1990:80) describes the aims of Latin American liberation theologians and practitioners. Both positions, furthermore, resonate with the call to restore the moral order of the world in Andean millenarian myths. The weight of Anrango's reflection thus rests on an already familiar religious message and a broader political awareness in the Andes.

The Political Community

Ritual not only moves people to think reflexively but can incite people to action (Turner 1995[1969]:129). This has certainly been the claim of ritual theorists throughout the decades of the 1980s and 1990s (see, for example, Raymond Firth 1981, Norman Whitten 1981, 1988, 1996; Michel de Certeau 1984, Peter Stallybrass and Allon White 1986, David Kertzer 1988, James Scott 1990, Catherine Bell 1992, and others), who have focused on the tremendous political mobilizing potential of ritual. In immediate context, Anrango seized the opportunity of a captive audience to communicate, through a particularly effective metaphor, the national indigenous agenda to broaden the bases of support for political action. In *The Ritual Process* (1995[1969]) and *Dramas, Fields and Metaphors* (1974:270), however, Turner systematically draws a correspondence between ritual, liminality, *communitas,* and the powers of the weak, linking ritual and politics in a structural (and not merely opportunistic) relation. The connection between ritual and politics is similarly advocated by Mircea Eliade (1963:71), who maintains that the strength, influence, and creativity of political, social, and economic movements that seek to improve social conditions ultimately reside in their fundamentally religious nature and in their expectation for restoring human happiness.

The vigorous contest over possession of the sign at the local level unfolds in a strategy of symbolic engagement and moral critique with stakes that are ultimately political in the sense that they call for profound social change. Beyond a local interpretation, in the twentieth and twenty-first centuries indigenous people have emerged on the modern national political stage as actors of consequence equipped with a powerful discourse aimed at filling the nation's moral void. The political rallying call of CONAIE, the Confederation of Indigenous Nationalities of Ecuador, throughout the 1990s, "*Ama Killa,*

Ama Llulla, Ama Shuwa" (Don't be Lazy, Don't Lie, Don't Steal), struck a chord with a nation eager to transform society and history for the production of a better life. Today these principles resonate through the Ecuadorian National Constitution (*Legislación Codificada* 2001:72—title III, chapter VII, article 97, no. 20) under the section on citizen rights, guarantees, and responsibilities.

Conclusion:
Threshold People of Imbabura

"Religious man attempts to remain as long as possible in a sacred universe . . .," writes Eliade (1959[1957]:13). The prominence of ritual celebration in the Imbabura area and the energy, creativity, and resources that Otavaleños pour into ritual activities suggest a concerted effort precisely toward this end.

Communitas, the spontaneous and self-generating condition of human intimacy achieved through ritual experience, is generally described as an ephemeral condition that "breaks in through the interstices of structure, in liminality" and exists "at the edges of structure, in marginality" (Turner 1995[1969]:128). The steady sequence of indigenous celebrations in the Imbabura area, however, is conducive to ritually invoking *communitas* with relative frequency. With every passage through liminality, as a ritual phase of collective transition through and emergence from indeterminacy, the group seems to build on an evolving experience of interrelatedness. Returning to Michael Bamberg's (1983:155, 138–41) language of cognitive scaffolding (introduction and chapter 2), I maintain that recurring ritual activity yields a "metaphorization continuum" that through annual recurrence bolsters the sense of shared understanding and intimacy necessary for developing creative and increasingly complex ways of seeing and experiencing the world. This collective and cumulative process of reflection and interpretation, and of embodied experience, is what Runakuna claim as *Ñawpa Yachaykuna,* the deep knowledge that emerges from ritual progression in space as movement through social change and as the unfolding of memory and historicity through mythic and mnemonic passage in time.

Through this process, the original conception of *communitas* as a transient or spontaneous phenomenon, a "moment in and out of time," gives way over time and through practice to a more enduring social condition. Turner (1995[1969]:132, 95) refers to this collective disposition as *normative communitas* and describes the people who sustain this heightened sense of

Mamita Carmen planting her field

interrelatedness as liminal *personae* or "threshold people." The threshold marks a point of entry or beginning. As *limen,* it captures a moment of sufficient intensity to begin to produce an effect. Poised at the crossroads of modern and metaphysical encounters, Runakuna come to embody this moment of transformation. Through their pursuit of meaningful universal dialogue (*rimarishpa*) in ritual and everyday contexts, they become human *chakanas*—points of passage, beginning, and *limen* at the heart of the moral and mythic community.

Appendix 1:
Glossary of Quichua and Spanish Words and Acronyms

achil taita—God. Also referred to as *pachakamak, taita diusitu, yayitu taitiku* (great good father).

acial—whip.

ahijado/a—godson or goddaughter.

alcalde—mayor. Can also refer to community members charged with maintaining order during indigenous *fiestas*.

alguacil—bailiff, constable.

alma—soul.

alpargates—sandals worn by Otavalan men and women.

el alto—upper moiety division, *hanan*. Juxtaposed to *el bajo*, or lower moiety.

ama killa, ama llulla, ama shuwa—don't be lazy, don't lie, don't steal.

amarun—constrictor such as a boa or an anaconda. Central symbolic concept in Amazonia and the Andes.

anaku—wraparound wool skirts. Generally dark blue or black in the Otavalo area.

apegado—people who are not kin but have become attached to a household and are treated as distant kin.

armay chisi—ritual bathing at sacred springs, waterfalls.

ASHIM—Asociación de Shamanes de Imbabura (Association of Imbaburan Shamans).

aumento—literally, increase. It indicates the obligation to return twice as much as one has taken (for example from a *castillo*) the following year.

aya—spirit.

Aya Uma—festival character that wears a double-sided mask and dances separate from the other dancers, oscillating between imposing order and causing chaos.

ayllu—traditional indigenous community. Community of kin and extended kin.

el bajo—lower moiety division, *uray*. Juxtaposed to *el alto*, or upper moiety.

las bases—the grassroots.

blanco/a—Spanish for "white."

blanco-mestizo—self-ascribed ethnic label for people of European and indigenous mixed descent. Many times this ethnic sector self-identifies simply as *blanco*.

blanqueamiento—ethnic and cultural "whitening."

brujería—witchcraft.

cabildo—community council.

cantón—canton. Territorial district within a province. Ecuador has twenty-two provinces subdivided into cantons, each with its own municipality. The province of Imbabura is divided into five cantons.

cargo—sequence of ritual obligations that a person assumes through his or her lifetime primarily through sponsorship of certain festivals. It is by fulfilling this social requirement that individuals gain respect and status in their community.

cariño—affection.

castillo—latticed frame made of cane stalks or thin wood. Decorated with fruit, bread, liquor, money, and live animals for the taking. Part of the tradition of the San Juan festivities in the Otavalo and Cotacachi area, also part of the Corpus Cristi celebrations in other highland areas. (On other public festival occasions, *castillo* also designates a latticed frame decorated with fireworks.)

chakana—cosmic intersection where the connections between divine and mundane correspondences are affirmed. Referred to sometimes as a cosmic bridge, ladder, or Andean steps.

chakiñan—footpath.

chakra—family field.

champús—sweet maize soup.

chapukamlla—mixing of food at the cemetery and at weddings.

chicha—maize beer consumed in quotidian contexts and especially served during festive rituals and other celebrations. Also referred to as *aswa* in quichua.

churu—conch shell. Instrument often used during ritual events to call upon *ayas* and *wakas*.

chusalongo—mischievous folk story creature with an enormous penis that seduces young women who venture to the mountain alone.

CICUJ—Comunidades Indígenas Católicas Unidas con Jesucristo (Indigenous Catholic Communities United with Christ).

comerciante—businessman or businesswoman.

compadre/comadre—fictive kin. The parents of one's godchild (*ahijado/ahijada*).

compañero—colleague. As it is used in indigenous organizations, the application of the term derives from comrade. In nonprofessional contexts *compañero* also means companion.

CONAIE—Confederación de Nacionalidades Indígenas del Ecuador (Confederation of Indigenous Nationalities of Ecuador). Indigenous umbrella organization created in 1986.

Coraza—festival character that appears at various festivals. The Coraza accompanied by a *paje* (his personal assistant) and a *loa* (generally a child that recites an acknowledgment). All three characters generally appear on horseback.

criollo—person of Spanish descent born in the New World.

diablo—devil.

difunto—deceased person, corpse.

dirigente—indigenous leader.

doble acial—backup whip. Often carried by the wives of San Juan dancers in their *kepis*.

ECUARUNARI—Ecuarunapac Riccharimui (Awakening of the Ecuadorian Indian), first indigenous highland regional organization created in 1972.

encuentro—encounter.

envidia—envy or jealousy.

fachalina—shawl or wrap worn by Otavalan women.

FEI—Federación Ecuatoriana de Indios (Ecuadorian Federation of Indians).

FENOC—Federación Nacional de Organizaciones Campesinas (National Federation of Peasant Organizations).

FICI—Federación Indígena y Campesina de Imbabura (Indigenous and Peasant Federation of Imbabura).

fiesta—feast, celebration, festival.

gallo fiti—ceremony where those who wish to accept sponsorship of the San Juan festival for the following year tear off the head of a rooster while it hangs from a cord, spilling the blood of the animal. *Gallo* is Spanish for rooster. *Fiti* is Quichua for cut. Also referred to as *arranque de gallo* (tearing of the rooster in Spanish).

gringo/a—foreigner. Mostly applied to Americans, but also to other foreigners, including Japanese tourists. Not necessarily a derogatory label and sometimes even used for expressing affection, especially in its diminutive form: *gringuito/a*.

hacendado—owner of large landholding.

hacienda—large landholding.

hanan/uray—upper and lower moiety divisions. In other parts of the Andes these concepts appear as *janan* and *urin*. Also referred to in Spanish as *el alto* and *el bajo*.

huasipungo—system of debt peonage. Indentured labor. Abolished in 1964.

indígena—indigenous person.

indio—pejorative term in Spanish for indigenous person.

inti—sun.

jari—man or male.

jatun—big.

kapak—great, supreme.

karay—to give, offer in charity, especially food. From the Quichua verb *karana*.

kawsanchik—plural inclusive form of "to live." Literally, "we live." Derived from the quichua verb *kawsana* (to live).

kepi—carrying bundle or backpack.

killa (quilla)—moon. Month.

kipa (quipa)—in back of, afterward. Quichua concept that designates both space and time, wherein the future lies behind us because we cannot see it. Juxtaposition to *ñawpa*: in front of, before.

kipu—a pre-Hispanic system of accounting and documentation.

kipukamayok—appears elsewhere as *quipocamayo;* keepers of the *kipus.*

kuichik—rainbow.

kulla (kolla, coya)—queen.

latifundio—large landholding.

latifundistas—large landholders.

madera de monte—dense wood from the uncultivated foothills. Sometimes used for making the handles of San Juan whips.

madrina—1. godmother, 2. female escort for a sports team.

makanakuy—combat or battle.

makiwatana or *manillas*—multiple-stranded bracelets made of pink coral and *coralina* worn by Otavalan women.

mayordomo—hacienda overseer.

mediano—ceremonial meal that generally includes hominy, potatoes, roasted guinea pig or chicken, and tostado.

mestizo/a—person of mixed Spanish and indigenous descent.

la migra—international immigration officers.

mindaláes—pre-Inka and Inka long-distance traveling professional merchants.

mishu—derogatory term that indigenous people use to designate white-mestizo people.

mita—institution of rotational labor under the Inka empire. Revived during the colonial era and described as a functional equivalent of slavery.

mitayos—workers conscripted for system of rotational labor under Inka and colonial administrations.

municipio—municipal government; city council.

muru—grain.

mushuk—new.

nina—fire.

ñakak—fat-extracting monster often described as a white man who hides in the shadows and attacks unsuspecting indigenous people. Also known as *pishtaku*, *kharisiri*, or *el operador.*

ñawpa—in front of, before. Quichua concept that designates both space and time, wherein the past lies in front of us. Juxtaposed to *quipa* (*kipa*)—in back of or afterward—which situates the future behind us.

ñawpa yachaykuna—deep knowledge rooted in the past conceived of in all of its dimension.

ñusta—young indigenous beauty queen.

obraje—colonial weaving factories.

ortiga—stinging nettle.

pacha—universal space-time; world or universe.

pachakutik—the transformation of space-time for a better life.

palanca—contacts or social leverage.

paro—national popular strike.

patrón/a—paternalistic master or mistress.

pawkar—tasseling of the maize.

pobre/pobrecito—poor person (diminutive added for affection). Also a term used to express pity. In Runa conceptions *pobre* can also be synonymous with *alma*, soul.

preparado—mixture of cologne and flowers generally left in people's patios as curses.

prioste—sponsor of a festival.

PSE—Partido Socialista Ecuatoriano (Ecuadorian Socialist Party).

el pueblo—"the people."

pueblo milenario—millennial people.

pukyu—spring.

puncha (punja, punlla)—day.

quipocamayo—*kipukamayok*, person versed in the interpretation and writing of the *kipus* (system of dyed and knotted strings that contained encoded information, equivalent of writing).

rama de gallos—an offering by a previous sponsor of a festival to the new *prioste* as an act of passing the *cargo*. The *rama* consists of two poles strung with six live roosters each.

raymi—ritual feast.

rezadora—prayer expert. Generally women but occasionally men (in this case, *rezador*).

rimarishpa—talking, dialoguing.

rosquita—dense, unleavened bread in the shape of a bracelet.

Runa—literally, fully human being. Self-designator for indigenous people. Pluralized as Runakuna.

sanjuanes—San Juan dancers who perform on the eve of the Saint John, and Saint Peter and Saint Paul festivals, and participate in the taking of the square on June 24–26 and again on June 29–July 1.

sanjuanito—music and dance characteristic of the Inti Raymi festival.

SIGNIE—Servidores de la Iglesia Católica de las Nacionalidades Indígenas del Ecuador (Servers of the Catholic Church of the Indigenous Nationalities of Ecuador).

taita—title of respect and affection combined either with first or last name when addressing an older indigenous man. It literally means father. The corresponding female title is *mama*, mother. Young adults are generally addressed respectfully as *tío* or *tía*.

tarpuy—to sow the earth in preparation for planting. From the Quichua verb *tarpuna*.

tienda—small grocery and variety store.

tinkuy—ritual fight or violent encounter performed in ritual context throughout the Andes.

tikray—half turn.

tola—burial mound.

toma—from the Spanish verb "to take."

la toma—short for *la toma de la plaza* (the taking of the square), symbolic act of material reappropriation, historical reversal, and territorial possession.

la toma de la plaza—the taking of the square. Symbolic act of reappropriation, historical reversal, and territorial possession.

tostado—unpopped, roasted corn.

trago—sugar cane alcohol.

tupaj amarun—the phenomenon of a boa constrictor's or anaconda's severed head and body growing together again, leading to the destruction and subsequent resurrection of an even more powerful constrictor.

tuparin, tuparina—to meet again or reencounter.

UNAIMCO—Unión de Artesanos Indígenas del Mercado Centenario de Otavalo (Indigenous Artisan's Union—Otavalo).

UNORCAC—Unión de Organizaciones Campesinas de Cotacachi (Union of Peasant Organizations of Cotacachi). Also referred to as UNORCIC. Second-tier indigenous organization representative of forty-three communities in the canton of

Cotacachi, with a total population of 16,500 people. Founded in 1977. Considered the oldest and most successful Ecuadorian case of extended indigenous representation in a city council. Committed to traditional class rhetoric and class strategies. Retains *campesinista* politics while simultaneously cooperating with CONAIE in national events and embracing most of the national Indian movement rhetoric (Pallares 2002:73, 76).

vacas locas—literally "mad cows"; a game wherein someone wears a festival cow costume, often with pyrotechnic horns, and participants attempt to snatch treats such as bread and fruit off its back.

viajero—traveler. Repeat return indigenous migrant.

víspera—the eve of a festival.

wacho(u)—planted rows of crops.

waka—sacred thing or sacred place.

wakcha—orphaned, widowed, or poor.

wakchu—individuals who for lack of parents or work lean on another for subsistence.

wallkas—glass-blown gold bead necklaces worn in multiple strands by Otavalan women.

warmi—woman or female.

watana—to tie.

yachak—one who knows. Shaman.

yaya—grandfather.

yumbo—warriors/healers from the lowlands. Festival character in Andean Ecuador that depicts lowland men and women from the eastern and western slope of the Andes.

Appendix 2:
Calendar of Festive Rituals in the
Imbabura Area

February–March

- Pawkar Raymi, Peguche, Carnaval Indígena (mid February to mid March migrating date).
- Carnaval, national celebration of water fights, fruit and flower parades (mid February to mid March).
- Spring Equinox (March 20)
  - Mushu Nina (New Fire). Indigenous ritual celebrated on the occasion of the spring equinox.
  - Offerings to sacred sites.
  - Miércoles de Ceniza (Ash Wednesday).

April

- Semana Santa (April)
  - Domingo de Ramos (Palm Sunday).
  - Wakcha Karay (Jueves Santo, Viernes Santo). Indigenous ritual celebrated on this and other occasions throughout the year. Offering to the poor or to the dead.
  - Cuadros Vivos (Stations of the Cross). Enactment of the Via Crucis on Good Friday.
  - Fanesca. Thick, symbolic soup made from tender grains, eggs, cheese, and salted dried fish. This soup is eaten during family feasts generally observed on Holy Thursday.
  - Domingo de Resurección (Easter Sunday).
  - Viernes de Despedida (Friday of Final Goodbyes). During this indigenous procession, saints' images from the community of San Pedro, Jesus de Nazaret, and the Virgen María from San José, approach each other slowly as if they were talking to each other. Then they distance themselves gradually. This is done three times until the final goodbye, where the images follow their own paths back to their respective communities.
- March through April is also the season for confirmations and baptisms because it is considered to be a time of purification and rebirth.

June

- Summer Solstice (June 21)
  - Inti Watana (*el amarre del sol*—Tying of the Sun). Indigenous ritual performed by *yachaks* at noon on the occasion of the summer solstice.
  - Offerings to sacred sites (performed by *yachak* organizations).
- San Juan (June 22–26)
  - June 22: midnight ritual bath at sacred water sites (Armay Chishi).
  - June 23: *víspera*—on the eve of the festival, *sanjuanes* visit the residences of kin and friends in a musical circuit that lasts throughout the night. "Taking of the house patios" in musical battles. Ritual drinking.
  - June 24: *largada de los sanjuanes* (departure of the dancers) from individual communities. *Toma de la plaza* (taking of the square, taking of the church). The entrance into the plaza is performed at noon. Cotacachi and Otavalo.
  - June 24: celebration of San Juan at the sacred site of San Juan Pogyo in Ilumán. Includes the *arranque del gallo* (tearing the heads off live roosters in acceptance of sponsorship of the *fiesta* for the following year); offerings by the *yachaks'* organization; communal dancing and eating; games such as the *palo encebado* (greased pole climbing) and *castillos* (castles with fruit, animals, money, and *trago*).
  - June 25: taking of the square at noon in Cotacachi and Otavalo.
  - June 26: taking of the square at noon in Cotacachi and Otavalo. *Llukshina* (departure of the dancers from the plaza and return to their respective communities). Occurs in late afternoon.
- San Pedro (June 28–July 1)
  - June 27: Armay Chishi (ritual bath at sacred springs, waterfalls). Ideally performed at midnight.
  - June 28: *la chamisa*. At approximately 4:00 P.M. on the afternoon of June 28, people traditionally gather leaves, twigs, sticks, and so forth along the streets and sidewalks in front of their homes and light fire to them. This is the *chamisa*. San Pedro is said to come from the north bringing cold winds, and the fire of the *chamisa* is supposed to warm him up.
  - June 28: *víspera*—on the eve of the festival, *sanjuanes* visit the residences of kin and friends in a musical circuit that lasts throughout the night. "Taking of the house patios" in musical battles. Ritual drinking.
  - June 29: taking of the square at noon in Cotacachi.
  - June 29: Wakcha Karay (offering to the dead, visit to the cemetery).
  - June 30: taking of the square at noon in Cotacachi.
  - July 1: dia de las mujeres—*warmi puncha*. Parody of the taking of the square by women in Cotacachi.
- July 1: Fiesta de Santa Lucia (Cotacachi).

July–August

- Fiestas Cantonales de Cotacachi (July 1–July 3). Celebrated in the central plaza of Cotacachi. Often overlap and conflict with the last day of the San Pedro festival.
- San Pedro, Peguche (migrating date). Celebrated sometime between late June and mid August. Involves costumed dancing in the *plaza* of Peguche.
- Virgen del Carmen, patron saint of drivers. Patron saint of Ilumán (July 16).
- Santa Anita, patron saint of Cotacachi (July 26). Widely known as the patron saint of students. Announced by an entrance of Corazas, festival characters that embody power.
- Virgen del Tránsito (August 1–15). Angry virgin who brings strong winds and earthquakes.
- June through August is also a season for weddings.

September

- Fiestas de la Jora, Cotacachi (beginning September). Nonindigenous popular festival. Jora refers to a special type of *chicha,* or corn beer, prepared during festivals.
- Fiestas del Yamor, Otavalo (beginning September). Nonindigenous popular festival. Yamor refers to a specially prepared *chicha,* or corn beer.
- Fall Equinox (September 22).
- Kulla Raymi, Tarpuy Raymi (mid to late September). Indigenous celebration in honor of women and the preparation of the soil for the planting season.

November

- Angel Kallpay Puncha (November 1). Children dress in white with colorful scarves (yellow, fuchsia, electric blue) on their heads and carry a bell. They are portraying the souls who travel widely and return to the communities for nourishment. This nourishment is both spiritual and physical. As the Angel Kallpay visits from house to house, people greet him with prayers and set a small table with bread, fruit, and eggs for the angel to eat.
- Finados (November 2). National holiday in observance of the dead.
- Wakcha Karay (November 2). Indigenous ritual offering to the dead.
- Virgen del Quinche (November 21).

December

- Novena. Nine days in preparation for the birth of Christ. Involves masses, prayer sessions, and private gatherings to sing Christmas carols *(villancicos)*.
- Noche Buena (December 24). Midnight mass.
- Navidad (December 25). Indigenous families prepare a special meal.
- Kapak Raymi (not observed until recently—or renewed observation).
- Winter Solstice (December 21).

- Año Nuevo (December 31). Costumed celebration where especially children dress up as the widows of the *año viejo* (the old year, represented in effigies of popular figures, politicians, and so forth). They pretend to cry and cry, and ask for money from passersby. At midnight the effigies are burned in the street. People jump over the flames for luck in the new year.

January

- Wakcha Karay (January 1). In addition to the four major celebrations of this ritual, Wakcha Karay is also practiced on Mondays and Thursdays of every week. Observance of the days of the dead on Mondays and Thursdays of every week is, moreover, salient in dividing the weekly cycle into days of danger, illness, and misfortune, and days of productivity and well being.
- Dia de los Reyes Magos (January 6). Represents the visit of the three wise men to the baby Jesus. Previously children received gifts on this day. Increasingly the practice has become to give and receive gifts on December 24 (Navidad, Noche Buena).
- Dia de los Inocentes (January 6). Costumed celebration. More generally, a day when people play jokes on each other. This Catholic tradition is said to derive from the biblical story that recounts that upon the news of Jesus' birth, Roman priests and ministers ordered that the Christ child be found and killed. To protect him, people played fools with the soldiers, offering no information on the child's whereabouts. Incensed and frustrated, the ministers gave an order to kill all of the innocents—children younger than one year.

Notes

Introduction: Otavaleños at the Crossroads

1. Luis Enrique Cachiguango (2000:307) cites the importance of the cardinal points in the cosmovision of nearby Cotama (twelve minutes north of Otavalo by bus, between Peguche and Ilumán). Appellation of the mountains from a geographically centric point in this community is as follows:

> To the South, which is commonly referred to as *wichai* or above, is Mojanda with its three lakes. To the North, known as *urai* or below, is Mount Aloburo, where, according to the elders, the ayas, owners of the riches there, live along lake Yawarkocha. To the East is the male mountain, Imbabura, at the foot of which is nestled lake Impakucha or San Pablo. To the West is the female mountain, Cotacachi, with lake Cuicocha.

This description alerts us to situational relativity of the mountains called upon as "ambassadors to *achilli taita* (God)." Depending on the site of the ceremony, different mountains are invoked. Also worth noting is the consistent pairing of the mountains with their respective lakes.

2. Ecuador completed its transition to a dollar currency in the year 2000, and the *sucre,* the former national denomination, was officially retired.

3. There is some disagreement regarding Uku Pacha among native Quichua speakers. Some Otavaleños gloss Uku Pacha as Hell. This interpretation, however, seems to reflect the influence of a superimposed Christian cosmology. People who adhere to this organization of the Andean cosmos tend to position human beings instead in Kay Pacha. Cachiguango's diagram is clearly one of many representations of the relation among time-spaces. Nonetheless, it is instrumental in teasing out native ideology from syncretic indigenous-Christian beliefs and for communicating clearly the process of interpenetrability and convergence of time-spaces.

Chapter 1: Uku Pacha—The World Below

1. *"Que las autoridades coloniales reconocían que los recursos y revitalización del 'inga' podían transformarse en elemento subversivo, muestra la prohibición, después de la sublevación*

de 1778 en Guano de 'que en las fiestas o funciones o yndios se haga por persona alguna la representación del inca, como inductiva del recuerdo de la Gentilidad, y otros gravísimos incombenientes que deben evistarse.'

2. " . . . *que no se representen en ningún pueblo de sus respectivas provincias, comedias u otras funciones públicas, de las que suelen usar los indios para memoria de sus dichos antiguos Incas . . .*"

3. I did, however, notice a deliberate shift in discourse among indigenous people away from *rescate cultural* (cultural rescue) and toward an emphasis on *refortalecimiento y revitalización cultural* (cultural strengthening and revitalization) during a follow-up visit in 2007.

Chapter 2: Return of the Migrants

1. I found no evidence of historical precedents to the festival prior to this date. Elsie Clews Parsons's (1945) detailed inventory of customs and practices in Peguche in the 1940s makes no mention of this celebration.

2. Latta (personal communication, 2/2007) reports that the *tumarina* ceremony is, in fact, a practice of long standing, though not in its current form. The *tumarina,* according to her informants, was a familial practice carried out in predawn hours within households, shielded from the critical gaze of the Catholic priest.

3. The number of *cabinas telefónicas* (calling booths) had increased dramatically when I returned to visit in 2007. In Otavalo there was a calling center and/or an Internet cafe literally every other block.

4. These organizational dynamics, which I observed in 1999 and 2001, may be changing, however. The Pawkar Raymi organizing committee incorporated as a legal entity in 2002. As Latta (personal communication, 2/2007) observes, introduction of the legal structure has created complications in the use of informal networks by overlaying issues of official administrators and their fiscal accountability to the non-profit entity.

5. This tendency stands in contrast to Billie Jean Isbell's (1978) ethnographic case study in highland Peru wherein the community of Chuschi protects itself from the outside world by closing in upon itself as much as possible.

6. This has been the case, for example, for the *fiesta del Coraza* in Cotacachi. This celebration traditionally took place twice a year—once in September and again in December. Sponsoring two festivals became financially difficult for a single *prioste,* and gradually people shied away from the responsibility inherent in this *cargo.* The festival in Cotacachi was last celebrated in the mid 1980s. The community of San Rafael (Cantón Otavalo, near Lake San Pablo), where the tradition originated, is one of the few places where the *fiesta* of the Coraza is still celebrated twice a year under its traditional structure (see also Butler 2006:132, 149–56; Salz 1955:201, especially 210 endnote 17).

7. An interesting reversal of the metaphor of "dirty Indians" used by wealthy *indígenas* in rejection of their poor cousins or neighbors, as described by Colloredo-Mansfeld (1999:209).

Chapter 3: Encuentros: Dances of the Inti Raymi

1. Originally translated to me in Spanish as ". . . *pisando duro, asentando con fuerza, carajo*" (stepping hard, stepping energetically, *carajo*), which corresponds to the action of stepping emphatically as the dancers say these words. In the text, I provide the exact translation from the Quichua, which I also heard on other occasions. Beyond its literal meaning, *churay* (put it there) carries a sexual connotation.

2. *Carajo* is a swear word in Spanish, pronounced *caraju* in Quichua, equivalent to "damn it" in English. It is often thrown in for emphasis in daily speech, political slogans, and popular songs.

3. When I returned for the festival in 2007, food vendors had been moved out of the park and into one of the side streets adjacent to the church of La Matriz. There were no longer any game operators. The vendors I spoke with said that it had been two years since the *municipio* had recommended that food stalls be moved out of the park owing to excessive fighting among the dancers and to ensure the safety of the vendors. There may, however, be an additional motive behind this shift in public spatial arrangement during the festival. Moving the food stalls cut down on the size of the audience in the main square. As Guerrero (1990:67) notes (although in a slightly different application) without spectators the *fiesta* loses its interest, its legitimacy, and its public.

4. Parsons (1945:124) offers a similar observation of women's intervention in the San Juan fights of the early 1940s and adds in a footnote that Karsten (1920:62) notes women's roles as buffers in drunken fights at Jíbaro (eastern Amazonian indigenous group) feasts.

5. For more detail, especially on the importance of saints' masses, preparations for the festival, the exchange of castles, and variability in customs from one community to another, readers should consult Ferraro (2000), Cachimuel and Cachimuel (1999), Cachiguango (1999), Cornejo (1995), and Díaz Cajas (1995).

6. 1. *kena*—six hole, vertical flute with an end-notched mouthpiece generally made of wood and sometimes made of PVC (plastic plumbing) pipe. 2. *melódica*—mouth piano with a recorder mouthpiece and approximately two keyboard octaves. 3. *bandolín*—rhythmic string instrument. 4. *charango*—rhythmic or melodic small string instrument with five courses of double strings. Traditionally made from an armadillo shell. 5. *rondador*—double-row reed panpipe.

7. I had not seen any representation or participation of Afro-Ecuadorians in the festival until I returned in 2007. In 2007 there were two Afro-Ecuadorian dancers among the indigenous *sanjuanes*. In addition, for the first time, I saw an Afro-Ecuadorian woman among the ranks of the national police assigned to the festival.

8. Though the Inti Raymi is an overt celebration of masculinity, it is important to note that women's behind-the-scenes contributions in terms of the preparation of food, beverages, and festival costumes are extremely important in ensuring the success of the event (Ferraro 2000:179).

9. Generally Otavaleño men wear their long hair in a tightly woven single braid that falls down their back. New fashions inspired in particular by the popular Andean music group Charijayac include unbraided mid-length ponytails.

10. Two poles strung with six live roosters each. The young men holding up the ends of each pole zigzag among their group at a constant trot. The wife of the person offering the *rama* carries a thirteenth rooster. The *rama* is offered to the new sponsor of the festival by a previous *prioste* in an act known as passing the *cargo*.

11. Although *indígenas* participated in military campaigns even before the wars of independence, since 1990 indigenous men from all over Ecuador have been recruited particularly actively into the ranks of the military. Selmeski (2007) documents that 65 percent of more than eight hundred recruits surveyed in Riobamba from 1999 to 2000 reported their families were "from the countryside." Fifteen percent of these identified their families as "indigenous." Discrepancy in the numbers may reflect ongoing reluctance to self-identify as indigenous in a racialized and often racist national social climate. Cecilia Ortiz (2006:78) documents that after the decade of the 1960s the military introduced practices of tolerance toward certain cultural aspects of indigenous recruits, (making special provisions, for example, for indigenous men to keep their ethnically distinctive long braids). This change was received favorably by *indígenas,* who began to approach the Obligatory Military Service as an opportunity for social mobility.

12. An understanding of the expense involved in wearing Otavaleño ethnic attire checks assumptions that dressing children in warm-ups and jeans necessarily indicates a trend toward westernization. Rather than corresponding to the aesthetic appeal of a particular fashion, the incentive to buy Western clothes often stems from economic limitations, inviting us to consider Colloredo-Mansfeld's (1999:214) conclusion that as "the burdens of participating in Otavaleño society mount . . . in the urbanized/suburbanized future of Otavalo, a clearly marked indigenous identity could become the property of the [indigenous] middle class."

13. Coba Andrade (1994:47) also documents a spiraling dance in Bolivar province—the "danza de la llaminga" performed in late June during the San Pedro festival. Unfortunately, he offers little interpretation of the pattern of the dance.

14. Whitten (1988:295) clarifies that "the current term comes to Quichua from the Spanish verb *topar*, which means 'to collide with, to run into or against.' "

15. The original number of horns or multicolored serpents is said to have been thirteen, in accordance with the lunar months. Today variations of twelve, for the solar months, and seven to represent the mystery of the rainbow or the mystery of the week, are prominent. On another occasion, at the Inti Raymi Festival in Urcuciqui (Cantón Cotacachi) in 2001, I saw the Aya Uma from the community of Gualapuro wrapped in a boa skin.

16. *Amarushina tuparin* translates as "boa constrictor–like encounter," or to meet like a boa constrictor or anaconda.

17. In 1984 Ilumán Bajo, along with other communities, fought to defend the sacred spring of San Juan Pukyu when they entered into a conflict over water rights with the city of Atuntaqui. It was to celebrate the final victory over water rights that in 1985 the festival of San Juan was transferred from the central plaza of the parish down to the spring. Resistance against the attempts of local government to infringe on resources upon which indigenous people depend, not only for their rituals but for their livelihoods, evokes broader, or references to cultural and religious impositions, and more recently to national and global influences. Contemporary experiences and recent history provide the substance for a broader rhetoric of resistance (Wibbelsman 2004:111–12).

18. Aside from contrasting obscenity and piety, festival depictions of priests often equate them with monsters. Orta (1998:175) notes that Aymara ascribe similarities between priests and *kharisiris* (*pishtakus*, fat-sucking monsters). Festival costumes in the Otavalo area similarly insinuate that the priest and the *pishtaku* are one and the same.

Chapter 4: Mythico-Religious Encounters—The Clash of Aciales

1. The presence of children in the dances shows their early socialization into the ritual experience. Children are, of course, guarded closely by their parents and whisked to safety the moment of the fights. In 2007 a "cultural day for children" had been integrated into the festival, with San Juan groups made up of preschool and elementary school children (accompanied by their teachers and adult musicians) dancing around the plaza on June 22. Even for the children's "taking of the square" there were police stationed at every corner.

2. Though the term *tinkuy* is used frequently in Imbabura, Emma Cervone (2000: 131) clarifies that *tinkuy* is actually an Aymara term, whereas in the area of Tixán, in the central Ecuadorian Andes, the Quichua term used is *pukllay* (game). Taita José Quimbo in the Otavalo area refers to the fights as *makanakuy* (fight, combat) or *tinkuy*.

3. In 2007 there were approximately two hundred national police at the festival.

4. The first day of San Juan, as Hassaurek (1997[1867]:308) describes it in 1863, was reserved for dances by whites or *cholos*. The fact that today indigenous dancers have taken over the first day of the San Juan and San Pedro celebrations as the *jatun puncha,* or the big day (and over the festival in its entirety as an indigenous event) can be interpreted as yet another act of incursion onto or counter-conquest of mestizo spaces.

5. In the past, blanco-mestizo residents would attend the festival as spectators, enjoying *aguardiente* (cane alcohol), ice cream, and *llapingachos y carnes coloradas* (potato patties and grilled meats—local culinary delights) from the edge of the plaza (see Collier and Buitrón 1949). However, writing at approximately the same time,

Parsons (1945:108) states, " . . . the White townspeople are said to be somewhat fearful of the Indians at this time because their usually submissive neighbors tend to be self-assertive and overbearing." Today, many consider the event too dangerous to attend or bring their families to watch.

6. This self-assertion, moreover, carries over to other things rural and indigenous underscoring the ethnic association with concepts of endurance in everyday discourse. On the occasion of a confirmation, I had to transport live chickens from one of the outlying communities to Otavalo by taxi. I expressed concern that they might die in the trunk of the car and offered to carry them on my lap. My *comadre* insisted that they would survive the trip, saying, "*Runita mismo es. Ha de aguantar no más.*" (They are Runa [indigenous] after all. They will surely withstand [the ride].)

7. A historical reference to white aversion to labor upheld in notions of ethnic cleanliness and fragility that conveniently prevented Spanish gentlemen and *criollo* ladies from exerting themselves—a colonial legacy that continues to justify relegating *indígenas* to the most dirty, backbreaking tasks.

8. Specifically, UNORCAC representatives "accompanied" (*acompañaron*) the widow. *Acompañar* carries connotations not only of attending an engagement but of a long-term social commitment. This term, for instance, is used when asking people to accept a commitment as *compadres* for a baptism or marriage, or to participate in helping a festival *prioste*.

9. Elsie Clews Parsons (1945:124) observes that in the early 1940s in Peguche men usually fought with their hands, "springing about in the wildest way, challenging the other or shaking off the women who [tried] to intervene." She heard people say that the men sometimes used sticks or stones, but reports that she never saw them doing this. Hassaurek (1997[1867]:307) describes an *arranque de gallos* during San Juan in Cayambe, and recounts how after tearing the roosters apart with their bare hands dancers proceeded to hit each other with the bloodied parts of the chicken. He describes that for the festival on June 29, people armed themselves with sticks and thick branches in anticipation of the annual battle. He documents that two or three men would be killed each year, and several others seriously injured (Hassaurek 1997[1867]:329).

10. Ferraro's (2000:179) observation that the relative invisibility of women in the male-dominated space of the plaza may, in fact, be the most evident sign of their power, manifests itself in this example, where the women of both moieties jointly evaluated and approved the mediator. Similarly in 2007, I observed how indigenous women positioned themselves close to national police, and it was they who instructed the police regarding what to do when fighting broke out in the main plaza.

11. Santiago Ortiz Crespo (2004:62) writes that historically the police would ensnare *indígenas* in their webs and find pretexts to arrest them, pointing out that the San Juan and Finados festival seasons were when the greatest number of incarcerations took place.

12. Hanan	Uray	Hot Spots
Topo: Turuku	La Calera: Cumbas Conde	Plaza de Cotacachi
Topo Grande	San Martín	El Ejido
Topo Chico	San Ignacio	
Santa Bárbara	Quitugo	
El Cercado	El Batán	
Morochos	San Martín	"ahí también se matan a bala," says Cornelio Orbes, director of UNORCAC
Perafán	Cumbas Conde	
San Antonio de Punje	Cumbas Conde	"también bala, toca mandar patrullero," says Orbes
San Pedro	Piaba Chupa Ashambuela	
Arambuela	Azaya	
Cuicocha	Guitarra Uko	
Imantag	Andabí	
Quitumba	Morlán	

Cumbas Conde joins San Martín, San Ignacio, and Quitugo to form a single front with La Calera. Turuku, Topo Grande, Topo Chico, and Santa Bárbara are part of Topo. (The community of Santa Bárbara has stopped participating since the *municipio* promoted a competition within the community.) The following comment was made about Ashambuela: "*Son los más jodidos. Son mestizos que no saben y se meten.*" (They are the worst. They are mestizos who do not know any better and get involved.) Tunibamba dances alone. This map coincides with the rivalries Angel Guandinango (1995:60) documents in his study of the Inti Raymi in the community of San Pedro.

Chapter 5: Conversations with the Dead

1. I collected several of these interpretations at an oral history encounter attended by storytellers, yachaks, midwives, and members of more than twenty Cotacachi communities. The event was organized by UNORCAC and took place at Jambi Mascaric in May 2001. Local researchers who facilitated the event included Rumiñahui Anrango, Carlos Guitarra, and Rosita Ramos.

2. I increasingly use the ethnic self-designations Runa and Runakuna (fully human being/s) in the latter sections of the book to signal Otavaleños' progression toward becoming reflexive beings through ritual practice and fulfilling their role as complete persons at the center of a universal dialogue.

3. Wörrle (1999:145) records a *curandera*'s (healer) description of epilepsy as a disease of children wherein the child lying in the hammock appears to be dead. The

curandera recommends a mixture of oil, rue (*ruda*), salt, and indigo (*añil*). "With these substances one proceeds to draw crosses on the forehead, palms, throat, chest, and soles of the child. On Tuesdays and Fridays when danger is more prevalent, the child should wear clothes dyed in this mixture for protection." It is significant that Tuesdays and Fridays, which fall immediately after the days dedicated to the dead, should be mentioned as particularly dangerous for children susceptible to losing their vital energy.

4. Gose (1994:124) suggests a symbolism of black and white during funerary practices and in afterlife accounts in Huaquirca, Peru, wherein black signifies death. In the Otavalo area, black guinea pigs are coveted by *yachaks* for healing rituals, also implying a connection between illness, death, healing, and the color black.

5. Weismantel (2001:xxv) briefly outlines the linguistic distribution of the terms— *pishtaco* in Peruvian Spanish, *ñakaq* in Quechua, and *kharisiri* in Aymara. In Ecuadorian Quichua these terms appear as *pishtaku* and *ñaqaq* or *ñakak*. Meisch (1997:290) also notes in the Otavalo region similarities with tales of the *chipicha* or *chificha*, who eats children.

6. *Mal aire* translates as "bad air" (I have also heard it referred to as *mal viento* "bad wind") and is characterized by pain in the extremities or the stomach. *Espanto*, fright, is a psychological affliction that renders children jumpy, easily scared after the trauma of presumably coming in contact with an evil presence. Parsons (1945:196) says that dogs and cats can also suffer from *espanto*, symptoms of which include loss of appetite, fatigue, nausea, and unquenchable thirst.

7. People in the communities seemed apprehensive about generosity devoid of vested interest. Long before we formalized our *compadre* relationship, when people asked why I was helping with the household or why they were helping me, Carmen and Segundo would respond, "*comadre mismo es*" (she is, after all, a *comadre*), turning potential suspicion into a recognition of due obligation.

8. Colloredo-Mansfeld (1999) and D'Amico (1993) comment on pejorative connotations of *mishu*, which is used in Quichua to designate mestizos. "Mestizos" normally self-identify as *blancos* (white).

9. In addition to the mestizo-indigenous ethnic segregation in cemeteries, Olivia Harris's (1982:57) analysis among the Bolivian Laymi reveals spatial divisions among indigenous graves according to ethnic group, moiety, and subdivisions within each moiety. She suggests that these divisions parallel the upper- and lower-moiety oppositions in the ritual battles (*tinku*), which are fought on All Saints Day and at most feasts throughout the year. I did not observe a similar arrangement of indigenous graves in the cemeteries in the Imbabura area. My attention to the more evident mestizo-indigenous segregation of the cemeteries may have obscured a more nuanced observation of divisions within the indigenous side.

10. When I returned in 2007 to Ilumán and visited the cemetery for San Pedro, I noticed a significant number of cement tombstones on the indigenous side. A friend

explained that the president of the community had declared that year that people should replace the wooden crosses with cement markers because the wooden crosses were falling apart. He also had a brick wall built around the cemetery to prevent grave robberies, because sometimes the dead are buried with gold and other precious things, and people had complained about looting.

Chapter 6: Stations of the Cross: The Eternal Return to Existence and Hence to Suffering

1. For narrative and analytic clarity, I disentangle my description of the living portraits from surrounding events, both of that same day (accompanying processions, Wakcha Karay, Catholic mass) and of the rest of the week. It bears reiterating, nonetheless, that, as with other rituals I describe, the performance of the Stations of the Cross, as well as the politics that surround it, are couched in a broader network of events.

2. The twelfth station presents the death of Jesus on the cross. In one version of the ritual representation, Jesus' body is removed from the cross in the thirteenth station, and in the fourteenth station he is laid in the tomb. In a different version, Jesus' body is removed from the cross and carried off for burial in the thirteenth station, and in the fourteenth station he rises from the dead.

3. Orta (1990) observes a similar and consistent turn of phrase in a Via Crucis performance in a Nicaraguan ecclesial base community. The repetition of "those who like Christ . . ." accentuates ongoing injustices, leading Orta to consider the Via Crucis a ritual of resistance. The ritual also involves asking for forgiveness, thus holding people accountable for "having allowed the injustice suffered by Jesus to continue today" (Orta 1990:81). Orta interprets the Via Crucis within a broader frame of Latin American liberation theology, whose members see themselves at the vanguard of a transformative social movement.

4. Anrango's specific targeting of corrupt bankers refers to the collapse of several banks beginning in March 1999, when the dollar fluctuated wildly above an unprecedented twenty thousand *sucres,* causing spiraling devaluation, and resulting in a federally mandated national "bank holiday" (*feriado bancario*). On Monday, March 8, 1999, personal checking and savings accounts across the country were frozen and the banks closed to the public to prevent withdrawals. This economic crisis was compounded by corruption and mismanagement. Corruption scandals that reached to the highest levels of bank management remained unresolved and many bank clients were never refunded their money. In subsequent years, the government funneled significant federal funds to try to rescue a number of the banks from bankruptcy. The crisis was experienced as all-the-more ruinous by middle and lower income Ecuadorians given the simultaneous cuts in social programs and benefits for the poor because of lack of funding and owing to International Monetary Fund (IMF) pressures for increased austerity measures.

References

Abercrombie, Thomas A.

    1998 *Pathways of Memory and Power: Ethnography and History Among an Andean People*. Madison: University of Wisconsin Press.

Adorno, Rolena

    1986 *Guaman Poma: Writing and Resistance in Colonial Peru*. Second Edition. Austin: University of Texas Press.

Almeida, Ileana, et al.

    1992 *Indios: Una reflexión sobre el levantamiento indígena de 1990*. Quito: ILDIS (Instituto Latinoamericano de Investigaciones Sociales) and Ediciones Abya-Yala.

Andrien, Kenneth

    1995 The Kingdom of Quito 1690–1830: The State and Regional Development. New York: Cambridge University Press.

Appadurai, Arjun

    1991 "Global Ethnoscapes: Notes and Queries for a Transnational Anthropology." In *Recapturing Anthropology: Working in the Present*. Richard G. Fox, ed. Pp. 191–210. Santa Fe, N. Mex.: School of American Research Press.

Armstrong, Robert Plant

    1971 *The Affecting Presence: An Essay in Humanistic Anthropology*. Urbana: University of Illinois Press.

Bakhtin, Mikhail

    1984 *Problems in Dostoevsky's Poetics*. Minneapolis: University of Minnesota Press.

Bamberg, Michael

    1983 "Metaphor and Play Interaction in Young Children." In *The World of Play: Proceedings of the 7th Annual Meeting of the Association of the Anthropological Study of Play*. Frank E. Manning, ed. Pp. 11–22. West Point, N.Y.: Leisure Press.

Barz, Gregory F.

    2003 *Performing Religion: Negotiating Past and Present in Kwaya Music of Tanzania*. Amsterdam and New York: Rodopi.

Bastien, Joseph W.

    1978 *Mountain of the Condor: Metaphor and Ritual in an Andean Ayllu*. Prospect Heights, Ill.: Waveland Press.

Bell, Catherine

1992   *Ritual Theory, Ritual Practice.* New York: Oxford University Press.

Botero, Luis Fernando

1991   "La Fiesta Andina: Memoria y Resistencia." *Compadres y Priostes: La fiesta andina como espacio de memoria y resistencia cultural.* Luis Fernando Botero, ed. Quito: Ediciones Abya-Yala.

Bricker, Victoria Reifler

1981   *The Indian Christ, the Indian King: The Historical Substrate of Maya Myth and Ritual.* Austin: University of Texas Press.

Buitrón, Aníbal and John Collier

1971 [1949] *El Valle del Amanecer* (The Awakening Valley). Otavalo: IOA.

Burke, Peter

1992   *History and Social Theory.* Ithaca, N.Y.: Cornell University Press.

Butler, Barbara Y.

2006   *Holy Intoxication to Drunken Dissipation: Alcohol Among Quichua Speakers in Otavalo, Ecuador.* Albuquerque: University of New Mexico Press.

Cachiguango, Luis Enrique

1999   "Yaku Mama: El baño y las peleas rituales del Inti Raymi en Cotama, Otavalo." In *Inti Raymipak Kawsay Sapi: La sabiduria andina del Inti Raymi en la visión de los Kichwa Kayampi-Otavalo.* Serie Intercultural Imba Sapi. Pp. 23–40. Ibarra: Centro de Estudios Pluriculturales CEPCU, Instituto Para el Estudio de la Cultura y Tecnología Andina IECTA/AYA UMA, Programa de Voluntarios de las Naciones Unidas VNU.

2000   "Wakcha Karai: una praxis de la religiosidad andina en Cotama, Otavalo (Ecuador)." In *Manos Sabias Para Criar la Vida: Tecnología Andina.* Juan van Kessel and Horacio Larraín Barros, eds. Pp. 301–12. Quito: Ediciones Abya-Yala, Chile: IECTA (Instituto para el Estudio de la Cultura y Tecnología Andina).

2001   *Experiencias de Revitalización Cultural en los Simbolismos y Praxis del Hatun Puncha Inti Raymi en Cotacachi.* Cotacachi: Reporte UNORCAC.

2004   "Tumay-Pacha/Pawkar-Raymi: La Ceremonia Festiva del Florecimiento de la Pacha-Mama" www.Otavalosonline.com (consulted 10/2006).

Cachimuel, José and Marcelo Cachimuel

1999   "El aumento, el castillo y los alimentos rituales en el Inti Raymi de los Kichwa-Otavalos." In *Inti Raymipak Kawsay Sapi: La sabiduria andina del Inti Raymi en la visión de los Kichwa Kayampi-Otavalo.* Serie Intercultural Imba Sapi. Pp. 15–19. Ibarra: Centro de Estudios Pluriculturales CEPCU, Instituto Para el Estudio de la Cultura y Tecnología Andina IECTA/AYA UMA, Programa de Voluntarios de las Naciones Unidas VNU.

Caillavet, Chantal

2000   *Etnias del Norte: Etnohistoria e Historia de Ecuador.* Madrid: Casa de Velázquez, Lima: IFEA (Instituto Francés de Estudios Andinos), y Quito: Ediciones Abya Yala.

Camacho, Juana

2006 "Good to Eat, Good to Think: Food, Culture and Biodiversity in Cotacachi." In *Development with Identity: Community, Culture and Sustainability in the Andes.* Robert E. Rhoades, ed. Pp. 156–72. Oxfordshire and Cambridge: CABI Publishing.

Campbell, Leon

1987 "Ideology and Factionalism." *Resistance, Rebellion and Consciousness in the Andean Peasant World 18th to 20th Centuries.* Steve Stern, ed. Madison: University of Wisconsin Press, 1987.

Carrasco, María Soledad

1976 "Christians and Moors in Spain: History, Religion, Theatre." *Cultures* 3 (1): 87–116.

Casagrande, Joseph B.

1981 "Strategies for Survival: The Indians of Highland Ecuador." In *Cultural Transformations and Ethnicity in Modern Ecuador.* Norman E. Whitten Jr., ed. Pp. 260–77. Urbana: University of Illinois Press.

Cervone, Emma

2000 "Tiempo de fiesta; larga vida a la fiesta: Ritual y conflicto étnico en los Andes." In *Etnicidades.* Andrés Guerrero, ed. Pp. 119–46. Quito: FLACSO.

Chacon, Richard, Yamilette Chacon, and Angel Guandinango

2002 "Blood for the Earth: The Inti Raimi Festival among the Cotacachi and Otavalo Indians of Highland Ecuador." Paper presented at the 2002 American Anthropological Association annual meeting. Cited with the permission of the authors.

Chandler, Daniel

2002 *Semiotics: The Basics.* New York: Routledge.

Coba Andrade, Carlos

1994 *Danzas y Bailes en el Ecuador.* Second Edition. Quito: Ediciones Abya-Yala.

Cohn, Bernard

1981 "Anthropology and History in the 1980s." *Journal of Inter-disciplinary History* 12 (2): 227–52.

Collier, John, Jr., and Aníbal Buitrón

1949 *The Awakening Valley.* Chicago: University of Chicago Press.

Colloredo-Mansfeld, Rudi

1998 "'Dirty Indians,' Radical *Indígenas*, and the Political Economy of Social Difference in Modern Ecuador." *Bulletin of Latin American Research* 17 (2): 185–205.

1999 *The Native Leisure Class: Consumption and Cultural Creativity in the Andes.* Chicago: University of Chicago Press.

Comaroff, Jean

1985 *Body of Power, Spirit of Resistance.* Chicago: University of Chicago Press.

Cordero, Luis

1989   *Quichua Shimiyuc Panca Diccionario Quichua.* Quito: Corporación Editora Nacional. Llactamanta Quillcac Tantanacushca.

Cornejo, Luis Alberto

1995   "La Fiesta de San Juan o 'Inti Raimi' en la Comunidad de la Bolsa." In *La Fiesta Religiosa Indígena en el Ecuador. Monographic Series: Pueblos Indígenas y Educación*, No. 33–34. Luz del Alba Moya, research coordinator. Pp. 65–74. Cayambe and Quito, Ecuador: Proyecto EBI, LAEB (Licenciatura de Lingüística Andina y Educación Bilingüe), Ediciones Abya-Yala.

Corr, Rachel

2000   *Cosmology and Personal Experience: Representations of the Sacred Landscape in Salasaca, Ecuador.* Ph.D. diss., University of Illinois at Urbana-Champaign.

2002   "Reciprocity, Communion, and Sacrifice: Food in Andean Ritual and Social Life." *Food and Foodways* 10:1–25.

Crain, Mary

1989   *Ritual, Memoria Popular y Proceso Político en la Sierra Ecuatoriana.* Quito: Ediciones Abya-Yala.

Crespi, Muriel

1981   "St. John the Baptists: The Ritual Looking Glass of Hacienda Indian Ethnic and Power Relations." In *Cultural Transformations and Ethnicity in Modern Ecuador.* Norman E. Whitten Jr. ed. Pp. 477–505. Urbana: University of Illinois Press.

D'Amico, Linda

1993   *Expressivity, Ethnicity and Renaissance in Otavalo.* Ph.D. diss., Indiana University.

de Certeau, Michel

1984   *The Practice of Everyday Life.* Berkeley: University of California Press.

Diamond, Stanley

1974   *In Search of the Primitive: A Critique of Civilization.* New Brunswick, N.J.: Transaction Books.

Díaz Cajas, Manuel

1995   "La Fiesta de San Juan en Ilumán." In *La Fiesta Religiosa Indígena en el Ecuador. Monographic Series: Pueblos Indígenas y Educación*, No. 33–34. Luz del Alba Moya, research coordinator. Pp. 57–64. Cayambe and Quito: Proyecto EBI, LAEB (Licenciatura de Lingüística Andina y Educación Bilingüe), Ediciones Abya-Yala.

Dillon, Mary, and Thomas Abercrombie

1988   "The Destroying Christ: An Aymara Myth of Conquest." In *Rethinking History and Myth: Indigenous South American Perspectives on the Past.* Jonathan D. Hill, ed. Urbana: University of Illinois Press.

Dirks, Nicholas

1994   "Ritual and Resistance: Subversions as Social Fact." In *Culture/Power/History.* N. Dirks, G. Eley, and S. Ortner, eds. Princeton, N.J.: Princeton University Press.

El Mercurio
November 24, 1990, Guayaquil.

Eliade, Mircea
1959 [1957] *The Sacred and the Profane: The Nature of Religion.* Translated from the French by Willard R. Trask. New York: Harcourt Brace Jovanovich, Publishers.
1963 *Myth and Reality.* Translated from the French by Willard R. Trask. World Perspectives, vol. 31. New York: Harper and Row.

Estermann, Josef
1998 Filosofía Andina: Estudio Intercultural de la Sabiduría Autóctona Andina. Quito: Abya-Yala.

Fallasi, Alessandro
1987 Editor. *Time Out of Time: Essays on the Festival.* Santa Fe: University of New Mexico Press.

Fernández Juárez, Gerardo
2000 "Entre lo 'abierto' y lo 'cerrado': Fracturas, tensiones y complicidades en torno a la salud en el espacio cultural aymara." In *Manos Sabias para Criar la Vida: Tecnología Andina.* Juan van Kessel and Horacio Larraín Barros, eds. Pp. 341–62. Quito: Ediciones Abya-Yala, Chile: IECTA (Instituto para el Estudio de la Cultura y Tecnología Andina).

Ferraro, Emilia
2000 "El costo de la vida: deuda e identidad en los Andes ecuatorianos. La fiesta de San Juan en Pesillo." In *Etnicidades.* Andrés Guerrero, ed. Pp. 147–200. Quito: FLACSO.

Firth, Raymond
1981 "Spiritual Aroma: Religion and Politics." *American Anthropologist* 83: 583–602.

Forment, Carlos
2003 *Democracy in Latin America 1760–1900: Volume I, Civic Selfhood and Public Life in Mexico and Peru.* Chicago: University of Chicago Press.

García Canclini, Néstor
1995 *Hybrid Cultures: Strategies for Entering and Leaving Modernity.* Translated by Christopher L. Chiappari and Silvia L. López. Minneapolis: University of Minnesota Press.

Garciagodoy, Juanita
1998 *Digging the Days of the Dead: A Reading of Mexico's Días de Muertos.* Boulder: University Press of Colorado.

Geertz, Clifford
1973 *The Interpretation of Cultures: Selected Essays by Clifford Geertz.* U.S.: Basic Books.
1986 "Making Experience, Authoring Selves." In *The Anthropology of Experience.* Victor Turner and Edward Bruner, eds. Pp. 373–80. Urbana: University of Illinois Press.

Glassie, Henri
   1982   *Passing the Time in Ballymenone: Culture and History of an Ulster Community.*
   Philadelphia: University of Pennsylvania Press.
Glucklich, Ariel
   2001   *Sacred Pain: Hurting the Body for the Sake of the Soul.* Oxford, Eng.: Oxford
   University Press.
Goody, Jack
   1977   "Against 'Ritual': Loosely Structured Thoughts on a Loosely Defined Topic." In Sally F. Moore and Barbara G. Myerhoff, eds., *Secular Ritual.* Pp. 25–35.
   Amsterdam: Van Gorcum.
Gose, Peter
   1994   *Deathly Waters and Hungry Mountains: Agrarian Ritual and Class Formation
   in an Andean Town.* Toronto: University of Toronto Press.
Gramsci, Antonio
   1971   *Selections from the Prison Notebooks of Antonio Gramsci.* Edited and translated
   by Quintin Hoare and Geoffrey Nowell Smith. New York: International Publishers.
Granovetter, Mark S.
   1973   "The Strength of Weak Ties." *American Journal of Sociology* 78 (6): 1360–
   80.
Guaman Poma de Ayala, Felipe
   1980 [1615] *El primer nueva corónica y buen gobierno.* Critical edition by John V.
   Murra and Rolena Adorno. Translation and textual analysis of Quechua by Jorge
   L. Urioste. 3 vols. Mexico City: Siglo Veintiuno.
Guandinango, Angel
   1995   "Fiesta Ritual de 'Inti Raimi' o Fiesta de San Pedro." In *La Fiesta Religiosa
   Indígena en el Ecuador. Monographic Series: Pueblos Indígenas y Educación*, no. 33–34.
   Luz del Alba Moya, research coordinator. Pp. 57–64. Cayambe and Quito: Proyecto
   EBI, LAEB (Licenciatura de Linguística Andina y Educación Bilingüe), Ediciones
   Abya-Yala.
Guerrero, Andrés
   1990   "La fiesta de San Juan: Una reconstitución ritual del universo simbólico en
   los Andes ecuatorianos." In *Nariz del Diablo* 16 (11): 53–70.
Guerrero Arias, Edgar Patricio
   1991   "La fiesta de la mama negra: sincretismo, cambio cultural y resistencia." In
   Compadres y Priostes: La fiesta andina como espacio de memoria y resistencia cultural.
   Luis Fernando Botero, ed. Quito: Ediciones Abya-Yala.
Guss, David M.
   2000   *The Festive State: Race, Ethnicity, and Nationalism as Cultural Performance.*
   Berkeley: University of California Press.
   2006   "The Gran Poder and the Reconquest of La Paz." *Journal of Latin American
   Anthropology* 11 (2): 294–328.

Halperin, Rhoda H.
 1984 "Polanyi, Marx, and the Institutional Paradigm in Economic Anthropology." *Research in Economic Anthropology* 6: 245–72.
Harris, Janet
 1983 "Pride and Fever: Two University Sport Promotion Themes." In *The World of Play: Proceedings of the 7th Annual Meeting of the Association of the Anthropological Study of Play*. Frank E. Manning, ed. Pp. 25–37. West Point, N.Y.: Leisure Press.
Harris, Max
 2003 *Carnival and Other Christian Festivals: Folk Theology and Folk Performance*. Austin: University of Texas Press.
Harris, Olivia
 1982 "The Dead and the Devils among the Bolivian Laymi." In *Death and the Regeneration of Life*. Maurice Bloch and Jonathon Parry, eds. Pp. 45–73. Cambridge, Eng.: Cambridge University Press.
Hassaurek, Friedrich
 1997 [1867] *Cuatro Años entre los Ecuatorianos*. Quito: Ediciones Abya-Yala.
Hill, Jonathan D.
 1988 "Introduction: Myth and History." In *Rethinking History and Myth: Indigenous South American Perspectives on the Past*. Jonathan D. Hill, ed. Pp. 1–18. Urbana and Chicago: University of Illinois Press.
Hoopes, James, ed.
 1991 *Pierce on Signs: Writings on Semiotic by Charles Sanders Pierce*. Chapel Hill: University of North Carolina Press.
INEC (Instituto Nacional de Estadistica y Censos)
 2001 Ecuadorian government census and statistics publication. Quito: República del Ecuador.
Isbell, Billie Jean
 1978 *To Defend Ourselves: Ecology and Ritual in an Andean Village*. Prospect Heights, Ill.: Waveland Press.
Jokisch, Brad
 1998 "Ecuadorian Emigration and Agricultural Change: The Persistence of Smallholder Agriculture in Lower Cañar, Ecuador," presented at the 1998 meeting of Latin American Studies Association, Chicago, September 24–26, 1998.
Kapferer, Jean-Noël
 1990 *Rumors: Uses, Interpretations, and Images*. Translated from the French by Bruce Fink. New Brunswick, N.J.: Transaction Publishers.
Karsten, Rafael
 1920 "Contributions to the Sociology of the Indian Tribes of Ecuador." *Acta Academiae Aboensis Humaniora* 1(3):1–75. Helsinki.
Kertzer, David I.
 1988 *Ritual, Politics and Power*. New Haven, Conn.: Yale University Press.

KIPU
1990   *KIPU: El mundo indígena en la prensa ecuatoriana*. Quito: Ediciones Abya-Yala.

Korol, Juan Carlos and Enrique Tandeter
1998   *Historia económica de América Latina: problemas y procesos*. Mexico: Fondo de Cultura Económica.

Kowii, Ariruma
1999a "Espiritualidad y Medios de Comunicación." Paper presented at the *Festival del video y film de los pueblos de Abya Yala*. Universidad Salesiana de Quito, June 17.
1999b "Simbología del Aya Uma." In *Inti Raymipak Kawsay Sapi: La sabiduria andina del Inti Raymi en la visión de los Kichwa Kayampi-Otavalo*. Serie Intercultural Imba Sapi. Pp. 20–22. Ibarra: Centro de Estudios Pluriculturales CEPCU, Instituto Para el Estudio de la Cultura y Tecnología Andina IECTA/AYA UMA, Programa de Voluntarios de las Naciones Unidas VNU.

Kyle, David
1999   "The Otavalo Trade Diaspora: Social Capital and Transnational Entrepreneurship." *Ethnic and Racial Studies* 22 (2): 422–46.
2000   *Transnational Peasants: Migrations, Networks, and Ethnicity in Andean Ecuador*. Baltimore: Johns Hopkins University Press.

Legislación Codificada
2001   *Contitución Política de la República del Ecuador*. Edición Universitaria. Actualizada a noviembre de 2001. Quito: Talleres de la Corporación de Estudios y Publicaciones.

Lipsitz, George
1994   *Dangerous Crossroads: Popular Music, Postmodernism and the Poetics of Place*. New York and London: Verso.

Macas, Luis, Linda Belote, and Jim Belote
2003   "Indigenous Destiny in Indigenous Hands." In *Millennial Ecuador: Critical Essays in Cultural Transformations and Social Dynamics*. Norman E. Whitten Jr., ed. Pp. 216–41. Iowa City: University of Iowa Press.

Males, Antonio
1989   "Past and Present of Andean Indian Society: The Otavalos." Translated by Joanne Rappaport. In *Who Needs the Past? Indigenous Values and Archaeology*. R. Layton, ed. London: Unwin Hyman. Pp. 95–104.

Manning, Frank
1998   "Celebrating Cricket: The Symbolic Construction of Caribbean Politics [Bermuda]." In *Blackness in Latin America and the Caribbean*. Arlene Torres and Norman E. Whitten Jr., eds. Pp. 460–82. Bloomington: Indiana University Press.

Meisch, Lynn A.
1987   *Otavalo: Weaving, Costume and the Market*. Quito: Ediciones Libri Mundi.

1997 *Traditional Communities, Transnational Lives: Coping with Globalization in Otavalo, Ecuador.* Ph.D. diss., Stanford University.

2002 *Andean Entrepreneurs: Otavalo Merchants and Musicians in the Global Arena.* Austin: University of Texas Press.

Mendizábal, Tannia

1982 "Informe Etnográfico sobre la Fiesta de San Juan en el Area de Cotacachi-Imbabura." In *La Fiesta Religiosa Campesina: Andes Ecuatorianos.* Marco Vinicio Rueda, ed. Pp. 346–58. Quito: Ediciones de la Universidad Católica.

Mendoza, Zoila S.

2000 *Shaping Society through Dance: Mestizo Ritual Performance in the Peruvian Andes.* Chicago: University of Chicago Press.

Miles, Ann

2004 *From Cuenca to Queens: An Anthropological Story of Transnational Migration.* Austin: University of Texas Press.

Ministerio de Turismo Ecuador

1/19/2006 www.ecuadorvirtual.com.

Mitchell, J. Clyde

1969 "The Concept and Use of Social Networks." In *Social Networks in Urban Situations: Analyses of Personal Relationships in Central African Towns.* J. C. Mitchell, ed. Manchester: Manchester University Press.

Moore, Sally F.

1975 "Uncertainty in Situations: Indeterminacies in Culture." In *Symbol and Politics in Communal Ideology: Cases and Questions.* Sally F. Moore and Barbara Myerhoff, ed. Ithaca, N.Y.: Cornell University Press.

Moore, Sally F., and Barbara G. Meyerhoff

1977 "Introduction: Secular Ritual: Forms and Meanings." In *Secular Ritual.* Sally Moore and Barbara Meyerhoff, eds. Pp. 3–24. New Haven, Conn.: Van Gorcum, Assen.

Moreno Yánez, Segundo

1996 *Sublevaciones* Indígenas *en la Audiencia de Quito Desde Comienzos del Siglo XVIII hasta finales de la Colonia.* Quito: Ediciones de la Pontificia Universidad Católica del Ecuador.

Moreno Yánez, Segundo, and José Figueroa

1992 *El levantamiento indígena del inti raymi de 1990.* Quito: FESO (Fundación Ecuatoriana de Estudios Sociales) and Ediciones Abya-Yala.

Municipio de Cotacachi

nd *Plan de Desarrollo del Cantón Cotacachi.* Cotacachi, Ecuador.

Murra, John

1946 "The Historic Tribes of Ecuador." In *Handbook of South American Indians,* vol. 2: *The Andean Civilizations.* Julian H. Steward, ed. Pp. 785–821. Washington: Smithsonian Institution.

Nora, Pierre
1997 *Les Lieux de Mémoire*. Paris: Gallimard.
Océano Grupo Editorial
2000 *Enciclopedia del Ecuador*. Barcelona: Océano Grupo Editorial, S.A.
Ohnuki-Tierney, Emiko
1990 "The Monkey as Self in Japanese Culture." In *Culture through Time: Anthropological Approaches*. Stanford, Calif.: Stanford University Press, pp. 128–53.
Orlove, Benjamin S.
1998 "Down to Earth: Race and Substance in the Andes." *Bulletin of Latin American Research* 17 (2): 207–22.
Orta, Andrew
1990 "Iconoclasm and History: Remembering the Via Crucis in a Nicaraguan Comunidad Eclesial de Base." *Nexus* 7 (supplement): 79–140.
1998 "Converting Difference: Metaculture, Missionaries, and the Politics of Locality." *Ethnology* 37 (2): 165–85.
2004 *Catechizing Culture: Missionaries, Aymara, and the "New Evangelization."* New York: Columbia University Press.
Ortiz, Cecilia B.
2006 "La influencia militar en la construcción política del indio ecuatoriano en el siglo XX." Special edition on *Populismo militar y etnicidad en los Andes*. Ed. Edison Hurtado. *Iconos Revista de Ciencias Sociales* 26: 73–84. Quito: FLACSO.
Ortiz Crespo, Santiago
2004 *Cotacachi: una apuesta por la democracia participativa*. Quito: FLACSO, Sede Ecuador.
Ortner, Sherry
1990 "Patterns of History: Cultural Schemas in the Foundings of Sherpa Religious Institutions." In *Culture through Time: Anthropological Approaches*. Stanford, Calif.: Stanford University Press, pp. 57–93.
Pallares, Amalia
2002 *From Peasant Struggles to Indian Resistance: The Ecuadorian Andes in the Late Twentieth Century*. Norman: University of Oklahoma Press.
Parsons, Elsie Clews
1945 *Peguche: Canton of Otavalo, Province of Imbabura, Ecuador: A Study of Andean Indians*. Chicago: University of Chicago Press.
Polanyi, Karl
1957 [1944] *The Great Transformation: The Political and Economic Origins of Our Time*. Boston: Beacon Press.
Quiroga, Diego
1999 "Razas, Esencialismos, y Salud." *Íconos* 7: 86–93.
2003 "The Devil and Development in Esmeraldas: Cosmology as a System of Critical Thought." In *Millennial Ecuador: Critical Essays in Cultural Transformations*

and Social Dynamics. Norman E. Whitten Jr., ed. Pp. 154–83. Iowa City: University of Iowa Press.

Ramón Valarezo, Galo

2002 "OSGs y Municipios: Desencuentro o complementariedad?" In *Construyendo Capacidades Colectivas: Fortalecimiento organizativo de las federaciones campesinas-indígenas en la Sierra ecuatoriana*. Thomas F. Carroll, ed. Pp. 413–26. Quito: RISPERGRAF.

Rappaport, Roy A.

1999 *Ritual and Religion in the Making of Mankind*. Cambridge, Eng.: Cambridge University Press.

Rasnake, Roger

1988 *Domination and Cultural Resistance: Authority and Power Among an Andean People*. Durham, N.C.: Duke University Press.

Reeve, Mary-Elizabeth

1988 "*Cauchu Uras*: Lowland Quichua Histories of the Amazon Rubber Boom." In *Rethinking History and Myth: Indigenous South American Perspectives on the Past*. Jonathan D. Hill, ed. Pp. 19–34. Urbana and Chicago: University of Illinois Press.

Reglamento Campeonato de Futbol, Pawkar Raymi "Peguche Tio"

2004 published online, www.Otavalosonline.com.

Rhoades, Robert E., ed.

2006 *Development with Identity: Community, Culture and Sustainability in the Andes*. Oxfordshire and Cambridge: CABI Publishing.

Rodriguez, Germán

1999 *La Sabiduría del Kóndor: Un Ensayo Sobre la Validez del Saber Andino*. Quito: Abya-Yala.

Rosnow, Ralph L., and Gary Alan Fine

1976 *Rumor and Gossip: The Social Psychology of Hearsay*. New York: Elsevier Scientific Publishing Company.

Rowe, William, and Vivian Schelling

1991 *Memory and Modernity: Popular Culture in Latin America*. New York: Verso.

Rueda Novoa, Rocío

1988 *El Obraje de San Joseph de Peguchi*. Quito: Ediciones Abya-Yala and TEHIS (Taller de Estudios Históricos).

Salomon, Frank

1981a "Killing the Yumbo: A Ritual Drama of Northern Quito." In *Cultural Transformations and Ethnicity in Modern Ecuador*. Norman E. Whitten Jr., editor. Pp. 162–210. Urbana: University of Illinois Press.

1981b "Weavers of Otavalo." In *Cultural Transformations and Ethnicity in Modern Ecuador*. Norman E. Whitten Jr., ed. Pp. 420–49. Urbana: University of Illinois Press.

1986 *Native Lords of Quito in the Age of the Incas: The Political Economy of North-Andean Chiefdoms.* Cambridge, Eng.: Cambridge University Press.

1999 "Testimonies: The Making and Reading of Native South American Historical Sources." In *The Cambridge History of the Native Peoples of the Americas. Volume III. South America. Part I.* Frank Salomon and Stuart B. Schwartz, eds. Pp. 19–95. Cambridge, Eng.: Cambridge University Press.

Salz, Beate R.

1955 *The Human Element in Industrialization: A Hypothetical Case Study of Ecuadorean Indians.* American Anthropological Association 57(6) part 2, memoir no. 85. Chicago: Research Center in Economic Development and Cultural Change.

Scott, James C.

1976 *The Moral Economy of the Peasant: Rebellion and Subsistence in Southeast Asia.* New Haven, Conn.: Yale University Press.

1985 *Weapons of the Weak: Everyday Forms of Peasant Resistance.* New Haven, Conn.: Yale University Press.

1990 *Domination and the Arts of Resistance: Hidden Transcripts.* New Haven, Conn.: Yale University Press.

Scott, John

2000 [1991] *Social Network Analysis: A Handbook.* Second Edition. London: SAGE Publications.

Selmeski, Brian R.

2007 "Sons of Indians and Indian Sons: Military Service, Familial Metaphors, and Multicultural Nationalism." In *Highland Indians and the State in Modern Ecuador.* A. Kim Clark and Marc Becker, eds. Pp. 155–78. Pittsburgh: University of Pittsburgh Press.

Selverston-Scher, Melina

2001 *Ethnopolitics in Ecuador: Indigenous Rights and the Strengthening of Democracy.* Coral Gables, Fl.: North-South Center Press at the University of Miami.

Sempat Assadourian, Carlos

1983 *El sistema de la economía colonial: el mercado interior regiones espacio economico.* Mexico: Editorial Nueva Imagen, S.A.

Seremetakis, Nadia

1994 *The Senses Still.* Chicago: University of Chicago Press.

Sherbondy, Jeanette

1992 "Water Ideology in Inca Ethnogenesis." In *Andean Cosmologies through Time: Persistence and Emergence.* Robert V. H. Dover, Katharine E. Seibold, and John H. McDowell, eds. Pp. 46–66. Bloomington: Indiana University Press.

Smith, Gavin

1999 *Confronting the Present: Toward a Politically Engaged Anthropology.* Oxford and New York: Berg.

Sorel, Georges

1999 *Reflections on Violence.* Cambridge, Eng.: Cambridge University Press.

Spalding, Karen
  1999 "The Crises and Transformations of Invaded Societies: Andean Area (1500–1580)." In *The Cambridge History of the Native Peoples of the Americas. Volume III. South America. Part I.* Frank Salomon and Stuart B. Schwartz, eds. Pp. 904–72. Cambridge, Eng.: Cambridge University Press.

Stallybrass, Peter, and Allon White
  1986 *The Politics and Poetics of Transgression.* Ithaca, N.Y.: Cornell University Press.

Stern, Steve J.
  1993 [1982] *Peru's Indian Peoples and the Challenge of Spanish Conquest: Huamanga to 1640.* Second Edition. Madison: University of Wisconsin Press.

Sullivan, Lawrence E.
  1988 *Icanchu's Drum: An Orientation to Meaning in South American Religions.* New York: Macmillan Publishing Company.

Szemiński, Jan
  1987 "Why Kill the Spaniard? New Perspectives on Andean Insurrectionary Ideology in the 18th Century." In *Resistance, Rebellion, and Consciousness in the Andean Peasant World, 18th to 20th Centuries.* Steve J. Stern, ed. Pp. 166–92. Madison: University of Wisconsin Press.

Tambiah, Stanley J.
  1985 *Culture, Thought, and Social Action: An Anthropological Perspective.* Cambridge, Mass.: Harvard University Press.

Taussig, Michael
  1987 *Shamanism, Colonialism and the Wild Man: A Study in Terror and Healing.* Chicago: University of Chicago Press.

Thurner, Mark
  2000 "Políticas campesinas y haciendas andinas." In *Etnicidades.* Andrés Guerrero, ed. Pp. 337–96. Quito: FLACSO.

Todorova, María
  2003 "The Mausoleum of Georgi Dimitrov as *lieu de mémoire.*" Paper presented at the Directions Seminar REEEC at the University of Illinois at Urbana-Champaign. Cited with the permission of the author.

Trouillot, Michel-Rolph
  1995 *Silencing the Past: Power and the Production of History.* Boston: Beacon Press.

Turino, Thomas
  1993 *Moving Away from Silence: Music of the Peruvian Altiplano and the Experience of Urban Migration.* Chicago: University of Chicago Press.
  1999 "Signs of Imagination, Identity, and Experience: A Peircian Semiotic Theory for Music." *Ethnomusicology* 43 (2): 221–55.
  2004 "Introduction: Identity and the Arts in Diaspora Communities." In *Identity and the Arts in Diaspora Communities.* Thomas Turino and James Lea, eds. Pp. 3–20. Warren, Mich.: Harmonie Park Press.

Turner, Victor

    1974 *Dramas, Fields and Metaphors: Symbolic Action in Human Society*. Ithaca, N.Y.: Cornell University Press.

    1985 *On the Edge of the Bush: Anthropology as Experience*. Edited by Edith L. B. Turner. Tucson: University of Arizona Press.

    1995 [1969] *The Ritual Process: Structure and Anti-Structure*. Hawthorne, N.Y.: Aldine de Gruyter.

Turner, Victor, and Edward M. Bruner

    1986 Editors. *The Anthropology of Experience*. Urbana: University of Illinois Press.

UNAIMCO

    2001 *Inti Raymi Plaza de Ponchos*. Advertising pamphlet produced by Unión de Artesanos Indígenas del Mercado Centenario de Otavalo. Otavalo: UNAIMCO.

UNICOBICI

    2000 *Plan de Desarrollo Local: Sumak Kausaita Maskankapak Ñan*. Ilumán: Union de Comunas y Barrios Indígenas y Campesinas de Ilumán y CODENPE, PRODE-PINE (Proyecto de Desarrollo de los Pueblos Indígenas y Negros del Ecuador Región Sierra Norte).

UNORCAC

    2001 Inti Raymi Workshop.

Uzendoski, Michael

    2005 *The Napo Runa of Amazonian Ecuador*. Urbana and Chicago: University of Illinois Press.

Varese, Stephano

    1996 "The Ethnopolitics of Indian Resistance in Latin America." *Latin American Perspectives*. Issue 89, 23 (2): 58–71.

Villamarín, Juan, and Judith Villamarín

    1999 "Chiefdoms: The Prevalence and Persistence of 'Señoríos Naturales,'" 1400 to European Conquest. *The Cambridge History of Native Peoples of the Americas. Volume III. South America Part 1*. Frank Salomon and Stuart B. Schwartz, eds. Pp. 577–667. Cambridge, Eng.: Cambridge University Press.

Vinicio Rueda, Marco

    1982a "Raíces Históricas." In *La Fiesta Religiosa Campesina (Andes Ecuatorianos)*. Marco Vinicio Rueda, ed. Pp. 69–96. Quito: Ediciones de la Universidad Católica.

    1982b "La fiesta religiosa en la religiosidad campesina." In *La Fiesta Religiosa Campesina (Andes Ecuatorianos)*. Marco Vinicio Rueda, ed. Pp. 21–44. Quito: Ediciones de la Universidad Católica.

Wachtel, Nathan

    1994 *Gods and Vampires: Return to Chipaya*. Translated by Carol Volk. Chicago: University of Chicago Press.

Walzer, Michael

    1994 "Multiculturalism and Individualism." *Dissent*. Spring Issue, pp. 185–91.

Weismantel, Mary

1998 [1988] *Food, Gender, and Poverty in the Ecuadorian Andes.* Prospect Heights, Ill.: Waveland Press.

1991 "Maize Beer and Andean Social Transformations: Drunken Indians, Bread Babies, and Chosen Women." *MLN* 106: 861–79.

2001 *Cholas and Pishtacos: Stories of Race and Sex in the Andes.* Chicago: University of Chicago Press.

Whitehead, Neil L.

2002 *Dark Shaman: Kanaimà and the Poetics of Violent Death.* Durham, N.C.: Duke University Press.

Whitten, Dorothea Scott

2003 "Actors and Artists from Amazonia and the Andes." In *Millennial Ecuador: Critical Essays in Cultural Transformations and Social Dynamics.* Norman E. Whitten Jr., ed. Pp. 242–74. Iowa City: University of Iowa Press.

Whitten, Dorothea Scott, and Norman E. Whitten Jr., editors.

1993 *Imagery and Creativity: Ethnoaesthetics and Art Worlds in the Americas.* Tucson: University of Arizona Press.

Whitten, Norman E., Jr.

1976 *Sacha Runa: Ethnicity and Adaptation of Ecuadorian Jungle Quichua.* Urbana: University of Illinois Press.

1981 "Introduction." In *Cultural Transformations and Ethnicity in Modern Ecuador.* Norman E. Whitten Jr., ed. Urbana: University of Illinois Press, pp. 1–41.

1988 "Commentary: Historical and Mythic Evocations of Chthonic Power in South America." In *Rethinking History and Myth: Indigenous South American Perspectives on the Past.* Jonathan D. Hill, ed. Pp. 282–306. Urbana: University of Illinois Press.

1996 "The Ecuadorian Levantamiento Indígena of 1990 and the Epitomizing Symbol of 1992: Reflections on Nationalism, Ethnic-Bloc Formation, and Racialist Ideologies." In *History, Power, and Identity: Ethnogenesis in the Americas, 1492–1992.* Jonathan D. Hill, ed. Pp. 193–218. Iowa City: University of Iowa Press.

2003 "Preface." In *Millennial Ecuador: Critical Essays in Cultural Transformations and Social Dynamics.* Norman E. Whitten Jr., ed. Pp. ix–xvii. Iowa City: University of Iowa Press.

Whitten, Norman E., Jr., Dorothea Scott Whitten, and Alfonso Chango

1997 "Return of the Yumbo: The Indigenous Caminata from Amazonia to Andean Quito." *American Ethnologist* 24(2):355–91.

2003 "Return of the Yumbo: The *Caminata* from Amazonia to Andean Quito." In *Millennial Ecuador: Critical Essays in Cultural Transformations and Social Dynamics.* Norman E. Whitten Jr., ed. Pp. 184–215. Iowa City: University of Iowa Press.

Wibbelsman, Michelle

2000 *Ecuadorian Indigenous Festivals: Sites of Cultural Innovation, Social Change and Identity Politics.* Masters thesis in anthropology. University of Illinois at Urbana-Champaign.

2004 *Rimarishpa Kausanchik: Dialogical Encounters: Festive Ritual Practices and the Making of the Otavalan Moral and Mythic Community.* Ph.D. diss. in anthropology. University of Illinois at Urbana-Champaign.

Windmeijer, Jeroen

1998 *Modern Traditions: The Otavaleños of Ecuador.* Amsterdam: Cuadernos del CEDLA.

2001 *De Vallei van de Rijzende Zon: Een studie naar de voorbeeldige Indianen uit Otavalo, Ecuador.* The Netherlands: Research School of Asian, African, and Amerindian Studies (CNWS) Publications, Leiden University.

Wogan, Peter

2003 *Magical Writing in Salasaca: Literacy and Power in Highland Ecuador.* Boulder, Colo.: Westview Press.

Wörrle, Bernhard

1999 *De la cocina a la brujería: La sal entre indígenas y mestizos en América Latina.* Quito: Ediciones Abya-Yala.

Zuidema, R. Tom

1992 "Inca Cosmos in Andean Context: From the Perspective of the Capac Raymi Camay Quilla Feast Celebrating the December Solstice in Cuzco." In *Andean Cosmologies through Time: Persistence and Emergence.* Robert V. H. Dover, Katharine E. Seibold, and John H. McDowell, eds. Pp. 17–45. Bloomington: Indiana University Press.

Index

Michelle Wibbelsman is a research fellow at the Teresa Lozano Long Institute of Latin American Studies at The University of Texas at Austin, and adjunct professor of anthropology at St. Edward's University (Austin). She has published articles in books and in journals such as *Latin American Music Review* and *Journal of Latin American Anthropology*.

The University of Illinois Press
is a founding member of the
Association of American University Presses.

Composed in 10/13 ITC Galliard
by Jim Proefrock
at the University of Illinois Press
Designed by Dennis Roberts
Manufactured by Cushing-Malloy, Inc.

University of Illinois Press
1325 South Oak Street
Champaign, IL 61820-6903
www.press.uillinois.edu